The Beaverbrook I Knew

# The Beaverbrook I Knew

Edited by Logan Gourlay

Quartet Books
London Melbourne New York

First published by Quartet Books Limited 1984
A member of the Namara Group
27/29 Goodge Street, London W1P 1FD

British Library Cataloguing in Publication Data

The Beaverbrook I knew
  1. Beaverbrook, William Maxwell Aitken *Baron*
  I. Gourlay, Logan
  070.4'092'4   DA 566.9.B37

  ISBN 0-7043-2331-1

Photoset by AKM Associates (UK) Ltd,
Southall, Greater London
Printed and bound in Great Britain by
Mackays of Chatham Ltd, Kent

# Contents

Illustrations

# Acknowledgements

I owe a large measure of gratitude to the contributors to this book for accepting me in my editing role, for responding to my invitation to write about the Beaverbrook they knew and, in some cases, for including material they may have been preserving for their own memoirs.

James Cameron, one of the most talented journalists to have worked for Beaverbrook, kindly gave me permission to use extracts from his book *The Best of Cameron* and I am grateful to him and his publishers, New English Library. I am grateful also to Alan Watkins and his publishers Hamish Hamilton for permission to publish an extract from his book *Brief Lives*, to Michael Foot and to his publishers Davis-Poynter for permission to use an extract from his book *Debts of Honour*, and to the Bodley Head for permission to publish an extract from *The Prerogative of the Harlot: Press Barons and Power* by Hugh Cudlipp. I add a special word of gratitude to him for turning his own editor's hand (a much more experienced and skilful one than mine) to the job of preparing his own extract for publication in this book.

My thanks are also due to Hutchinson, publishers of *Strange Street* by Beverley Baxter; to Heinemann, publishers of *Headlines All My Life* by Arthur Christiansen; and to Weidenfeld & Nicolson, publishers of *Beaverbrook: A Study in Power and Frustration* by Tom Driberg — for permission to publish extracts from those books. I must thank also the BBC and Anthony Howard who gave me permission to publish extracts from the television programme 'Lord Beaverbrook' in the series *Reputations*, which he wrote and presented.

I am indebted to the Centre for the Study of Cartoons and Caricature at Kent University without whose help and co-operation the selection of Beaverbrook caricatures and cartoons could not have been published.

Finally my warmest thanks go to Paul Keegan of Quartet Books for his valuable editorial assistance in preparing this book, and in particular to Naim Attallah, whose publisher's imagination produced the idea for this book, and whose publisher's patience made its completion possible.

Logan Gourlay, London, 1984

# Preface

When I was a film and theatre critic for one of the Beaverbrook newspapers, I was sometimes told by producers and directors that I was making the mistake of aiming my criticisms at a production I thought should have been attempted rather than confining them to what was actually intended and offered.

I fear that this book may bring similar criticisms, so let me anticipate them by pointing out that I did not set out presumptuously to produce a biography of Beaverbrook and then change course, realizing the task was beyond my capacities as it would have been. However, although there have been three biographies of Beaverbrook, I felt that he had such a remarkably long, colourful and eventful life that there were still some interesting events to be recorded and many anecdotes as yet unpreserved in print. And who better to record the events and relate the anecdotes than the people involved, those who knew him and worked with, and for, him over the years? Hence *The Beaverbrook I Knew*. It is intended to be no more than a companion volume to the full-scale biographies, an anecdotal supplement to the authorized work by A. J. P. Taylor, who, I am happy to say, has contributed some newly minted words to this book.

To add some historical balance and perspective, I have also included extracts from books by three men, now dead, who were closely associated with Beaverbrook in their journalistic careers – Beverley Baxter, Arthur Christiansen and Tom Driberg.

The Beaverbrook who emerges from a compilation of this kind cannot, of course, be the complete man: inevitably pieces are missing from the mosaic but a few new ones may be added: although the portrait cannot be a comprehensive one, fresh light is thrown, I hope, on some parts of the subject.

As Beaverbrook himself would have wished, there has been no

attempt to remove, or conceal, any of the warts. He genuinely liked the
Graham Sutherland portrait (reproduced on the dust jacket) which
brilliantly revealed those warts that lay below the surface. Indeed
Beaverbrook described it, when it was first delivered to him by
Sutherland's wife, as 'a work of genius'.

Among Beaverbrook's critics, there are some who think that the
Sutherland portrait was not sufficiently frank and revealing, who
might even consider it flattering. They consign him to a canvas
depicting dystopia – as a brother of Beelzebub, if not Beelzebub
himself. There are a few, however, as this book shows, who viewed
Beaverbrook if not as smilingly ingenuous as the portraits that adorn
the lids of chocolate boxes, then at least as charming and benevolent
as the Father Christmases who wink at the world on glossy wrapping
paper.

A compiler of a recent book about Charles Dickens pointed out that
some of the contributors who had known Dickens well could not agree
about the colour of his eyes. To some they were blue; to others brown.
Beaverbrook, I'm sure, would be delighted to know that people are still
disagreeing, as they do in these pages, about the colour of his
character, the true shade of his immortal soul. In moments of self-
honesty, his own choice would have veered undoubtedly towards
black – or at least a dark Calvinistic grey.

When he chose his title, 'Beaverbrook', he called my brother Max and my mother and myself into the library which was his sacred place and he discussed for a long time what he was going to do, and then he said: 'Well, there was a little brook next to our home in Newcastle off the Miramichi River and the beavers used to come into this little brook and I used to feed them. I think I'll call myself Beaverbrook.'

> Janet Kidd, Lord Beaverbrook's daughter, speaking on the BBC2 programme 'Lord Beaverbrook' in the *Reputations* series, written and presented by Anthony Howard and broadcast on 28 June 1981.

# The Rage
# Hugh Cudlipp

'I am the victim of the Furies,' wrote William Maxwell Aitken, Baron Beaverbrook, to a friend. 'On the rockbound coast of New Brunswick the waves break incessantly. Every now and then comes a particularly dangerous wave, smashing viciously against the rock. It is called The Rage. That's me.'

One of his friends said, 'Everything that anyone said about Max is true – the best things and the worst things.' Andrew Bonar Law, whom he manoeuvred into No. 10 Downing Street, called him 'a curious fellow'. He played a decisive part in making David Lloyd George Prime Minister, but Lloyd George said no man in any party trusted Max. When he appointed the Canadian as Minister of Information in 1918, the severest critic was Lord Salisbury: he described Aitken to backbenchers as 'a very wicked man', and when challenged by Edmund Goulding to justify the gibe, merely added, 'Oh, ask anyone in Canada.' For fifty-five years, with few estrangements, Winston Churchill enjoyed Max's boisterous companionship and acknowledged his energy, confidence and ability to get things done in a crisis, but Churchill was sorely taxed by Beaverbrook's tantrums as Minister of Aircraft Foundation in 1940, his bullying and bickering and threats of resignation. Clementine Churchill considered that Birkenhead, Beaverbrook and Brendan Bracken, over the years, brought out the worst in Winston and she deplored their influence.

Cabinet ministers of other parties, who had to endure Beaverbrook in coalition during the Second World War, some in silence, expressed their views in due course. To Clement Attlee, he was 'the man in public life most widely distrusted by men of all parties; he had a long record of political intrigue and political instability, with an insatiable appetite for power'. Ernest Bevin settled for 'the most dangerous man in British public life'.

Lord Reith, who exhibited the Christian virtues ostentatiously in public and confided his darker thoughts to his diary, reserved a special place of hatred in his heart for The Rage: 'What a dreadful man he is; one of the worst I ever met. Evil he seems . . .'

Harold Macmillan had no illusions about the more 'distasteful aspects' of Beaverbrook's character, yet learned, as his Under-Secretary at the Ministry of Supply, 'to appreciate the extraordinary gifts of this strange and wayward genius'.

In Fleet Street, Beaverbrook was regarded less horrifically than in Westminster. His whimsicality and eccentricity were accepted by journalists with favour. The omnipotence and omnipresence of the driving force behind his publishing empire were apparent before one even crossed the threshold. He was demanding, exacting, tyrannous, vindictive and malicious, yet all or most of the excesses of the master journalist were forgiven by the men and women who worked for him because of the success of his publishing enterprise and his impish sense of fun. My personal experience of his capacity for encouragement of the young is no doubt typical of many.

Halfway through the war he said would never happen, in 1943, I was ordered, as a seconded infantry officer, to London by air for three days (to receive my next orders) after the advance of the Desert Rats from El Alamein to Tunisia. 'Why not tell the country what you've been telling me about the campaign?' said Grigg, the Secretary of State for War. 'I'll ring the MOI.' On the morning after my performance for the captive, blacked-out audience of the BBC, Beaverbrook phoned me: 'D'ya know who this is? The Prime Minister and I listened to your Eighth Army broadcast last night and Winston thought it was great stirring stuff. Goodbye to you.'

He approached me at the end of the war to join the *Express* organization, and then, when I was unemployed for two hours just before Christmas 1949, immediately invited me to what he called 'the sunny side of the street'. The Fleet Street edifice, veneered in black glass, where the *Express* newspapers are still produced, faces south.

The speed with which he acted was one of the attractive aspects of the man. I had telephoned Arthur Christiansen, the Editor of the *Daily Express*, to inform him that the tone of the correspondence between Harry Guy Bartholomew and myself in the rival newspaper group indicated my imminent departure. Christiansen phoned Beaverbrook at his winter retreat in Montego Bay, Jamaica. Within two hours I had joined the *Express* organization and within six hours a cable reached me from the Beaver:

IT IS WITH ENTHUSIASM THAT I WELCOME YOU TO OUR HOUSE WHERE
YOU WILL BE HAPPY AND CONTENTED. I HAVE SOUGHT YOUR COMPANION-
SHIP FOR LONG

BEAVERBROOK

His intention was that I would eventually follow John Gordon as
Editor of the *Sunday Express*. He twice appointed me Editor but
omitted to tell John Gordon – another interesting facet of his
character.

When I arrived, on my first visit as an employee, at his top-floor
apartment at Arlington House near the Ritz, overlooking Green Park,
he said, 'Hugh, bring your chair over here. Not there – here!' The accent
was a pleasant, soft and persuasive Canadian twang. I learned on other
occasions that it could easily become harsh and domineering when
raised in anger. We sat opposite each other and the invitation to 'Come
closer' was repeated until our knees touched. The siting of the chairs
was a matter of meticulous stage-management. The lighting seemed to
play upon his face alone. He was not apparently expecting me, with
uplifted right hand, to swear by Almighty God to speak the truth, the
whole truth and nothing but the truth (according to the policies of
Lord Beaverbrook), he was silently exhorting me to see the truth in his
face. He narrowed the lids of his eyes and peered into mine; having no
alternative I peered steadfastly back. The prophet was casting his spell
on a newcomer half his age. He was administering a mute oath of
allegiance. Or was Mephistopheles promising to show Dr Faustus all
knowledge and all experience in return for his immortal soul? Or was it
a ritualistic absolution from my sins of the past when, in some
unthinking moment, I had doubted his dictum of Empire Free Trade?

Halfway through the two-minute ordeal I prided myself that lesser
men might have cracked, sobbed fitfully, and confessed that, under the
influence of government hospitality, they had indeed commended the
British Council for sending Welsh harpists and long-haired poets to
Istanbul, or thought in their ignorance that the United Nations was a
noble concept, or kissed the faded hem of the Fabian Society, or shaken
Earl Mountbatten of Burma by the hand. Had I at last acquired the
artifice of silence, or was I mesmerized? No word was spoken, and I was
therefore able to concentrate upon the remarkable head twelve inches
or less away from me. It was round, with a mouth so broad that it
seemed to reach his ear on each side, like a melon chopped but not
severed by a machete. The brow and the lines dividing the cheeks from
his nose and upper lip were deeply furrowed. The skin was leathery,
permanently tanned from the sunshine of Montego Bay and Cap d'Ail,

where he took his asthma and friends for the winter. The eyes were piercing and his features immobile for the first minute of the seance. I noticed that the collar of his shirt was slightly frayed and his tie loosely knotted. The second minute was occupied with a display of his range of moods, all facially expressed: doubt, suspicion, anger, ruthlessness. It is all magnificently captured in Graham Sutherland's portrait. The final expression, the most startling of all, transformed the Three Wise Monkeys – 'Hear no evil, see no evil, speak no evil' – into one Wise Monkey reversing their policies. Then the mouth broke apart in a pleasing puckish grin and the eyes opened wide and he laughed.

'Hugh,' he said, 'have you seen my electric rum-cocktail mixer? Jamaican rum and West Indian limes. The limes are absolutely paramount.' I had passed the loyalty test and within a few months was appointed to the inner circle of the Policy Committee, the sanctum where the chosen few were vouchsafed untrammelled freedom to agree with what the master said.


William Maxwell Aitken had three careers in his lifetime. The first, as a financier in Canada, made him a millionaire by the age of thirty. In the second, as a politician in Britain, he exerted influence behind the scenes rather than achieving personal success in Parliament. In the third, he became a multi-millionaire newspaper proprietor. His appointment as a Cabinet minister in the 1914 war sprang from his friendship with Bonar Law and David Lloyd George, and from his propaganda performance for the Canadian forces in Europe. His three ministerial appointments in the 1939 war were the result of his friendship with Churchill, his drive and ability as an organizer and his fame as a Press Baron. His political career from 1910 to 1918, however, was a self-contained phase of his life with no relation to his subsequent high jinks as a newspaper owner.

The approaching armistice in November 1918 released him from Westminster to launch his third and most explosive career as a newspaper proprietor in Fleet Street. In November 1916, at Blumenfeld's suggestion, he had bought the controlling shares of the *Daily Express*, inheriting its debts and committing himself to further expenditure on newsprint. As always, he sought advice and hesitated before he moved. Lord Rothermere, while warning him of the financial risks and personal effort involved, told him to go ahead, thus creating the greatest competition Northcliffe's *Daily Mail* ever faced. Northcliffe himself was less encouraging, seeking to frighten him off:

N: How much are you worth?
B: Over five million dollars.
N: You will lose it all in Fleet Street.

Beaverbrook was nearly forty when he set his hand to establishing his newspapers as permanent institutions that would assure his influence and preferably make a profit. The heady wine of newspaper power was pleasing to his palate. His newspapers became the absorbing passion of his life. To the *Express, Daily* and *Sunday*, he devoted his energy, cunning, leadership and ideas, and he knew that the only way through was to achieve an excellence that would dwarf the records set by Northcliffe.

The *Daily Express* developed as a human-interest paper in pursuit of the *Daily Mail*, which was visibly weakening under the control of the first Lord Rothermere after Northcliffe's death in 1922. The *Sunday Express*, when it got its second wind after four years, offered well-advertised, circulation-raiding, big-name series, lapsing rarely to the level of Mrs Thompson's love letters to the murderer Bywaters, and rising occasionally to H. G. Wells's record of his journey to communist Russia. Financial scandals were a speciality, fascinating the chief shareholder more than the readers. The policy of both papers was to avoid raw sex and the sordid, and to peddle romanticism and escapism, ever yearning for the good and glittering life of High Society – beyond the reach of its readers but now within the grasp of the proprietor.

The *Sunday Express* was long in the doldrums with a mortality rate among its early editors equalled only by Rothermere's *Daily Mail*. The biggest flop in the chair was James Douglas, the same Douglas who later made his name on the same paper as the apostle of spontaneous moral indignation. He upbraided Lord Dawson of Penn, royal physician and Lloyd George's as well, for defending birth control, which moved Lloyd George to write to Dawson: 'When Beaverbrook holds up hands steeped in the blood of slaughtered commandments to express horror at your speech, it beats the record for disgusting hypocrisy.' Beaverbrook was happy to foist sanctimonious nonsense on his middle-class readers while conducting his private life as a parody of the unctuous Douglas dictum.

In 1922, he announced that the *Express* stood for 'More life – more hope – more money – more work – more happiness – the creed which is going to redeem Great Britain from the harsh aftermath of war and set her feet once again on the path to prosperity.' Who was against more life, hope, money, and happiness, then or now? He chose the cosy course of being furiously anti-Labour in any election and naggingly anti-Conservative when the Conservatives were in government.

The editorial excellence of the products was not conspicuous until John Gordon from Dundee became Editor of the *Sunday Express* in 1928 and Arthur Christiansen, from Lancashire, of the *Daily Express* in 1933. Beaverbrook needed these two professionals who knew how to organize the flow of news, how to present the goods in the super-market, and sustain an atmosphere of perpetual suspense. They buttressed the Beaver as a newspaper tycoon until he became a fully fledged journalist himself, and he paid them well to do so.

As an impresario Beaverbrook assembled around him a galaxy of writers and cartoonists without equal in the newspaper world: Hannen Swaffer; David Low, licensed to caricature the boss and his policies in his cartoons; Valentine Castlerosse, the gossip-writing Irish viscount nurtured by the Baron and described by Lady Astor as 'Beaverbrook's Buttons'. There were H. V. Morton (*In the Footsteps of Christ*), J. B. ('Beachcomber') Morton, James Agate, Sefton Delmer, Osbert Lancaster, Giles, Nathaniel Gubbins, Strube and his 'Little Man' and dozens of book, film and theatre reviewers.

Frank Owen was Beaverbrook's 'ghost' on economic policy, and the brilliant, subtle George Malcolm Thomson, still now writing books at the age of eighty, wrote the boss's articles and editorials on foreign affairs. Beaverbrook persuaded Arnold Bennett, Bertrand Russell and the acid pessimist Dean Inge to become his contributors as well as H. G. Wells. Inge wrote regularly in the *Evening Standard* on the imminent collapse of Christian civilization and Bennett reviewed books in an elegant weekly article. To be mentioned even disdainfully by the master was the foundation of many a novelist's career. Rayner Goddard also wrote for the *Evening Standard* on crime and punishment while sitting as Lord Chief Justice. When my brother, Percy Cudlipp, was editing the Beaver's *Evening Standard* in the inter-war years, the anonymous contributors to its Londoner's Diary included Robert Bruce Lockhart, Harold Nicolson, Malcolm Muggeridge and Randolph Churchill.

The Beaver's success as a journalist was that he had the same insatiable curiosity as Northcliffe and Luce. His newspapers knew what was going on, but apart from the news of the day, large areas of which were presented without bias, the readers could never be sure *they* knew what was going on. Political news and opinion were subject to the chief shareholder's fiat. The personal beliefs of the writing journalists who laboured near the sun were shrivelled by its heat. They wrote with the courage of his, Beaverbrook's, convictions, and wrote in his style, influenced by American newspapers and magazines and, curiously, the Old Testament. They consoled their consciences with an easy cynicism and a fat cheque. But, hell, it was fun for them.

The Beaverbrook familiar to the British public and the publishing world emerged as soon as his newspapers were successful. He knew a millionaire need never be lonely; he also found that newspapers opened more doors than cement or steel. Politicians, industrialists, film magnates, famous writers, actors and actresses, and the darlings of Society were at his beck and call and he was the glamorous host. People of real talent or true independence in public life were impervious to Beaverbrook's law, but only the foolish or the brave went out of their way to insult the *Daily Express*, the *Sunday Express* or the *Evening Standard* and to make an enemy of him. Who wouldn't be a Press Baron in London rather than a company promoter in Montreal or a bonds salesman anywhere in the world?

With his wife Gladys and his sons and daughter parked away at Cherkley, he enjoyed the Roaring Twenties as a playboy with a purpose. The powerful, the promising, the storytellers, the witty and the beautiful were welcome at his table; he did not suffer the foolish or the plain. He became a figure in the social scene, flitting between Deauville and Monte Carlo with his guests. He became a racehorse owner, acquired a yacht, and multiplied his millions by an entry into the film industry. These were the roisterous years in the Beaverbrook saga, and his sexual track-record was not the least of his accomplishments; he did not spend all his energy on money-making. Alan Wood, an Australian who became a *Daily Express* war correspondent in 1943 and stayed in the group as a policy writer, made a shrewd observation on these affairs.

It seemed that Beaverbrook would take a special delight in tumbling the pride of society women. One of his journalists was a little disconcerted on one occasion, on being summoned to get some instructions, to find Lady — sitting on his lap, caressing his face with her hand the whole time Beaverbrook talked. Another editor complained that what annoyed him most, on being woken early in the morning by Beaverbrook shouting criticism down the phone about something in the paper, was to hear feminine laughter in the intervals of Beaverbrook's sallies, and to realize that the performance was simply to amuse some girl with him.

Mr Wood took the solemn view that a public man's private life should be treated as his own affair, but before hurrying on to other aspects of Beaverbrook's career he did record for posterity this romantic interlude:

> The talk of the town was to touch on several of Beaverbrook's affairs, beginning with a musical-comedy actress who had taken part in a film made about the time of his period as Minister of Information. She described him as her best lover since Little Tich (her first). She liked to describe his habit of giving a great shout of laughter every time, and it was gossip about this affair which largely accounted for Beaverbrook's later unpopularity in provincial Ashton-under-Lyne, where Lady Beaverbrook was idolized. [From *The True History of Lord Beaverbrook* by Alan Wood, Heinemann, 1965]

The forgiving Gladys sent signals of distress when he overtly made Mrs Jean Norton, a noted beauty, his regular mistress and attendant at social engagements, and one event, in those playboy years, caused distress to Beaverbrook himself. In December 1927 his wife died from heart failure at forty-two. Sir Thomas Horder broke the news and it is said that The Rage cried like a child. The letters that passed between them in the final years give evidence of her enduring love for him and of his sense of guilt. He railed against the doctors for forbidding him, to avoid excitement, to visit her as she was dying. He erected an illuminated cross at Cherkley 'to remind me that I'm a Christian', he told Hannen Swaffer. 'She had a beauty, a poise, and a judgement which would have recommended her to any society in Europe at the most critical moment of that society . . . She was essentially womanly, and being womanly she was incredibly understanding. She made allowances easily and generously.'

Lady Beaverbrook died at Stornoway House, a residence of some elegance near St James's Palace. Her 'My Lord dear Lord' and 'My Beloved One', as she endearingly addressed him in her domestic notes, had acquired the property in 1924 when she had complained of her isolation at Cherkley in the weekdays between the weekend parties.

William Maxwell Aitken's character was enigmatic or complex only to those who took him at his own valuation or were well rewarded to pretend to do so. The aura of Old Testament prophet was sustained throughout his life in Britain by his biblical allusions and quotations:

> I hoped to see the British Empire united in one economic unit. Again and again the prospect seemed almost realized, but on every occasion the golden gates closed on it.

I have touched the ivory on the golden gates with my fingertips, but I have never got within.

The temple of success is based on the three pillars of Health, Industry and Judgement.

How long, O Lord, how long must we listen to those who give us false counsel and persuade us to walk in ways that bring us to low estate and bitter humiliation? How long must we submit to this leader, Mr Baldwin?

They became tedious, but who dared say so?

Only the credulous believed that there was any deep religious conviction. He had learned the Bible like a parrot in his father's Presbyterian church and studied the good book for oratorical rather than spiritual inspiration throughout his life: it was an ingredient of the personality he decided to project. He wrote *The Divine Propagandist*, setting out his own thoughts on the meaning of Christ to mankind, but the moral force of His life and His teaching had no discernible impact on the private or public life of the author of that slim volume. As soon as his Presbyterian mumbo-jumbo is taken at its real and not its face value, the man behind the tanned, furrowed mask becomes comprehensible. Aitken was the political equivalent of Edward G. Robinson in the film *Little Caesar*. To an uncanny degree he physically resembled the stocky, growling Hollywood actor; they had the same jaunty walk, and in their moments of rage their nasal accents were similar. Indeed, Ronald Neame, casting his film *The Magic Box*, tried to get Robinson to play the Beaverbrook part. Little Caesar was a small-time hoodlum and Lord Beaverbrook was a company promoter, politician, and newspaper tycoon, but they shared a determination to get to the top by any means at hand.

Max's political perception was acute, and mischievous. His support was invaluable, and mercurial. His mental gifts were adulterated by his addiction to intrigue. He liked to be the 'honest broker' with a foot in both camps, negotiating a peace that suited himself. Hugh Kingsmill called him 'Robin Badfellow' and few praised him without qualification. The menace of the man, with his roaring personality and his talent for communication, was the unreality of his causes. The public would have been hoodwinked had they bought his newspapers for political guidance instead of for entertainment. Imperial economic unity, or Empire Free Trade, was an impracticable pipedream. Splendid Isolation from Europe was a panacea that scared the feathers off even the most senile of ostriches. The rest of his policies were transient attitudes, dictated by expedience or headline heroics, that sprang from his basic misconceptions. Percy Cudlipp, when editing the *Evening Standard*, observed to me in a moment of disillusion: 'No cause is really lost until we support it.'

Beaverbrook's vendetta against Stanley Baldwin was an example of the use of his newspapers to stalk and seek to destroy a public man who would not bend to his will. The vehemence of his denial that there was ever a vendetta was the sort of ruse that led people to call him enigmatic or complex. It was a lie, with the evidence in his newspapers and public speeches.

His major disservice to his country and to Western civilization was the deployment of his newspapers for five decades in the cause of Splendid Isolation. It was the basis for his jeering onslaughts against the League of Nations and the United Nations, and against the individual advocates, like the pre-Suez Anthony Eden, of any semblance of international co-operation. His gospel was a national menace during the rise of the European dictatorships, unique in its reckless disregard of current evidence, history, and even of common sense. When the only shield against Germany's diplomatic and then military aggression was collective security, his newspapers preached salvation in going-it-alone. He advocated rearmament, but sought to sell his readers and the country the myth that Britain was safe so long as it kept its nose out of Europe's business.

The folly of Splendid Isolation culminated in Beaverbrook's personal assurance to his readers that 'there will be no war'. In the year of Munich, 1938, his newspapers were peddling the twin policies of appeasement and optimism while paying lip-service to rearmament. The poster at the front of the sandwich-board Messiah said 'Rearm', the poster at the rear said 'Relax'.

In his headline, 'There will be no war', Beaverbrook, not for the first time or last time held his readers in contempt. At editorial conferences where the braver of his executives and leader writers expressed their misgivings, he always replied: 'If we're right, everyone will praise our foresight. If we're wrong – nobody will remember.' Dead men tell no tales, but those who did survive remembered.

'There will be no war' was the most dishonest and indefensible of the *Express* campaigns, the subject of angry criticisms long after the war was over. 'There will be no war' suited the advertisers who knew their customers would be less likely to buy new motor cars, furniture, carpets and cooking stoves if in a few months' time they might be dented by bomb blasts, covered in rubble, or blackened by incendiaries. In the spring of 1939, a visitor to Stornoway House observed men digging a hole in the garden, preparing a private air-raid shelter for the occupant, which for some reason was never completed. In the autumn of 1940 Stornoway House was shattered and burnt out by a German bomb.

Beaverbrook's contribution to the war effort as Minister of Aircraft Production and in other Cabinet appointments, sustaining Churchill, does not concern us in this study. Here was the verdict of the man who appointed him:

All his remarkable qualities fitted the need. His personal buoyancy and vigour were a tonic. I was glad to be able sometimes to lean on him. He did not fail. This was his hour. His personal force and genius, combined with so much persuasion and contrivance, swept aside many obstacles.

Critics niggled that the instant production of planes was the fruit of plans he had inherited rather than initiated. When Churchill referred to Beaverbrook's 'magic', a Cabinet minister said the principal stock-in-trade of a magician was illusion. But he produced results and exuded confidence in the darkest hours of the struggle for survival. The propagandist aspect was vital.

After twenty-one successive months of what he called 'high adventure' as Minister of Aircraft Production, he was again the maverick, pressing in his newspapers for support of Stalin's insistence on an immediate Second Front, an invasion of Germany in the west to relieve the pressure on the Eastern Front. Operation Overload of 1944 could not have been launched in 1942 and Beaverbrook knew it. In a BBC broadcast six months before he resigned as minister in February 1942, he told the British people that 30,000 more tanks were essential before the Western Front onslaught could be unleashed. Rommel rolled the British Army back to Egypt; hardly an auspicious omen. The bloody failure of the raid on Dieppe in the summer of the same year silenced the belligerent Second Front civilians, and Beaverbrook's return to the Cabinet in September 1943 silenced him and his newspapers.

There were many victims of Beaverbrook's vengeance. Ernest Bevin, as Minister of Labour in Beaverbrook's Aircraft Production days, had to pay for his intransigence. Geoffrey Dawson, Editor of *The Times* and Baldwin's crutch during the Abdication Crisis, was frequently scorched. Earl Mountbatten of Burma was in a category of his own as the target of a Beaverbrook vendetta.

We began with the proposition that 'everything anyone said about Max is true – the best things and the worst things'. There is abundant evidence for the worst, and less for the best. Harold Macmillan, who had contact with him at stages of his own career, in and out of office and occasionally serving under him in a ministry, is an impressive witness because he neither praises nor condemns wholeheartedly:

> Beaverbrook sometimes seemed almost a Jekyll and Hyde ... If there were aspects of his character which repelled, there were others that were intensely attractive. While I served him and until the end of his life I received from him nothing but kindness ... Perhaps I was fortunate, but this was my experience. [ From Harold Macmillan, *The Blast of War*, Macmillan, 1967]

Others were less fortunate. One repellent diversion of Mr Hyde was his persecution of the second and last Sir John Ellerman, a shy, sick recluse whose interest in life was the scientific study of rodents but who also happened to be Britain's richest man. His wealth, his business activities, his hobby, his houses, his journeys were the subject of persistent scrutiny in Beaverbrook's newspapers. He was rarely newsworthy and hated publicity, yet he could not put his head outside a door without being pursued by reporters and photographers on the Beaver's payroll. Ellerman in an agonizing talk with me – 'All those millions, and this persecution by the press, are driving me crazy. I can't stand it any more' – said the cause of the vendetta was a quarrel Beaverbrook had had with his father. Beaverbrook told me he had never known Ellerman's father, never had had a business conversation with the son, or any relationship with him whatsoever. He merely had the pleasure of his acquaintance, nothing more; Ellerman was 'a short stout little Jew, he didn't attract anybody or please those he came in contact with'.

The *Express* newspapers were as enterprising as their rivals in expanding sales by the lavish coverage of glamorous or poignant royal events. In the intervals between they were noted for their waspish comment, inspired by the chief shareholder. Whacking Mountbatten was some recompense for having been whacked himself by the late King George V, and occasionally it was implied that, as the uncle of Prince Philip, the Earl Mountbatten was a sinister influence behind the throne. Beaverbrook's newspapers were tediously vigilant in exposing any whiff of inefficiency or discourtesy on the part of the palace, though the errors were occasionally those of officials. It was the fashion of the time (less so now) to attribute sin to the advisers as if the royals were their puppets on a string. The advisers were taken to task by Beaverbrook's newspapers for selecting the wrong date for the coronation of the present Queen, to suit the convenience of Her Majesty and her consort rather than that of the readers of the *Daily Express*. The criticism of Prince Philip moved him to refer to the *Express* as 'that bloody awful newspaper'. Any columnist writing for Beaverbrook's newspapers, including John Gordon, knew that he could come in from the cold by a spontaneous fit of anger about a new lick of paint on the royal yacht *Britannia*. 'Why wasn't the allowance paid to Prince Philip made public?' 'What is the Queen really worth?' [relating to her private fortune] – the royal finances were a recurrent theme, the best years of the lives of many a city editor and economic expert were wasted on that inconclusive probe. 'No', Beaverbrook would say, 'it must be more than that', and resurrect the subject a few months later as if it had never been mentioned before. The nagging of the royals was unjust to them and distasteful to his readers, but what did that matter? There was no reason known to Beaverbrook why royal blood should not be spilled in a vendetta; the fact that they could not reply was their concern, not his.

Beaverbrook had the same freedom of speech in his newspapers as any stump orator on a soap-box at Hyde Park Corner, no more, no less. It was his own affair when he squandered his gunpowder on foolhardy campaigns. It was everybody's affair when he used his influence, whether unwittingly or from some Machiavellian or merely mischievous motive, to weaken national resolve and resistance.

The Empire Free Trade bubble created havoc in the Conservative Party, otherwise it caused no more harm than the activities of the Flat Earth Society or the spotters of unidentified flying objects. The potential danger of his policy for Splendid Isolation was limited by the common sense of the British public rather than by any lack of energy or skill on his part as a propagandist. 'There will be no war' was at its best an irresponsible gamble and at its worst a cruel deception. Beaverbrook was telling his American friends in private that nobody knew *when* the blow-up would come; concurrently, his newspapers were assuring their readers that a blow-up would not come because Germany was not ready for war and could not come because even if Hitler himself wanted war his generals would not allow it. The slogan appeared in the *Daily Express* a few weeks before the outbreak. The European dictators could not have hoped or prayed for a more efficient

Fifth Column in Britain than that created by the principal Press
Barons, aided and abetted by the appeasement policy of *The Times*.
Beaverbrook considered it 'the duty of newspapers to advocate a policy
of optimism in the broadest sense'; it was not, therefore, their duty to
tell the truth.

When war did come there was no hint of contrition from the leading
deceiver, no attempt to make amends. The man who said there would
be no war was soon embarking upon campaigns that, had they
prevailed, would have ensured there would be no victory. Perversity is
a mild explanation of his opposition to expanding the British Army
when war was declared and to buying American planes; as soon as he
was Minister he ordered American planes on a vast scale. He beat the
drum in favour of the pettiest discontents, and his incitement to the
public to revolt against wartime food rationing bordered on sedition.
Opinion surveys conducted by Mass Observation showed that a large
majority in all classes was decidedly in favour of rationing, more so
after the *Daily Express* campaign than before it.

It would be pleasant, but it is difficult, to absolve the Beaver from
any charge of cant. The man who told Churchill in a letter that he had
created all the big trusts in Canada, asking him not to tell anyone else,
became in Britain the vociferous champion of the 'small man' in
business, insisting on free competition, pillorying the Co-op and the
chain stores for pushing the High Street shopkeepers out of business.
'Instinctively,' he declared in his newspapers, 'I am on the side of the
little man and against the great big fellow. I am on the side of the little
minnow against the great big trout. I am on the side of the little pig
against the big bad wolf. I am on the side of the little trader and against
the Co-operative Society.'

Beaverbrook approached death with some reluctance and delay but
with his accustomed histrionic majesty: 'The days of our years are
three score and ten. I have passed the allotted span. Every hour further
is a bonus to me from the Almighty.' Some bonus: it lasted another
fifteen years. There may have been some reluctance on the part of the
Almighty to speed his parting from the earth.

At this stage of his life there was some jocularity among the friends
of the Old Testament prophet about his future. H. G. Wells had earlier
expressed the view that if Max got to Heaven he wouldn't last long: 'He
will be chucked out for trying to pull off a merger between Heaven and
Hell . . . after having secured a controlling interest in key subsidiary
companies, of course.' Randolph Churchill said: 'It would be damned

ungrateful of him if he *didn't* believe in Hell, seeing that they've been getting the place ready for him specially all these years.'

Beaverbrook acted the final scenes with superb artistry and no noticeable humility. He read the Bible even more diligently as he contemplated the Life to Come, quoting this as a favourite passage: 'God shall bring every work into judgement, with every secret thing, whether it be good, or whether it be evil.' He knew that Elijah was carried up to Heaven in a whirlwind (II Kings 2:11), and would not have been surprised if some such exit was in store for him. He did not, to the end, lose his puckish sense of fun, nor did he conceal his uncertainty as to his destination. I was present at the Positively Last Farewell Performance of William Maxwell Aitken, Baron Beaverbrook. A banquet was staged at the Dorchester Hotel on 25 May 1964 to celebrate his eighty-fifth birthday. Lord Thomson of Fleet, another ebullient Canadian and the proprietor of *The Times*, was the host. There were six hundred of us, of all ages and most professions, happy or proud for one reason or another to be at the last gathering of the tribe, regarding the guest of honour either with awe or, with quali- fication, affection. I was able to reflect, like Harold Macmillan, that I had received nothing from him but kindness, knowing others were less fortunate. Nobody present, I reckon, has forgotten the nerve- tingling atmosphere of the occasion, as spellbinding as the last act of a Verdi opera without the need for scenery or music or lighting effects. The compelling personality of the man, now physically frail and dying, was undiminished. Everybody knew, including Beaverbrook, that it *was* the last performance, but not, far from it, the Death-bed Repentance. He arrived at the hotel in a chair, walking to his place on the arm of his son, bracing himself for a display of oratory equalled in my experience only by Lloyd George, Winston Churchill and Michael Foot. We heard his definition of the good journalist: 'First, he must be true to himself. The man who is not true to himself is no journalist. He must show courage, independence and initiative. He must also, I believe, be a man of optimism. He has no business to be a pedlar of gloom and despondency. He must be a respecter of persons, but able to deal with the highest and the lowest on the same basis, which is regard for the public interest and a determination to get at the facts.'

The timing of his sallies and asides was professional, the voice strong, the grin whimsical, the gestures dramatic. His theme was 'The Apprentice' – an apprentice to finance in Canada, to politics in England and to journalism in Fleet Street. He had thought that at last he would be master, fancy-free, instead he became 'the slave of the black art', never to know freedom again. The peroration was perfection:

'This is my final word. It is time for me to become an apprentice once more. I have not settled in which direction. But somewhere, sometime soon.'

There was a brief silence while the audience shuffled to its feet, uproarious applause, and then an emotional rendering of 'For He's a Jolly Good Fellow'.

Beaverbrook returned to Cherkley that night and died two weeks later on 9 June. His son, Max Aitken II, told me that his father, just before he became unconscious, handed over to him a box of papers he described as secret. Young Max, accompanied by George Millar, the Beaver's secretary in charge of his private office, took the papers to the hillside near Cherkley and set fire to them.

# The Baron
## Beverley Baxter

The pleasant little English train pulled up at the station at Leatherhead, some twenty miles from London, and I found a car waiting to take me to Cherkley Court, Lord Beaverbrook's country house.

There is something peculiarly satisfying about being met by a car. I have never lost the desire to purr when I emerge from a station and a waiting chauffeur touches his cap and takes my suitcase. To me it gives a far greater sense of luxury than driving the entire distance by car. I cannot explain it and at any rate it is probably not worth explaining.

Cherkley Court lies in the country at the end of a mile-long driveway, and its terrace, guarded by cypress trees, looks down on a Surrey valley, giving the illusion that one is gazing at it from an airplane. There are lawns, gardens, bridle paths, a pool lovely enough to hold the body of Ophelia, birds that welcome the dawn and the lovely music of the wind in the leaves. There are also innumerable telephones, for is this not the home of Baron Beaverbrook, the British Hearst, the man who challenged Northcliffe, the king-maker, the Cabinet-buster, the Puck and the Caliban of British Public Life? How often the leaves of the trees have trembled to the sound of that ringing voice from the verandah, while the servants and secretaries darted about in appropriate commotion.

It was nearly dinnertime when I arrived on that Saturday night and I went at once to my room to change. The operation had been half completed when his Lordship burst into the room and shook hands.

'Are you being looked after all right?'

I assured him that it was so.

'What did you think of the *Express* today?'

I told him.

'What did you think of the *Mail*?'

I told him.

'I see. You don't read the papers very carefully, do you?'

I said I didn't suppose so.

'Did you read George's speech in *The Times*?'

It is a little difficult to stand in one's underwear and meet such an onslaught with perfect poise. I began to realize why certain ministers always wore silk hats in the House of Commons. They were an aid to morale. Besides, who was George?

'It was a very good speech, sir, I thought.'

Beaverbrook frowned. 'It was a great speech. It will do the Government a lot of good. Where were you born?'

So George was Lloyd George. That was something. And lucky I had said it was a good speech. Oh, yes. Where was I born?

'Toronto.'

'Come down when you're ready,' he answered and went out. The air which had been vibrating subsided and I finished dressing. It also seemed to have turned warmer.

I went down a little early and found one guest already there studying the titles of the innumerable books that lined the massive room. I bowed to him and wondered where I had seen his face before. He was an odd-looking man in his middle fifties, with the unmistakable appearance of a provincial, but the assurance of a metropolitan. His untidy moustache almost, but not quite, covered his mouth, which in turn almost, but not quite, covered a set of indecisive teeth that seemed as if they might drop out at any moment. There was puckishness, humour and intelligence in the face and there was a pleasing shyness that mellowed a natural air of combativeness.

'Are you spending the ... weekend – with Max?'

His voice was high-pitched and staccato, but at the word 'weekend' he was seized with an extraordinary stammer. His eyes half closed and his mouth stayed open without a sound. After a pause that was anguishing, the remaining words come out and his eyes opened wide.

'Yes,' I said.

'Are you a Canadian?'

'Yes.'

'Well ...' again the stutter, 'Canadians are an extraordinary people, aren't they?'

I began to feel like Alice in Wonderland. Did no one in the house ever do anything but ask questions?

He took a book from a shelf and handed it to me. It was by a much-married author for whom I have always felt a great affection.

'Have you read it?'

Another question.

'It's terrible,' he said. 'It's awful. It's the worst book . . . ever written.'

When he had completed the stammer he chuckled so infectiously that I found myself laughing in sympathy.

I asked him if he knew Lord Beaverbrook well. After all, if it was to be a game of questions I might as well enter in.

'Do I know Max? Does anybody? He's a . . . remarkable fellow. He's a great man, an astonishing fellow. I'm very fond of him. Of course he's a card.'

He resumed his study of the books. I sat down and inadvertently hummed some tune or other.

'Do you play the piano?' he asked.

'A bit.'

'Come and play duets with me Monday . . . at five o'clock.'

This was becoming ridiculous. Who was he, where did he live, and was it possible that people still played duets?

The door opened and a man of slightly Jewish features, a sensuous mouth and a carefully cultivated moustache came in. He carried himself like one who naturally walked on a crimson carpet. Wealth, taste and power had marked him for their own.

'Look at that view,' he said, in a guttural but pleasing voice. 'I always say that America is the place for the young man, but here in England is where a man may always live in happiness.'

'Were you born in America?' I asked, deciding to get in the first question.

'No, I was born in Germany, but I have been here most of my time. A great country, England. The greatest country in the world. The nation that can stand against the centralized will of the English people has not yet been created.'

A radiantly beautiful woman came in and apologized for being late. She had lovely fair hair, a perfect complexion and her face mirrored the sweetness and simplicity of her soul. She came over to me at once.

'You are Beverley Baxter, I suppose?' she said. 'I'm Lady Beaverbrook.'

I shook hands and liked her enormously. 'You have met Arnold, haven't you?'

'Oh!' My eyes must have widened. 'Is that Arnold Bennett? He's asked me to play piano duets with him.'

'Really?' She laughed at my air of reverence. 'He's a dear,' she said.

'And who's the other chap talking to him now?'

'That's Otto Kahn.'

Late that night Beaverbrook and I sat alone by his fireside and talked until long after midnight. To my astonishment I found a mind richly stored in literature and history and a gift of picturesque and incisive language that made it impossible ever to let the mind wander.

He had humour, too, and the rare power of being personal, of showing that he was acutely conscious of the other's presence. He had a memory like a mouse-trap. It seized on its morsel of fact with a snap and literally never let go. He could summon the exact wording of a poem he had not read for years. I have seen him suddenly accosted by some Canadian acquaintance of thirty years back. Beaverbrook would take one look at him, the vein of his forehead would swell, and then he would say: 'How did your Uncle John get on when he sold his farm? And where's that no-good cousin of yours?'

Sometimes I think his memory was responsible for his violent fits of depression. The ability to forget is part of the art of living. Beaverbrook could never look back upon the pleasantly blurred meadows of the past. Every blade of grass, every thistle, every rabbit hole was as vivid as on the day when his feet had trod among them. How much happier the nature of Arthur Balfour, who once declared with self-revealing humour: 'I never forgive . . . but I always forget.'

It is easy to talk to a man with whom your destiny is resting. It is easy to listen to him. A philosopher once said: 'If a man would talk with his wife with the same interest as he talks to his employer, how few marriages would fail.'

And although Beaverbrook and I were destined to exasperate and savage each other many times in the years to come, let me state now that I have never met anything finer or cleaner than his zeal for youth, his delight in taking a younger man and giving him a chance for a successful career. He has had many failures, and sometimes, in trying to blow the young frog into the size of a bull, he has brought disastrous consequences to the frog. But he never lost his faith in youth nor ever hesitated to give the verdict to talent over mere experience.

At two o'clock he told me his highly revised version of the story of King David, picturing him as the Lloyd George of his time. After that I went to bed and slept soundly.

Next day Winston Churchill, Lord Birkenhead and Bonar Law came to lunch. Arnold Bennett had gone back to town (after confirming our piano duet appointment), and Otto Kahn had drifted off to see some neighbouring mogul.

Here was conversation to remember. It was politics with the lid off. I was learning for the first time the apparent recklessness of politicians' talk when not on duty. I did not know then that English politicians hit hard, but not always fair. Private conversation is 'out of bounds'. What one says at a luncheon party, like what the soldier said, is not evidence.

That night Beaverbrook asked me if I played tennis. I admitted that tennis was one of my minor accomplishments, whereupon he said: 'Come and play at Roehampton in the morning.'

When we arrived at the Roehampton Club he introduced me to 'Cardie' Montagu, the financier, who was to be his partner, and to a well-built, bucolic young man named Lionel Tennyson, who was to partner me.

'Are you any relation . . . ' I began with a natural awe.

'To the bloody bard?' interrupted the Honourable Lionel cheerfully. 'Yes. I am his grandson.'

Just before the first set began, Tennyson called out to Montagu: 'I'll have ten pounds on this set. Baxter, you will take half?'

'Certainly,' I answered.

Beaverbrook and Montagu won.

'We'll have twenty pounds on the last set,' said Lionel. 'That suit you, Baxter?'

My parched mouth uttered an acquiescence. Then something happened. Beaverbrook, who had played an accurate game all morning, went utterly wild. With a face of hot determination, he rushed at every ball, hitting it wildly out of the court or into the net; he collided with Montagu and poached on every shot but his partner's service. It was a terrible performance, and bad as I was, we won a love set.

'That's all square,' said Tennyson. Montagu looked at Beaverbrook with eyes that were eloquent.

When we were driving to town, Beaverbrook said: 'Now listen to me. Don't make a damned fool of yourself. Montagu is a rich man. Tennyson is a gambler and runs his own finances his own way. You were going to lose your whole week's salary. Look what I had to do to prevent it.'

That afternoon I played duets with Arnold Bennett. As I suspected he took the treble and I the bass.

# The Little Man
# Lady Mary Clive

I was twenty-six when I was first summoned to the presence of Lord Beaverbrook.

'Did he make a pass at you?' asked my sisters as soon as I returned home.

'Oh no,' I replied. 'He is *much* too old.'

That was in 1934 when – I can hardly believe it – he was barely fifty-five. Very, very ancient he seemed to me. People said that in the past he had done disgraceful things, but it was all long ago; now, in the sunset of his days, he was brimming over with benevolence and idealism.

We became acquainted because I was writing for the *Evening Standard*. Being painfully shy, I did not find journalism a congenial occupation but the pay was wonderful and there was a shortage of girl journalists and so, under various pseudonyms, I struggled away. Then, out of the blue, came the command that I should go round to Stornoway House. At that time I knew practically nothing about Lord Beaverbrook except that he was a sort of ogre with a voice that was irresistible to mimics, and that in the office he was referred to as 'the little man', and I was appalled at the prospect of having to ring his doorbell.

The name Stornoway suggests storms and wrecks, but it turned out to be a dignified mansion in a quiet cul-de-sac near St James's Palace, and I was effusively welcomed by a most affable small goblin whose clothes had a slightly clerical look, who wore little black boots and who did not even talk in the Beaverbrook voice. We sat in large armchairs in a stately saloon under a curiously disconcerting portrait of the late Lady Beaverbrook in evening dress, and he gave me tea and sugar-cakes and entertained me with gossip and scandal and the story of the private life of Captain Wardell, the manager of the *Standard*.

Elderly people tend to soliloquize, but he talked *to* you, and so skilful was his flattery that, although completely at sea, I soon began to feel that I had never enjoyed a tea party so much. Presently he rang up Captain Wardell and said that I must write about films. Captain Wardell objected to this but agreed that I could become a reporter, after which Lord Beaverbrook, who by now had assumed the harsh, rasping voice which was so easy to imitate, began ticking him off for something which had appeared in the paper and for 'being too hard on Thomas'. He then smacked down the receiver and was as nice as pie to me in his other voice. I was, of course, all ears, and felt that I had been vouchsafed a glimpse of Fleet Street with the lid off.

After that I was sent for quite often and he always treated me with punctilious formality as though he were playing at being an old English nobleman entertaining a duchess. I never got to know him any better or found out what went on in the rest of the house or sorted out the nameless slaves who answered the bell and took away scribbled messages and brought him notes which were then crumpled up and thrown on the floor. Secretaries scurried to and fro with arms full of papers, and occasionally friends drifted through who belonged to a tough, smart world which I had read about in gossip columns.

Sometimes we sat side by side on his balcony, looking down on the populace disporting themselves in Green Park or hurrying down the path from Piccadilly to the Mall. Like Napoleon, he felt that his life had been a romance, and the memory of his former insignificance obviously added to his enjoyment of riches and power. He cherished the idea that he came of Scottish farming stock and that an understanding of farming and the countryside ran in his blood. Moreover, his father had been a Presbyterian minister and so the Almighty was to some extent his property. However, there were limits to his sentimental fancies, and when I suggested that his father must have been proud of his success, he said, 'If he was, he showed it by developing a pronounced taste for living in expensive hotels.' Lord Beaverbrook clearly had a very soft spot for his granddaughter Jean, and he was sometimes bothered by the bickerings of his domestic staff as are ordinary mortals; otherwise life at Stornoway House seemed to be completely unreal.

Stimulating though his company might be, it cannot be denied that he was a tyrant and a bully and that he liked to cause embarrassment. He introduced me to his daughter with the words: 'This is m'daughter. She der-rinks.' And I was once summoned so late in the morning that I imagined that lunch was intended, but when lunchtime came, a beautiful lady appeared, and I faded away sheepishly.

I remember also a large and glittering dinner party. The men were either politicians or journalists and the women were worldly and clever – the modern version, perhaps, of a political dinner in a Victorian novel of high life. I was near Aneurin Bevan who was slightly fuddled and making up to an elegant socialite in pale mauve satin. Suddenly Lord Beaverbrook shouted down the table, 'Nye! Nye! You're impotent, aren't you, Nye!' Bevan, famed for his ready wit, was completely nonplussed and could only bluster something to the effect that the very reverse was the case. Lord Beaverbrook brushed his protests aside. 'Gar! It's no good you pretending. We all know you're impotent.'

On the other hand, one had to avoid saying anything which might make *him* look foolish; his entourage hesitated to correct him and one was constantly being brought up short by his ignorance of the most ordinary matters. When he proposed that I should write a series on little-known London beginning with Hampton Court, I mumbled some bogus excuse rather than explain that Hampton Court was old hat.

His passion for interfering and meddling was never long in abeyance, and he once asked me which items I turned to first when I opened the *Express*. I tried to be honest and said Beachcomber, the gossip column and so on, and he duly wrote this down and sent it off to the Editor, who was hardly likely to alter his layout because of my whims. Next morning I watched myself reading the *Express* and discovered that I began on page one and, with much skipping, went straight through to the end. So much for market research.


I think that after that first summer our friendship rather languished, but I know that in 1935 I was invited to stay at Cherkley, Lord Beaverbrook's house in Surrey. Unfortunately I had a previous engagement and regretfully refused. To refuse such an offer was almost a sin against the Holy Ghost and I was not invited again until 1939. This time I accepted with alacrity, and in my usual state of curiosity and trepidation, I set out.

Cherkley was a large Victorian villa standing in its own grounds. The garden was clearly unloved and the edges of the drive were being planted with sheets of St John's wort, that useful but dingy ground-cover, which Lord Beaverbrook preferred to call rose of Sharon, as though it were a rare blossom brought from afar. The lawn was half-mown, suggesting that the mowing-machine had given offence and been suddenly sacked. There was a kitchen garden ('I've got green-

houses. Why do I have to buy peaches?') and a covered swimming-pool
into which water spouted from a replica of the Brussels manikin which
would have put me off bathing even if the weather had not been too
cold. But the really odd feature of the place was a giant floodlit cross.
This was somehow invisible during the day, and when I caught sight of
it through the window during dinner it gave me quite a turn, as no
doubt it was meant to do.

As for the house, the rooms were large and light and equipped with
mildly modern furniture, adequate but sparse. There were few knick-
knacks and the general effect was that a clearance had been made
before spring-cleaning. The food, however, was delicious.

The three other guests were all male. The most conspicuous was
Lord Castlerosse, an enormously fat, humorous Irishman who wrote
an urbane column in one of Lord Beaverbrook's papers. I had come
across him some years before and then I had thought him the most
amusing man I had ever met, but now he seemed in low spirits and he
did not add much to the liveliness of the party. There was also a quite
young gossip columnist, who if one had not known that he was the
eldest son of a peer, one might have taken for a newspaperman in an
American film. The third was a Member of Parliament, W. J. Brown,
quite human and jolly.

In the course of the weekend, other people came and went, and I
remember some Canadians who had known Lord Beaverbrook in
former days and were not in the least in awe of him; they seemed to
think the whole set-up a joke and even dared chaff him about the
half-mown lawn. With them was a Canadian flapper who was crossed
in love and took a bolshie line about everything. After inspecting the
stables, she wondered loudly why the horses were such a poor lot: 'One
would have thought that Lord Beaverbrook . . .'

At some point there was an inrush of smarties headed by the ex-Lady
Castlerosse whom I examined with interest as she had the reputation
of being a fashionable courtesan. She was slim and trim with neat
golden hair like a picture in *Vogue*, and she was wearing the perfect
outfit for a cold summer afternoon: her dress was white silk, so simple
that it could have been run up by her maid but immaculate as an arum
lily, and over it was a a cape of wolf's fur, which was the very latest
fashion from Paris. Her object in descending on us, Lord Beaverbrook
informed me later, was to enlist his aid in preventing Lord Castlerosse
from marrying again – just the sort of intrigue he enjoyed – and while
they whispered in a corner I made conversation with an elderly
playboy called Sir 'Scatters' Wilson who cracked saucy jokes and said
he'd love to know 'what Max and Valentine and you get up to in the

evening', which took me by surprise as it had not crossed my mind that two such geriatrics could get up to anything.

What we actually did after dinner was to watch films in a very nice little cinema attached to the house. The pictures were the sort which are shown at children's parties. One, if I remember rightly, was called *The Boyhood of Abraham Lincoln*, and the other, *They Had to See Paris*, was a farce with people running up and down the steps of the Eiffel Tower. Afterwards Lord Beaverbrook put us through a serious grilling. Which did we think the finer film? It was a difficult point to decide and sycophantically we reached the conclusion that they were both so excessively fine that it was impossible to choose between them.

The most enjoyable bit of the weekend were my tête-à-têtes with Lord Beaverbrook, who never ran short of gossip. He was particularly amused, I remember, because his daughter-in-law had run off with a drummer – a *der-rummer*! – though I am not sure whether he meant a bandleader or a commercial traveller. He mentioned that he was trying to make up his mind whether to take Lord Castlerosse with him to the West Indies. 'As your court jester?' I hinted. 'No, no,' he said. 'He's not funny any more. But there was a time when no duke, no king, no emperor had a finer court jester than I had in Lord Castlerosse.'

We went for a wet walk together and then we sat for two hours in his bedroom which was fitted out with anti-asthma apparatus and looked like the engine-room on a ship. He was suffering very badly from asthma. In fact he seemed so dilapidated that I reckoned that his earthly career was nearly ended. For me this session was somewhat of an ordeal as the room was asphyxiating, but I politely stuck it out.

As a further entertainment – and he was quite right, I found it fascinating – he invited me into his library while he rang up the son of Bonar Law regarding some writer who wanted access to the Bonar Law papers which were in Lord Beaverbrook's keeping. 'But Dick,' he kept saying, 'we don't know what's in them. There could be *anything*.' Dick seemed to be extraordinarily obtuse. 'But Dick, you don't understand. If it was someone like John Buchan of course I'd let him see them. But we know nothing about this man and there's only one thing written on his face. And that is *der-rink*.' Compared to my family who would hardly telephone the butcher if there was someone in the room, he seemed wonderfully indiscreet, but on reflection I realized that it was simply that he could distinguish between what mattered and what did not. When he had a blackmailing call put through to the drawing-room, he knew just what he was doing. 'Have you ever been successfully blackmailed?' I asked. 'No, no,' he growled, and then with a chuckle, 'Yes, once. Mrs . . .' (I forget her name and the story).

Once he took me for a drive in his car. It was an open sports model, bright red and very small and we bulged over the top. Lord Beaverbrook wore a black hat with a high crown like a wizard and we must have presented a curious spectacle as we proceeded in fast spurts. He owned some downs nearby, and we careered over bumpy tracks, in and out of the gorse bushes and all among the holidaymakers who were star-scattered on the grass. He probably saw himself as the lord of the manor graciously surveying his domain and when the car stalled, as it did every now and then, he would lean out and shout to the nearest courting couple, 'Having a good time?' The courting couples, far from touching their forelocks, merely gazed in silent horror at the extra-ordinary little figure with the rasping voice and the wizard's hat, probably imagining he was some sort of inspector of morals.

As a bedside book, I was given the poems of Thomas Campbell and told they were very fine. In the old days, Campbell had figured largely in school anthologies and I had learnt by heart 'Hohenlinden' and 'Ye Mariners of England' and many others, and it seemed strange to be reading them again in these very different surroundings. To be honest, I was surprised how good they seemed; their swinging rhythms and clanking rhymes were comforting in a dotty world. I saw, too, why Lord Beaverbrook liked them: among other things, Campbell was a Scot.

In the morning I delayed getting up as long as I decently could so as to make the day shorter. I was more or less dressed but had not put on my stockings when there came a knock at the door, and when it opened, instead of the housemaid to fetch my breakfast tray, there stood, like a music-hall turn, Lord Beaverbrook in jodhpurs and Lord Castlerosse in a striped bathrobe. Once again I was completely at a loss and had the feeling of acting in a play without having had even a glimpse of the script.

Blessed Monday came at last and I drove back to London with Mr Brown, MP, and I can still recall what a lovely morning it was and how cheerful and relaxed we, or at least I, felt. Naturally our main topic of conversation was our host, and after laughing at his idiosyncrasies and shaking our heads over his legendary wickedness, we agreed that we 'liked him as a cove', which perhaps meant no more than that he knew how to flatter us.

Then came the war.


Early in 1940 I met Lord Beaverbrook toddling down the street. True, he was not far from home but it seemed strange to see him by himself without henchmen and telephones. However, he was very friendly and

invited me to a large dinner party at Stornoway House where were
gathered the usual collection of politicians and journalists. This
was during the 'phoney war' and Lord Beaverbrook asked the
assembled company what the mood of the country was: negotiated
peace or fight to a finish? He obviously wanted us to agree to the
former, and though everybody managed to say something different, I
think I was the only person who said that the mood of the country was
to fight to the finish. I had been mixing with what might be called a
cross-section of *ordinary* people, at an ARP post, a Red Cross depot and
in canteens, as well as seeing my usual friends, and I had never heard
anyone suggest such a thing as a compromise. Considering the
enthusiasm with which Churchill's indomitable speeches were
subsequently received, it would appear that I was right, which prompts
the reflection that top people are often completely out of touch with
the rest of us.

I went to live in the country and Lord Beaverbrook passed out of my
life till 1957 when I got a letter from him inviting me to stay in his villa
in the south of France – I could travel out in his aeroplane.
Alternatively, would I come to lunch? Remembering the claustrophobia
of that weekend in Surrey I had no hesitation in refusing the south of
France. 'Suppose I go instead of you?' suggested my teenage daughter.
But I also remembered those exhilarating tête-à-têtes in
Stornoway House, so I put on my best clothes and went up to London
for the day.
    Lord Beaverbrook was now living at the top of a forbidding and
fortress-like block of flats, and ascending in the lift, I was jittery as
ever. He was by this time seventy-eight but he did not seem to have
aged to any noticeable degree; in fact he seemed in rather better health
than at Cherkley. With him was a lady who looked like a beautiful
foreign spy but might have been an art dealer. She soon faded away
sheepishly, and I wondered if she had been expecting lunch.
    The flat was a surprise. At Stornoway House the only noticeable
picture had been the portrait of Lady Beaverbrook, but here the walls
were covered as thickly as could be with large paintings which he had
bought for his gallery in Fredericton, and he showed me round with
justifiable pride, though not without complaints about the dishonesty
of dealers. I was too nervous to see them clearly, let alone enjoy them,
but I do remember that, railed off at the end of one of the rooms, there
was a smashing Gainsborough. Then he took me on to the roof, which
commanded a bird's-eye view of our old friend Green Park as well as a

distant prospect of a good deal of the rest of London.

Lord Beaverbrook was in his most courtly mood: 'Is your grouse done as you really like it, Lady Mary?' I felt that I had only to say the word and it would be whisked away and replaced by another, better grouse. He exerted himself to amuse me and was entirely successful. On the shelf he might be, but he had not lost his most attractive characteristic: his zest for life. Once or twice he made a gratuitous dig at the Queen – he must have found it very annoying to have no finger in the Buckingham Palace pie. And he revealed small worries: for instance, his chef was being temperamental; but I suspected that his main trouble was that most of his contemporaries were dead and that ambitious young men looked elsewhere for patronage. The constant telephone calls, formerly so imperious, were now slightly plaintive as he endeavoured to find someone with whom to spend the evening.

Time flew by and I left with regret. Next day my home circle was impressed by the arrival of a large bouquet from Interflora, and on that happy note our acquaintance closed. He lived another seven years but we did not meet again.

# The Species *Salientia*
# Lord Blake

What I write about Lord Beaverbrook is entirely off the cuff. I rely on memory, that most fallible of guides, especially as the period is between twenty and thirty years ago. It is therefore impression, not history. I first met him in the winter of 1950/51 – January, I think. He was anxious to find a biographer for his curiously incongruous hero, Andrew Bonar Law who had bequeathed to him all his political and private papers. Bonar Law had died in 1923 and the original plan had been that his youngest son, Dick (later Lord Coleraine), should write the book, but time had slipped by. He wrote a couple of chapters but by 1950 had decided that he did not wish to do it. Lord Beaverbrook's first choice was Hugh Trevor-Roper (now Lord Dacre of Glanton) who had won well-deserved *réclame* by his best-selling study, *The Last Days of Hitler*. He was a close friend and colleague of mine at Christ Church, Oxford. He decided that this was not his field of history and asked me whether he could suggest my name as an alternative. I agreed, for it sounded an interesting task.

At this stage I had never actually published anything, but I was engaged in editing the diaries of Field Marshal Earl Haig, and I had already written a long introduction – it took up some fifty pages in print – filling in the biographical and political background. I was asked to send the typescript to Lord Beaverbrook. A few days later I was met at Paddington by Tom (later Sir Thomas) Blackburn, one of the principal executives of Express Newspapers, and driven down on an icy-cold evening to Cherkley, Lord Beaverbrook's country house in Surrey near Leatherhead. The house is one of remarkable hideousness both outside and inside. It is an imitation of a French château, and the décor of the rooms in those days reminded one of the worst taste of the 1920s. The house had beautiful gardens and a splendid view, but naturally enough these were invisible on a January night at six o'clock.

My first impression of Lord Beaverbrook was how small he was. He resembled a sort of impish frog. Some years later when he allowed his portrait by Graham Sutherland to be exhibited, a critic observed that this was a generous act since it made the sitter 'look like nothing so much as a toad bottled in methylated spirits'. Frog or toad there was certainly something of the species *Salientia* about his appearance. He possessed, however, a restless vitality which was anything but toadlike, and he launched straightway into a discussion of my piece. 'I like it,' he was kind enough to say. 'It's very well written, but you're quite wrong on one point. The Asquith coalition of May 1915 had nothing to do with the shell shortage.' And he proceeded to a lengthy discourse about the timing of events, which certainly convinced me that he was right in the view that the real cause of Asquith's decision was not the alleged lack of shells on the Western Front but the resignation of Admiral Fisher, the First Sea Lord. In fact it is all in the first volume of Beaverbrook's *Politicians and the War* – a book which, I am ashamed to say, I had not read at that time.

At the end of our conversation it seemed to be understood that I would write the biography and start work as soon as I was clear of the Haig book. I was driven back to London where I had a dinner engagement, feeling somewhat bewildered and wondering just what I had let myself in for.

My next encounter with the great man is one that I can date with some precision. I was invited to lunch on 21 April that year. It was a very warm day and there was a large party which included, among others, Brendan Bracken. The food and wine as always at Cherkley were delicious – at that time Lord Beaverbrook had a Dutch chef of genius. After lunch most of the guests either departed or wandered around the garden. I remained behind sitting in the sun on the terrace with Beaverbrook and Bracken. The subject of the freedom of the press somehow came up, and the two potentates began a sort of cross-talk evidently for my benefit. Beaverbrook declared that it was essential to leave editors with complete freedom and never interfere. 'I have no idea what is going to be in the *Sunday Express* tomorrow,' he said. 'It will be as entirely fresh to me as to any of the readers.' 'I entirely agree,' Max,' said Brendan Bracken. 'I never interfere in the *Financial Times* [which he effectively controlled in those days]. The Editor must be free to make up his own mind.' And so on . . . I listened drowsily till there was the sound of the french door being opened, and the butler came out bearing a piece of ticker tape on a silver salver. Cherkley was wired to Fleet Street, rather like a London club. He went up to my host and said, 'There's a message, my lord.' Beaverbrook looked at it. It was the

news that Aneurin Bevan and Harold Wilson had resigned from
Attlee's Cabinet. The terrace had at least two telephone lines. Before I
could draw breath, Beaverbrook was telephoning instructions on the
treatment of this startling development to John Junor (now Sir John),
the Political Correspondent of the *Sunday Express*, and Bracken was
doing the same to a man called Grimes who, presumably, had a similar
role on the *Financial Times*. When they had finished – and it took
quite a time – they resumed their discussion of editorial freedom as if
nothing at all had happened.

My edition of Haig's diaries came out in autumn 1952 and caused
something of a minor sensation in France because it revealed for the
first time the very adverse opinion which Haig had had of the French
army. General Juin declared that the diaries must be *'apocryphes'*, for
Haig was a great gentleman who could not have written such stuff, and
Duff Cooper (Lord Norwich) was pressed to resign the chairmanship of
the Travellers' Club in Paris because he had reviewed the book
favourably in the *Continental Daily Mail*. Beaverbrook was far from
displeased with all this publicity. It made him feel that he had backed
the right horse. Meanwhile I had been working on the Bonar Law
papers from the time that my editorial task on Haig had finished –
from, I suppose, the spring of that year. The papers were at Cherkley
and I spent large parts of the Oxford vacations there during 1952 and
1953. I was married in the summer of 1953 and thereafter got
permission to take away some of the boxes of paper to work on them
at my house in Oxford. I continued to see Beaverbrook regularly,
but there was something to be said for not being in Cherkley all
the time.

He was a fascinating source of reminiscences, and his memory was
very good. Whenever I had occasion to check it, either with that of
others or with written documents, he was usually right. He had, of
course, lived through the very period I was writing about. He had
played, as a young Conservative MP, quite a part in the elevation of
Bonar Law to the leadership of the Conservative Party in 1911. He had
been at the heart of affairs as long as Law had been, but when Law
resigned in 1923 (to die a few months later) after one of the briefest
premierships in British history, Beaverbrook ceased to be in the centre
of events. Baldwin did not like him, and the feeling was reciprocated.
Apart from a brief flurry during the Abdication Crisis of 1936, he did
not return to the inner ring till Churchill, an old friend, became Prime
Minister in 1940. So I was listening to someone talking about the most
exciting years of his life, a millionaire Canadian adventurer who had
taken the entirely legitimate advantage of friendship with the only

Canadian-born Conservative leader in British history to move into the top circles of the political world.

Beaverbrook was intensely interested in the recent past and was himself no mean historian of the events in which he had participated. *Politicians and the War* (1928–32), *Men and Power* (1956), *The Decline and Fall of Lloyd George* (1963) will always make fascinating reading for those who are concerned with the history of political manoeuvre and intrigue. He gave me excellent advice about how to write. I remember three points. The first was never to wait till you have accumulated all the evidence, before you set pen to paper. 'You can get bored by research,' he said, 'and the subject becomes dead.' How right he was! I have passed this piece of advice on to every doctoral student who has come my way, but it is seldom taken. The second was to tell the tale in the proper chronological order and give plenty of dates, never jump forward, leap backwards or analyse thematically. This is easier to say than to do, and there are some occasions even in a biography when one simply has to depart from strict chronology. Nevertheless, as a general aim the advice is right. If it is possible to describe events in the right order, the reader will find the narrative far easier to follow. One should never forget that history is also a story.

The third point he made, which might seem to contradict the second, was that one should not, when actually writing one's book, necessarily begin at the beginning. 'Begin at the period which interests you,' he said. 'You will have to rewrite it all anyway.' The early life of Bonar Law is not very exciting and so I plunged into the battle for the leadership in 1911. I soon saw why he gave this advice. The leadership crisis was the first moment at which Beaverbrook exercised – or thought he had exercised – major political influence. He wanted to see my draft chapter and talk about it. But his advice was valid none the less. There is a lot to be said for starting to write a biography with a chapter on the period which seems the most interesting and stimulating. It can give that 'take-off' which every historian needs, and he was quite right to say that everything has to be rewritten.

Beaverbrook was a great acquirer of historical papers. Those of Bonar Law had come to him by inheritance, but he bought many others. The Lloyd George papers were among the most important, and while I was engaged on Bonar Law, the late Frank Owen was busy on Lloyd George. I was not encouraged to meet him. Beaverbrook liked to deal separately with the historians on whom he conferred his patronage, and since he was certain to find out any transgression of this unexpressed rule, I made no attempt to talk to Owen, nor did he to me. His biography of Lloyd George has been underrated. It is often slapdash and inaccurate but it has vitality and vigour, and it conveys more successfully than most books the extraordinary personality of one of the greatest prime ministers of the twentieth century. However Mr A. J. P. Taylor's criticism that it only 'scratched the surface of the vast Lloyd George material' is quite right.

Beaverbrook was disappointed with it. He was also, though for different reasons, disappointed with my book, *The Unknown Prime Minister*, which appeared in October 1955. He hoped for a more dramatic picture of his old friend, but in fact Bonar Law was not a dramatic figure and Beaverbrook himself had failed to depict him as such in *Politicians and the War*. If he could not it was unlikely that I could. Anyway it would not have been true. Then there was the great row about whether Asquith kept Law, who had come out on urgent political business, waiting at his country house on that Whitsun Bank Holiday morning in 1916 while he finished a rubber of bridge with three ladies. This was what Beaverbrook told me Law had told him, and I put it in the book. Beaverbrook had had the proofs and made no objection. The Asquith family was convulsed. Lady Violet Bonham-Carter wrote a furious letter in *The Times*, and the ensuing correspondence occupied 112 inches of column space. Beaverbrook did not want to be drawn in. He advised me not to reply, and was annoyed when I did. Eventually he wrote a letter which effectively torpedoed Lady Violet and ended the correspondence. But he did not thank me for obliging him to do so. I was now definitely out of favour. However, this is the risk one runs in dealing with such a mercurial character. It had all been great fun while it lasted, and I will never cease to be grateful to him for the opportunities which he gave me.

# The Lovable Degenerate
# Lady Diana Cooper

When asked what I felt and still feel about Lord Beaverbrook, the answer is I loved him most dearly. I met him under the wing of a humorous friend called Claude Lowther, who was the owner of a magnificent ruin called Hurstmonceux. Sir Herbert Beerbohm Tree was there as a guest and said to the tourists who came for architectural culture in the afternoon: 'Pick all the flowers you like for your homes.' To which Claude Lowther parried: 'And when in London you'll all get free tickets at His Majesty's Theatre.'

Max Aitken was older than me, yet younger than most adults, but already bitter tongues were against him. I and my friends found him delightful, witty and unique.

Later came the First World War and to our surprise Max became an Olympian of our humble circle, all important, deeply involved in the press and politics. But he was always ready to talk of his early youth and his clerical father who had left his homeland for Canada, and of his Calvinist upbringing. I remember his recitation of one of his childhood's hymns:

> I know that God is wrath with me
> For I was born in sin.
> My heart is so exceeding vile
> Damnation dwells therein.
> Awake I sin, asleep I sin,
> I sin with every breath.
> When Adam fell
> He went to Hell
> And damned us all to death.

'Beautiful, isn't it?' he always added.


Life and the war took their cruel course. Came the happy day when I got married, and Max gave me a grand Rover car and we often stayed in his house at Leatherhead, Cherkley, and all the notables were there. And if they were not, Albert the butler was told to ring up Lloyd George and tell him to come round as soon as possible, and round he came.

All his lady friends – and, alas, there were too many – got £100 on his birthday and he would take these ladies and their lady's maids on trips as far as Buenos Aires or Berlin, in overwhelming luxury.


Came an awful day when my husband was fighting him over the St George's division of Westminster. The opponent was a man of straw put up by the *Daily Mail* and the *Daily Express*. My mother and Lady Cunard used to grace the opponent's meetings carrying the *Daily Telegraph* and, whenever either Lord was mentioned, would cry in unison 'Degenerates, they are both degenerates!' Duff won, but in doing so made some small 'bloomer'. Max's fondness for me caused him to call his *Express* Editor and tell him to suppress the gaffe. 'Mr —, do you love your wife?'

'Yes, Lord Beaverbrook.'

'Well, I love Lady Diana Cooper, so leave the passage out.'

I loved Max to his end and miss him with all my heart.

# The Evil Adventurer
# Cecil King

I came into Fleet Street in 1922. At that time the *Daily Mail* was, by a long way, the leading popular newspaper but Northcliffe, its creator and its real Editor, had died a few weeks earlier. It was now edited by Tom Marlow, who had been the titular Editor for many years. He had no ideas beyond continuing to churn out Northcliffe's *Daily Mail* but deprived of Northcliffe's vitality and flair. I was in the *Daily Mail* office at that time and remember hearing that Marlow had admonished one of his reporters, saying, 'Young man, don't you realize the *Daily Mail* is read in Park Lane!' The *Daily Mirror* had had the world's biggest sale in 1917 but by this time was in decline.

The *Daily Express*, founded by Pearson in 1900, had been bought when in very low water by Max Aitken, a young Canadian. He had made a large fortune in Canada by methods severely criticized by Canadians, but had made an impact on political London by winning an unpromising by-election for the Conservatives. He had had no training in journalism, but proved to be a born editor. He made no attempt to copy the *Daily Mail*, but created a new paper unlike its competitors. I seem to remember that he concentrated on excellent sport and well-informed gossip. Politically he was all for the Empire, but the most enduring quality of his newspaper was its optimism. However depressing the news, the *Daily Express* would find a bright side. I think it was this that caused him to print the headline 'There will be no war this year or next' three weeks before the outbreak of the Second World War. The paper was a kind of morning cocktail buoyed up by Beaverbrook's overflowing vitality. The news in his paper was not reliable and the opinions expressed in its leaders were often absurd, but that didn't matter, it didn't affect the escapist world into which *Express* readers were introduced.

I remember years later someone saying that articles on holidays in the *Express* told its readers how to arrange them on the Riviera while the *Mirror* told them how to make the most of their holidays at Clacton. *Daily Mirror* readers *were* going to Clacton or its equivalent, *Daily Express* readers were *not* going to the Riviera – it was just something to dream about.

I don't think Beaverbrook's newspapers ever had any political influence. They reflected the whims and intrigues of the proprietor, not the aspirations and interests of the readers. His influence in politics was personal, obtained by the lavish use of his money and by personal contact. He obtained the *Evening Standard* when the *Daily Express* was well established and he founded the *Sunday Express*, a highly successful paper to this day, edited for long years by John Gordon, a hypocrite nauseating even by Fleet Street standards. The *Evening Standard* came to Beaverbrook by way of commission on a deal he negotiated, selling the dying Hulton's newspapers to Rothermere. It was never a financial success as it sought to be the evening newspaper for the West End of London, not for the metropolis as a whole. But it was useful for planting stories – true or untrue – that suited Beaverbrook's purposes at that time.

Beaverbrook's arrival in the top political echelon came with his association with Bonar Law, a dull Canadian who became the compromise leader of the Conservative Party in 1911 and briefly Prime Minister in 1922. Like Beaverbrook, he too was born in New Brunswick. It was this association that got Beaverbrook a peerage in 1917 – a step up which Beaverbrook regarded as the greatest blunder of his life.

In spite of this, he had moments of aspiring to the prime ministership during the Second World War, but it never seemed to me that he had the slightest chance, with or without a peerage. His strength was in backstairs intrigue. His main political plank was Empire Free Trade – a policy which sounded good but was quite bogus. His association with Churchill really dated from the thirties when Churchill, who never attempted to limit his expenditure to his income, was short of money. This was supplied, at any rate to some extent, by Beaverbrook, Rothermere and, no doubt, others.

As the 1920s merged into the thirties, the *Express* asserted its supremacy as the top-seller of the popular newspapers. The *Mirror* appeared to be on its way to the cemetery and the *Daily Mail* made the fatal mistake of copying the *Express* instead of pursuing what is now the *Daily Telegraph* readership. The *News Chronicle* and the *Daily Herald* were so dull that they appealed only to those who had similar political views. And so to the *Daily Mirror* revolution of 1934. It was extremely fortunate that the rival newspapers treated the *Mirror* with derision until it was too late, while my uncle, Rothermere, told me the new *Mirror* would land me in jail.

I suppose it was in 1938 that I was invited to dine with Joseph Kennedy, then the US Ambassador in London. Signing the visitors' book with me was Beaverbrook, whom I had not seen before. He said to me, 'Well, young man, you have made your impact on Fleet Street' – or words to that effect. I remember this episode because I had not thought of myself in that light.

The next time I met Beaverbrook face to face was after the last war, perhaps in 1952. I was on a boat going to New York. It soon appeared that one of the other passengers was Lord Beaverbrook. We often met as we walked about the ship, but Beaverbrook never showed the slightest sign of recognition though he must have known by that time who I was. However, as we neared the American coast I had a note from Beaverbrook to say that he had heard I was on board and would do himself the pleasure of calling on me in my cabin. This seemed to me a preposterous idea, so I shot back a note to say that I wouldn't hear of his calling on me, but I would call on him at the hour mentioned in his note. I did so and we exchanged some polite conversation, in the course of which he invited me to dine with him in his hotel that evening. When I got there I found that we were a party of three, Beaverbrook, myself and Ben Smith, famous in 1930 as the 'Wolf of Wall Street' and later responsible for financing Garfield Weston's entry into the British market. In the course of the dinner Ben Smith suggested that we should vote for Eisenhower in the presidential election, which was to take place next day. He said he was a power in the Democratic Party and that it would be quite easy to arrange for us to vote. I declined, pointing out that, if I was photographed coming out of a polling booth, I should never hear the end of it. Ben Smith thought it would make a good story when I got home to be able to boast that I had actually voted in an American presidential election. Afterwards I wondered if Beaverbrook would have arranged for a photographer to be present if I had been foolish enough to accept the invitation.

To meet, Beaverbrook was a hideous little man with a curious face that seemed wider than it was long. I found it hard to believe that anyone could find him attractive, his money apart. But I came to the conclusion that most people are pretty limp and here was a man who exuded vitality, and made them feel more alive than usual. I have plenty of vitality of my own – though of a very different kind – and had no need of any boost Beaverbrook might have given me. Another facet of Beaverbrook's character which was important was that he was essentially an adventurer. Brendan Bracken was an adventurer, pure and simple: Beaverbrook was the same but also a man of far greater ability than Bracken. This adventurer element was what, I think, appealed to Churchill who, in his early years, was himself something of one also.

Looking back over the inter-war years it has seemed to me that the four outstanding personalities in British public life were Lloyd George, Churchill, Birkenhead and Beaverbrook. Though Beaverbrook operated in a more restricted area than the two Prime Ministers, he had a more pervasive influence – perhaps for that reason. But his influence was destructive and, in my view, evil. I do not mean by that adjective that his sexual morals were not those supported by his newspapers, nor am I referring to the means by which he may have amassed his fortune. The common or garden sins of mankind are due primarily to weakness of character, but to be evil implies to me that there was a positive, active intent. In his newspapers he favoured disorder rather than order, he seemed to take pleasure in humiliating and corrupting his young men, preventing them from breaking loose by absurdly over-paying them. On one occasion, for instance, he interviewed his staff while sitting on the lavatory seat. A conspicuous example of corruption was the fate of Frank Owen, one of the two or three most promising young MPs of his day.

Beaverbrook was also given to vendettas conducted through the columns of his newspapers. The best known of these was his campaign against Mountbatten. In the course of a film about the navy that came out during the last war, the front page of the *Daily Express* with the headline saying there would be no war this year or next was photographed floating about in the sea. This incident was not introduced by Mountbatten who had no responsibility of any kind for it. But Beaverbrook decided it was an act of malice by Mountbatten and sniped at him on any possible occasion for years and years. Esmond Rothermere told me that he was with Beaverbrook on one occasion when Beaverbrook held forth at length on the inadequacies of his son Max – and Max was the third man present. Towards the end of the war I was talking to Stafford Cripps and Beaverbrook's name cropped up – at the time they were in the same Cabinet or had recently been so – and I was interested to see Cripps positively shuddering as he mentioned Beaverbrook's name.

For seven years I was chairman of the Newspaper Publishers Association and for many years before that had been a member of the council, representing my newspapers. The perennial problem before the London newspaper publishers was uneconomically high wages and massive over-manning. As the print unions always acted together, the only way the proprietors could hope to stand up to them was to stand together also. But whatever pledges were made or undertakings signed, when the crunch came it was the *Express* that broke the united front. At an earlier stage in the history of the *Express*, Beaverbrook calculated that he could afford to meet the extravagant demands of the unions while his rivals could not, but of course in the end the *Express* finances were as embarrassed as everyone else's. It is amusing watching the struggles of *The Times*'s management whose problems stem from when they usually supported the *Express* in acceding to ruinous wage demands.

I bore no ill will towards Beaverbrook. The only ground on which we met was the popular press and my *Mirror* thrashed his *Express*. From my point of view, Beaverbrook's claim to fame lies in the fact that he was the first evil man to figure in British public life for a very long time.

# 'Billikens'
# Barbara Cartland

Lady Diana Cooper once described Lord Beaverbrook as 'a strange, attractive gnome with the odour of genius about him'. To me, he exuded the unmistakable vitality of success which seemed to vibrate in the air around him.

In 1923 I was trying to write a novel in between dancing all night. At a party I met a young reporter on the *Daily Express* who suggested I should contribute to the gossip column which had become an important feature on the paper. He said he would pay me five shillings a paragraph, which was to me a lot of money and I felt I was rich!

After I had written for the *Daily Express* for a few months and also contributed several articles which brought me in two or three guineas a time, the telephone rang and I was told that Lord Beaverbrook would like to see me. A car was sent for me to go to a small, unimpressive house called the Vineyards near Hurlingham.

I thought when I first saw him that he looked like a lucky talisman we had carried in the war – the God of Good Luck – called 'Billikens'. He was certainly very lucky for me for he taught me how to write, and I believe it is entirely due to him that I have been so successful with my books and the thousands of articles I have done over the years.

Max was fascinating because he seemed omnipotent, enigmatic, and had a strange dynamic vitality which was mesmeric, but he was human with many frailties.

No one had been impressed when he bought the *Daily Express* at the end of the war for the sum of £17,500. In fact, his friends told him that he had wasted his money, and any more that he poured into the newspaper would be 'buried in Fleet Street'. But the *Daily Express* fully expressed the ebullient, relentless, mission-laden personality of its owner, and it became the most widely read daily newspaper in the world.

Max was forty-four when I met him, and although it took me time to discover it, he was passing through a particularly difficult and unhappy period in his life.

Bonar Law, 'the unknown Prime Minister' to whom he had been private secretary and whom he had loved, had died, and Max said to me once, almost savagely: 'Do you know what it's like to watch someone you know dying slowly, day by day, to know that you cannot help them, that you can do nothing for them? Have you any idea what it's like to sit there wanting to give them a part of yourself, a part of your life, some of the years you still have to live, and knowing you are helpless?'

Another time he said to me of Bonar Law: 'He would have been the greatest Prime Minister we've ever had, but – he died in my arms.'

I didn't know then how Bonar Law had once tried to take his own life when he had retired to the south of France. It was before he knew he had cancer of the throat and he sent for Max, or rather he told him what he had tried to do, and Max abandoned everything to go to his friend, but was still powerless to help him: 'I watched a man die!'

He was to say it over and over again because it had happened just a few months before I came into his life.

Years later when I wrote the story of Metternich the great Austrian statesman, who all his life had searched for the ecstasy he had felt in his first love affair, I thought of Max. The two men were totally unlike each other in every way, except they both had the same magnetic power and both searched for a perfect, ideal love they knew once.

Max, I am convinced, measured all men he met by what he had felt for Bonar Law. When sometimes he believed in them for a short while and they failed him, he hated them because they had revived within him the hope that he would once again love and trust a man who would become, for him, another hero.

But Max was too vital a person to spend his life looking back into the past.

He never told me what an important part he had played in politics or about the magnificent job he performed in war propaganda for the Canadian forces. One tribute to his success in comparison to other propandists was shown in the *Punch* cartoon of someone asking a British Tommy: 'Why do we never hear what you are doing?'

'Oh, I only appear on the casualty lists,' was the answer.

Max had stood as a Parliamentary candidate for Ashton-under-Lyne – a Manchester seat. He was a stranger to England and he had only ten days to win the seat. His opponent was a local man. Max got in with a majority of 196.

His new triumph, however, seemed at first a cul-de-sac. He was not liked in the House of Commons. Like other great reporters, he was too dynamic for that mellow complacent atmosphere.

Max learnt to speak, he studied politics and politicians, he studied England and the English with his perceptive, superhuman concentration. By 1923 he became a power but he never tried to popularize himself. He was content to pull the strings with others gaining the acclamations. He was always looking forward, trying out the new, attempting to change the traditional and the conventional in both big things and small.

Just before I met him he employed craftsmen who were making new designs in furniture for him. With his money he could have bought the most fabulous treasures in the world, but instead he encouraged a few obscure workmen to create for him something no one else possessed.

When I met him, he had suddenly come to the decision that he should know more about music. As the Vineyards was very small, the musicians who played oboes, harps, cellos and violins were usually forced to do so in the garden. Although they did their best, the conversation was usually so interesting that nobody listened to the poor players.

I remember a night when a Russian choir had arrived in England to be met at Southampton and rushed by car to the Vineyards to sing for a dinner party of eight. As they stepped into the dining-room, Max, in one of his most puckish moods, had a film of Russian life taken immediately after the Revolution thrown on to the wall behind his chair. It was a propaganda film and there were various horrifying close-up shots of children crawling with lice and dying of starvation.

The Russians, who could not speak English, were stunned, and Lord Birkenhead whispered to me: 'We'll all get a knife in our back at any moment!'

As is inevitable with anyone as vital as Max, people disparaged his arrogance, his impetuosity, his ruthlessness, his impatience, his intolerance and his habit, which increased as he grew older, of sucking a person dry, like an orange, and then chucking him aside. But his perceptive, painstaking mind was always looking towards new horizons.

His worst fault was that, to those he disliked, he was vindictive to the point of absurdity. The two men he tried to destroy for no apparent reason were Anthony Eden and Lord Mountbatten. He used all his power as a Press Baron against them; his newspapers were instructed to attack and disparage them continually.

Later Max was polished in a great many ways by the Honourable

Mrs Richard Norton who was one of the great beauties of the twenties, and who really loved him. But in 1924 he let his valet buy him clothes at Harrods – rather badly fitting, nondescript navy-blue suits – and his shoes, bought in the same way, had thick soles.

He was also at the time indifferent to food and wine, though he changed over the years. His two great friends, Lord Birkenhead and Winston Churchill, were always complaining: 'Where did you get this claret, Max?'

'The grocer's, I think.'

'It tastes like it!'

As a boy, Max had been horribly teased about his looks until, while playing with the idea that everything around him should be beautiful, he was not interested in himself. Yet he said to me: 'A man wants to spread his tail like a peacock!'

He had been deprived of love in his childhood, and I think what he remembered most was wanting to escape, of being ashamed of being so poor, although later he used to boast about it.

One thing he told me, which was very revealing, was about a big dance which was held in Newcastle, New Brunswick. Max, young, ambitious and studying law, wanted to be present. He was told by a friend that, as a law student, he would get an invitation.

He hired a tail-coat, white shirt and tie and waited, and he told me how finally he had contacted his friend and complained that he had not yet received the precious card which would admit him.

'I'm sorry,' his friend had replied, 'you can't go after all. They have learned that in the past you sold newspapers in the streets. We cannot have newsboys at this assembly.'

I knew by his voice how much it had hurt him.

'What did you do?' I asked.

'I went home,' Max replied, 'and put on that dress-suit. I stood in front of a mirror. I looked at my reflection and I said to myself: 'The day will come when they'll be glad to ask me to their goddamned assembly!'

That was the secret!

When Max was made Minister of Supply in 1941, Lord Privy Seal, Lend-Lease Administrator to the USA, and Chancellor of the University of New Brunswick in 1947, he was still showing that 'goddamned assembly' exactly what they had missed.

# 'The Old Bastard'
# David Farrer

My introduction to Lord Beaverbrook came through that best of all gossip columnists, the first William Hickey, alias Tom Driberg.

'Would you like a job with Beaverbrook?'

'Good God, no.'

'It might be amusing.'

'You know what I feel about the old bastard!'

Tom persisted. 'He's looking for an Oxford graduate to be his social secretary.'

'I can think of nothing more ghastly.'

But Tom would not be gainsaid. 'At least go and see him. It'll be fun.'

So I yielded. An appointment was arranged, with the man my parents regarded as the arch-enemy of the middle classes – and a bore at that. I went out of curiosity, with no intention of accepting any job.

And then everything changed. At my first meeting with him, I felt the magnetism of his personality, and before the interview was over, I had received my first dose of his extraordinary power to charm when charm was the order of the day.

'Did that fellow Driberg tell you about the job?'

'That I would be your social secretary, arrange your dinner parties, that sort of thing.'

He grinned impishly. 'Dinner parties when there is a war on?'

'Then what *am* I supposed to do?'

'I want a *political* secretary.'

With those words he had me hooked. Exciting vistas opened; inwardly I turned from a surly watch-dog guarding my supposed principles into a puppy eagerly watching a bone. I also accepted the job.

But at what salary? When I got home I rang up Driberg. He was ill. 'Please, it's very urgent.'

Tom came reluctantly to the phone.

'Tom, how much salary should I ask?'

'Goddamn it, Beaverbrook's just asked me how much he should offer.'

The result was to me highly satisfactory. He was, so far as I was concerned, a generous employer.

The next six-and-a-half years were the most exciting of my life. You could say many opprobrious things about Max Beaverbrook, but you could never call him dull. I lived with him through his heyday. Anecdotes abound. To one man, he paid the utmost attention: my senior secretary, George Malcolm Thomson. On one occasion I fell ill with water on the knee. Beaverbrook wrote:

Dear Farrer,

    I am so sorry to hear that you have water on the knee.

    I am just as sorry to say that I have water on the eye.

    And I hope that you will soon be well enough to come back and help poor Thomson who cannot keep his water in the right place.

Then there was his valet, the inimitable Nockels, whom he inherited from Princess Arthur of Connaught, and of whom Beaverbrook was somewhat in awe. Nockels lost no opportunity of reminding his employer of his pedigree. On one occasion, as we drove to London in the Blitz, the car's windows were blown out, together with Beaverbrook's private papers. 'Nockels,' screamed Beaverbrook, 'get them quick.' 'My Lord, I am not a Spitfire.' But he collected the papers.

In my first six weeks with Beaverbrook, it was plain sailing, but the storm clouds were gathering. They broke in the first week in May. The Chamberlain government was tottering; the cry 'Churchill for Prime Minister' was loud in the land. Churchill consulted Beaverbrook, who gave him the advice 'Say nothing.' It was wise counsel, but then hell broke loose. Churchill wanted Beaverbrook in his government. Beaverbrook screamed blue murder. 'Never, never,' and every time he screamed, Thomson and I grew more certain that the real answer was yes. And so it turned out, and the Ministry of Aircraft Production was born. It was a stormy birth, launched in Beaverbrook's large mansion, Stornoway House, facing Green Park. He quarrelled with the Civil Servants from the Air Ministry who were foisted on him, he promoted business friends, and out of it all emerged a team that was to win the Battle of Britain.

My part in all this was minimal. I drafted answers to his enormous mail, while Thomson dealt with the most important letters. There was a rule that my letters had a little 'f' at the top, and his bore the signal 'T'. On one occasion the Master pressed my bell. I had gone home; Thomson deputized. 'Where,' demanded Beaverbrook, 'is little "f"?' The answer came pat. 'F's f—ed off.' The Minister's full council, including Beaverbrook, rocked with laughter.

The Battle of Britain was won in the British skies in September 1940, and its chief architect was Beaverbrook. Almost at once began his series of resignation letters, fourteen of them before the end of the year. They were ignored and I think he meant it thus. But then Churchill stopped turning the other cheek. The fifteenth letter was accepted and Beaverbrook was sent off to America on an ill-defined and unofficial mission vaguely concerned with oil. The argosy set forth – Beaverbrook, Nockels and myself – ending up in due course at a seaside resort in Georgia, good for the Master's asthma. He was acutely aware that he was sailing under false colours. Then came a summons from Roosevelt in Washington. I was told to book seats on the Atlantic Express from Jacksonville.

'Sorry, no seats.'

'I'm speaking for Lord Beaverbrook.'

'It can be arranged.'

So we duly presented ourselves at a wayside station, only to be greeted by a very long train crammed with serving troops – and at the end a totally empty coach, into which we were ushered. Somehow Nockels bundled 'the Lord' into his sleeper without his noticing, settled him down and then rushed up and down making the noises of people taking their seats. It worked, and worked again next morning. We kept him in bed just long enough. He never knew. If he had, we would have been sacked.

The purpose of the Washington visit was twofold. The other reason was to connive with Roosevelt – these two disparate men had a deep mutual respect for each other. The connivance was over the speech Beaverbrook was to make at a banquet to be given in his honour by the Newspaper Proprietors Association of America. The subject was 'The Second Front'.

I had been working hard at this speech. I'd produced what I thought was a rather splendid peroration: 'Nor shall the sword sleep in my hand.' At the last moment this was omitted: 'They'll give me a lot to drink and I shall end up: "Nor shall the shord shleep in my hand."'

The speech created a sensation newswise, but did not alter the course of history one iota. The Second Front was not on and I think he knew it. He had a love for lost causes.

The evening, however, had its aftermath. Nockels grew weary of looking after the Beaverbrook cronies who had been asked to listen to the speech in Beaverbrook's suite. He retired to bed. His master was furious and when he returned to his suite there was a blazing row. But shortly afterwards the two men faced each other in their pyjamas. Beaverbrook handed over a note: 'I could not possibly manage without your help. The simple fact is that I have a great affection for you, and will never think you rude or rough.' Beaverbrook at his best. He couldn't do without Nockels and he knew it.

He couldn't do without Churchill either, but Churchill did not lightly forgive the 'Second Front' treachery. Beaverbrook returned to England in the doghouse. His great days were over, never politically to return. The dream of high office – perhaps even the highest – vanished into limbo. No office awaited him on his return to London. He returned to semi-retirement as a power in the land still, but from a distance, from his mansion in the country, Cherkley, from which he pontificated as a Press Baron, urging for a Second Front. I remember a particularly effective entreaty from the town hall (I think) in Birmingham.

And then suddenly the music changed. One day he turned to me – we were driving from Cherkley to London – and said 'Farrer, Churchill has been a great Prime Minister. He saved the country. But now he should go, he's outlived his usefulness. What we want now is a Prime Minister who can make peace.' I made some sort of protestation, and he dropped the subject. But what did this remarkable pronouncement portend? Had the great supporter of the Second Front – 'Strike out, strike now' – suddenly reverted to the old pre-war appeaser? Or was he again wearing the phantom crown? Was *he* the man who would lead the country safely on the paths of peace? Or was it just the random utterance of a man whose every nerve tingled with frustration? His mind was never easy to read. Perhaps at that time he really was indulging in a pipedream. In any case I did not need to worry, for I knew by then that, at a word from Churchill, the dream would vanish and 'like an insubstantial pageant faded, leave not a wrack behind'.

The winter of Lord Beaverbrook's discontent seemed to drag endlessly on. But if winter comes, can spring be far behind? It came suddenly. We were told that Churchill had offered him 'a glass of brandy and a job'. He was to be Leader of the House of Lords. But nothing of the sort. Instead Churchill took Beaverbrook with him on an ill-defined visit to Washington. I was to go with him.

So far as he could, Beaverbrook kept out of both Churchill's and Roosevelt's way during this Washington parley. He felt, and was, a fish out of water. His first experience of playing this role landed him, however, with an enormous snub. On the first weekend he got an invitation from the President to join him and Churchill for the weekend. It fell to me to ring Harry Hopkins refusing the invitation. Back came the reply: 'Tell Lord Beaverbrook that the President is not accustomed to having his invitations refused'. Queen Victoria could not have been more regal. Beaverbrook went.

But there was a happier sequel. Churchill went home, leaving Beaverbrook behind, probably not knowing what to do with him 'and he needs a rest'. Beaverbrook spent the weekend with Roosevelt. As they boarded the presidential train, the President gave a sigh of relief. 'Now there's no Winston to interrupt I can get busy with my stamp album.'

But when Beaverbrook returned from his 'rest', nothing happened. Summer merged with autumn ... and then suddenly in October he was appointed Lord Privy Seal, but without a seat in the Cabinet. He was a lion with his teeth at least partly drawn, but a valuable ally in time of need.

As Lord Privy Seal he was summoned, with me in attendance, to hold the Great Man's hand when Churchill was convalescing in the Villa Taylor at Marrakesh from an illness that very nearly laid him low. On the eve of his recovery and departure, the French military attaché gave a painful farewell party. Beaverbrook arrived late. An animated group, led by Lady Diana Cooper, whose husband, Duff, was our ambassador to de Gaulle, was busily gossiping in French. Beaverbrook hovered uneasily; it was obvious he had no French. Lady Diana beckoned him forward, and it became clear that everyone spoke fluent English. The situation was saved. The next morning Beaverbrook said to me: 'Tell me, Farrer, how long would it take a man of my age to learn French?'

Back at Beaverbrook's new office, the stately Gwdyre House in Whitehall, there were alarums and excursions, but we were a backwater. Officially Beaverbrook was allotted the problem of international civil aviation, much of which depended on the vexed question of something called 'cabotage'. What cabotage really meant was never clear, or at least not clear to Beaverbrook, but it seemed to threaten British interests, so in the House of Lords he attacked it vigorously. Cabotage, he exclaimed in rich Canadian accents, must be fought tooth and nail. But 'cabotage' came out as 'sabotage' and, ear-trumpets raised to the charge, elderly peers exclaimed: 'Sabotage! Disgraceful! Shame!'

During the waning years of his ministerial career, Beaverbrook remained close to Churchill but, it must be confessed, of little consequence in Cabinet. He did, however, have access to the secret telephone known as 'the green line'. Over this, one afternoon Churchill and Beaverbrook conducted a hilarious dialogue listened to shamelessly by their private secretaries.

That morning, in the earlier editions of the *Evening Standard*, there had appeared a cartoon by Low which was highly unflattering to the Prime Minister. Beaverbrook was nervous and felt guiltily responsible – unnecessarily, since he had not been shown it in advance, and after all he was always telling fellow ministers that he never interfered with his newspapers. But still, on that same morning, unknown to him, Churchill had received a particularly insulting cable from Stalin. About three o'clock in the afternoon, one of Churchill's private secretaries came on the phone.

'Is your master in?'

'Yes, just back from lunch.'

'The Prime Minister wants to speak with him. Will you scramble?'

I pressed the button, and I am afraid remained with my ear glued to the receiver. The following conversation then took place:

CHURCHILL (in rich post-prandial voice): Max, that fellow Uncle Joe . . .

BEAVERBROOK (on tenterhooks and mishearing): Don't worry, Prime Minister, don't worry.

CHURCHILL: What are we going to do about him? He's sent me . . .

BEAVERBROOK (interrupting): Don't worry, I'll sack him tomorrow morning.

CHURCHILL: What are you saying?

BEAVERBROOK: I'll sack him. He shall never appear in my newspapers again.

CHURCHILL: What are you talking about? I said Uncle Joe.

BEAVERBROOK (after a pregnant pause, flatly): Oh.

D-Day came and, with great reluctance, Beaverbrook joined Churchill's caretaker government. In the ensuing election, his advice was usually wrong and his interventions unfailingly ill chosen. Many a Tory candidate had come to regard him as 'mad, bad and dangerous to know', particularly Brendan Bracken, whom he proclaimed before a huge audience to be 'the greatest First Lord of the Admiralty since Nelson'. Unfortunately Nelson had never been First Lord of the Admiralty.

With the Labour victory in July 1945, Beaverbrook's active political life came to an end, and fifteen months later I resigned as his secretary. Now Beaverbrook was not accustomed to employees leaving him, but so far as I was concerned he treated me with the utmost kindness. In fact, after I had outlined my future plans, he picked up his receiver and said to his General Manager, 'Mr Robertson, Mr Farrer is joining and investing in the firm of Secker & Warburg. I want my newspapers to give that firm all the backing and assistance they can.' And they did. Is it strange that I retain a deep affection for the most remarkable man I have ever worked for?

# The Characteristic Mixture
# Sir George Middleton

From Pearl Harbor until the end of hostilities in the last war, the problems of petroleum supplies to the various theatres of war were becoming more and more complex and often acrimonious. The needs of Europe, civilian as well as military, competed with those of the Far East. The Americans and British had different priorities. The British wanted as much 'sterling' oil (Iran, Iraq, Trinidad) as possible, but almost all the available transport was US-controlled 'dollar' tankerage. The services vied among themselves. National loyalties conflicted, while the military and civilian authorities seldom saw eye to eye. Finally the major oil companies were pursuing their own individual interests and jockeying for position in the post-war world. Some kind of ground rules had to be established.

It was felt that wartime co-operation at all levels was a reasonable basis on which to build and that talks should be held in Washington. Into this highly charged, and indeed Byzantine atmosphere, there arrived as the British delegate, Lord Beaverbrook, the champion of free trade and imperial preference. It must have been a situation after his crusading and mischievous heart.

The UK petroleum representative at the Washington embassy was the immensely experienced Sir Harold ('Tim') Wilkinson, on loan from Shell. For the proposed talks I was detailed to be general factotum to look after Lord Beaverbrook's comforts. Telegrams then started to fly and the first request was for an adequate supply of an acceptable brand of French champagne. No easy thing in those days and the best that Lord Halifax's cellars could provide was angrily turned down as undrinkable.

The question of secure communications then arose, secure not from the outside world but from other sections of the embassy and from other departments in London. Not even the embassy cypher staff was regarded as suitable and Lord Beaverbrook said he would have to deal with the problem personally on arrival. Cars, secretaries and office accommodation were all needed on an exclusive, instant and top-level basis. Lord Halifax was fairly Olympian about it all. The lower ranks were full of foreboding.

Lord Beaverbrook, when he arrived, was, I believe, his characteristic mixture of charm, hustle, egotism, suspicion and persuasiveness. I think he must have got the remaining best of the champagne. He arranged lines of communication through the US Navy Department, the combined Chiefs of Staff, the embassy, the Military Mission and probably several others. He could then send simultaneous and contradictory accounts of meetings. From Tim Wilkinson's office came the sounds from behind closed doors of explosive discussion, noisy argument and what sounded like violent, if unarmed, combat. Tim, I seem to recall, resigned several times a day.

Throughout this, it was not too difficult to deduce that Lord Beaverbrook's mission, in his own eyes, was to ensure that there should be no agreement, and indeed he succeeded in sowing sufficient mutual distrust to ensure this. But at the end of each day the magnetism somehow worked, exhausted smiles appeared and he could make everyone believe that something useful had been achieved. Only Lord Halifax remained totally unconvinced. He must have seen the mission as being deliberately made to fail. He is said to have remarked at the end of it that 'as long as I am here I shall see to it that Max never, never, comes back to Washington in any capacity'.

On his return to the United Kingdom, Lord Beaverbrook spoke against the proposed agreement in the House of Lords. It was never ratified in the United States, and died of inanition in about 1947.

# The Tougher Man
# Derek Dempster

It said in the note: 'Mr Dempster. BOAC were late getting my newspapers to me today. Find out why and if they're at fault, give them hell.'

There was no signature; nor any indication whence it came. And because it was a carbon copy on white flimsy paper torn into a ragged strip about two inches wide, I was tempted to take it as a hoax – some kind of initiation for a new boy, which I was in the autumn of 1952, when I joined the *Daily Express* as Air Correspondent.

Basil Cardew, the Motoring Correspondent, whose desk faced mine, quickly disabused me. 'You'll get one of those from time to time,' he said, 'usually when the Beaver's in Cap Ferrat or Nassau, and he's narked about something. He's in Nassau at the moment.'

Freddie Gillman, BOAC's Director of Public Relations, was quick to get me an answer. The Nassau-bound Stratocruiser carrying the Beaver's papers had been diverted because of engine trouble. I was able to cancel my booking for BOAC's hot seat in hell.

Having read Orwell's *1984*, the directive kindled a feeling that here was Big Brother in person, waggling his tentacles at me, right across the Atlantic. At the same time, it intensified the excitement I felt at being one of Arthur Christiansen's tautly managed team – Arthur Christiansen, the Editor, my Boss, and the Lord God Beaverbrook's ambassador on Earth.

The Beaver never contacted me directly again. But I was not forgotten.

In the summer of 1953, France was on the brink of civil war. The Beaver was at Cap Ferrat and, although he did not want to leave, it was clear that he would have to if the shooting started and all public services, especially the telephone, stopped. Indeed, Christiansen said he would have to be rescued, and within hours of assigning us to the job, Basil Cardew and I were speeding across France in Basil's pale blue Jaguar.

It was a brand-new Mk VII. Actually, the model itself was so new and coveted that it was still turning heads. Its image was absolutely right for the sort of Pimpernel mission we had been sent on. As we closed on Paris, where we were to pick up further instructions, I already had a mental picture of the front page that would tell the story:

BEAVERBROOK IN DARING RESCUE

'Lord Beaverbrook was plucked yesterday from his Mediterranean-pine-fringed home at Cap Ferrat, on war-torn France's famous Côte d'Azur, in a rescue almost as daring in concept and execution as the abduction of deposed Italian dictator, Benito Mussolini, by German airborne troops from a partisan mountain stronghold in 1944.

'He was flown out of Cannes Flying Club under the armed insurgents' noses in a small plane piloted by *Express* Air Reporter Derek Dempster after an attempt to reach Italy by road with *Express* Motoring Reporter Basil Cardew was thwarted by the warring factions.

'Lord Beaverbrook, seventy-eight, looked little the worse for his ordeal.

'"After six hours of interrogation by a bunch of ignorant soldiers and two days dodging around road-blocks, I need a shave," he said, as he stepped on to the tarmac at Genoa Airport.

'The plan to get Lord Beaverbrook out of France was put into action last Monday when it was realized that civil war was imminent. Basil Cardew and Derek Dempster were picked for the job because of their motoring and flying expertise.

'Driving one of the new Mk VII Jaguars, the two *Express*men raced through France last Tuesday in an attempt to reach Cap Ferrat before the balloon went up. They made good time to the town of Sisteron in the southern Alps, but from then on were hampered by armed rebels, army patrols and the police.

'Because Dempster is bilingual – he was educated in France – they were able to joke and talk their way through the road-blocks and reach their goal.

'By then, however, the frontier between Menton in France and Vintemiglia in Italy had been blocked by rioting mobs, and the two reporters had to fall back on plans they had already worked out in anticipation.

'Several roads wind through the mountains behind Monte Carlo into Italy. Discreet inquiries had indicated that one of them – scarcely more than a track – was passable and unlikely to be patrolled. The frontier post it passed by was seldom manned.

'While Cardew drove Lord Beaverbrook over the twisting trail, Dempster was to get hold of an airplane and stand by at Cannes airfield in case the Jaguar was turned back. Although he had used the airfield frequently and knew it well, it was a tall order. But luck was with him. A disorganized mob had taken over and Dempster, by now dressed in the pale blue overalls and beret of a French mechanic, convinced the guards that he had instructions to check the engine of one of the aircraft. The pilot would be along soon with the proper authorization to fly an English milord out of France.

'It did not take him long to find a suitable plane with enough fuel for a two-hundred-mile flight, nor to find out that the owner would not mind a bit if he borrowed it.

'He had been shot.

'Meanwhile, Cardew and Lord Beaverbrook had run into a military road-block and were held for questioning. By the time they were released, it was too late to break curfew.

'The plan had allowed for contingencies like this, so that Dempster was not surprised when the pale blue Jaguar swept into the airfield early yesterday. It then took just a few words from Lord Beaverbrook to persuade the guards to let the party through.

'Forty minutes later, the six-seater plane touched down in Genoa, eighty miles away.

'As for Cardew's Jaguar, His Lordship promised to buy him a new one.'

There was little sign of impending strife on the streets of Paris when we arrived. Sydney (Bill) Smith, the *Express* Bureau Chief in France, who was co-ordinating our mission, and his delectable number two, Joan Harrison, thought the political pressures might be contained.

By now, however, I was beginning to question the validity of our dash into France, fun though it was, and asked Bill over dinner: 'Would it not have been easier to get the Beaver into a motorboat at the foot of his own garden and sail him twenty miles down the coast to San Remo?'

'Of course,' he replied. 'But it would only make a couple of pars in the paper. The Beaver himself was probably first to spot the dramatic story potential of sending two *Express*men to the rescue, and Chris went along with it.'

I yielded inwardly to a moment of despair. 'Here I am again, on

Gullible's travels. Why didn't I think of that? This is no way for a self-respecting journalist to be!' But I soon consoled myself with the thought that Basil Cardew had been an *Express*man since long before the war, and he had not twigged – or if he had, he wasn't telling.

As Bill and Joan predicted, the pressures were contained: fingers eased off triggers. Basil and I never got beyond Paris. We had three splendid days there – by courtesy of His Lordship.

I met the Beaver only once. It was in the lobby of the *Express* building in Fleet Street, as I arrived for work. Chris introduced me.

He was smaller than I had imagined. His movements, too, were slower than I had thought they would be. But there was a glint in his eyes. 'We meet at last,' he said. There was a pause, as he looked me over. 'You've got to be tougher with your copy. Do that and you've got a big future with the *Express*!'

Tougher? Before I could ask him to explain, he had turned on his heel and was heading for the lift.

Surprisingly, the meeting diluted my fear of the Old Man. He had cooler breath than the dragon of my imagination – at least, that's what I thought then.


On Sunday, 10 January 1954, a BOAC Comet jet airliner disintegrated nineteen minutes after taking off from Rome, en route for London. It crashed into the Mediterranean near the islands of Elba and Monte Cristo. All thirty-five aboard perished.

As Air Correspondent, I was naturally interested in the possible causes of the disaster and I agreed with BOAC's decision to ground the Comet fleet.

Over the next few weeks all seven of BOAC's Comets were stripped down and minutely examined. Not one of them gave the engineers a clue about what had actually gone wrong 30,000 feet above the Mediterranean on that fateful Sunday. Indeed, the fifty or more modifications made to each of the aircraft were based on speculation.

My information came from one of the Comet fleet engineers – an old chum – so that throughout February Arthur Christiansen went along with my view that the aircraft should stay grounded until BOAC, the makers, De Havilland, and the Royal Aircraft Establishment at Farnborough had discovered exactly what had caused the disaster.

One evening early in March, as I was about to close my desk and leave for home, however, leader writer Tony Cutbill brought me the 'Opinion' column galley proof. He had written a strong, fallacious attack on Sir Miles Thomas, Chairman of BOAC, taking him to task for keeping Britain's pride of the air out of the air. Because of the tacit understanding with Christiansen I was surprised.

'We can't print this,' I said, pencilling a cross over the piece, and explained why.

'It's what Chris told me to write', he replied.

Unusually, Christiansen was absent from his office. His secretary was not sure when he would be back. So I left, after instructing Tony to tell Chris that I did not agree with the leader and that it must be spiked.

Tony did just that, but the piece was printed nevertheless, unleashing BOAC's lawyers and putting me on the mat.

Chris was pretty rough. 'You're not employed to dictate *Express* policy,' he told me. 'As the air reporter your job is to make sure the facts we print are correct.'

I complained vigorously that I had not been properly consulted and argued that as the expert, I had a duty to protect the paper from appearing foolish – and that meant expressing opinions designed to mould policy.

'Either you tow the line and stick to reporting facts,' he replied tersely, 'or you'll have to find another job.'

I chose to leave immediately, with three months' money, rather than work out my contract.

On 23 March BOAC's Comets went back into service. Meanwhile, Colin Valdar, who left the features editorship of the *Daily Express* to become Editor of the *Sunday Pictorial*, had invited me to be his Air Correspondent. Then, on 8 April, another BOAC Comet disintegrated – this time over the Bay of Naples – and gave me a double-page spread in the *Pictorial*.

Tragic though it was for the victims and British aviation, the accident vindicated my stand at the *Express*. It was not until several years later, however, that I learnt how directly the Beaver had been involved in my downfall.

Soon after retiring, Arthur Christiansen took me to lunch. It had been more than six years since I had seen him, so the invitation came as a fascinating and total surprise. There was no beating about the bush. Chris came straight to the point when I joined him at the bar of Peter Evan's Eating House in Fleet Street.

'I've had you on my conscience for a long time,' he said, 'and I wanted to tell you how sorry I was that we parted company as we did.'

Lord Beaverbrook had insisted that the attack on BOAC should be published, and was then furious when he got egg all over his face on the following day. He held me responsible and was adamant that I be fired. 'I had no other choice,' lamented Chris.

I had followed the Beaver's advice and been tough. But I was tough with the wrong man: he was tougher.

# Penny Wise, Pound Foolish
# Arthur Christiansen

I am always asked, 'What is it like working for Beaverbrook?' Usually my questioners provide their own answers before I can get a word in edgeways: 'It must be hell.'

It is hell – and it isn't. On the days when you think it is going to be hell, it isn't, and on the days when life seems serene, it turns out to be hell. During the Battle of Britain I was invited to lunch in the boardroom of *The Times*. Another guest was Sir Charles Craven, who used to be branded by the socialists as 'Merchant of Death No. I' because he was Managing Director of Vickers Armstrong, the giant armaments firm. We were introduced, and his handsome, bronzed face puckered in pain as Major J. J. Astor (later Lord Astor of Hever) explained that I was the youngest editor in Fleet Street, and had been running Beaverbrook's top paper for seven years. 'Good God,' said Craven, 'I don't think I will live for seven years if your boss doesn't change his ways. I'm working for him at the Ministry of Aircraft Production. He called me at two o'clock this morning and at half-past eight he was on the telephone again to get a progress report. I told him that I had hardly had time to put my head on the pillow, and he didn't seem at all happy. "Neither have I," he said. "Get a move on, Charles." Does he go on like that with his newspapers?'

'You'll get used to it,' I replied. But actually I never did. No week, no day, no hour conformed to any pattern, except that the telephone constantly rang. Wherever Beaverbrook went, the telephone followed. Even when he was sunning himself on the porch of Cherkley, his home in the Surrey Downs, there was a telephone at his side. When he went to America he telephoned for news directly the *Queen Elizabeth* cast off from Southampton. 'Where's my son Max?' he asked me. 'I expect he's quite near me in Cowes Roads on his yacht by now. Get him to call me.' When the ship got out of his range for calls to England, he telephoned the New York office.

Leading articles, feature ideas, news stories, gossip paragraphs, criticism and praise flooded over the telephone hour by hour. My rusty shorthand was inadequate for the task. Sometimes, if I knew what was coming, I would put my secetary on to a parallel line, but even she could not get anything like a verbatim of the torrent which at its peak reached a good 400 words a minute. That was a pity because the richness of Beaverbrook's oratory and the coherence with which he talks represents tailor-made journalism. Yet if I called him back to check a phrase, it had gone from him as surely as though it were a note of music that had vanished into the air.

I write about the days before the Dictaphone and the Soundscriber; now every word can be taken down on tape and transcribed. 'Am I on the machine?' he asks with sudden caution when he is about to launch a violent diatribe; or 'Put me on the machine,' when he feels a leading article welling up.

Work goes on in all circumstances. A notebook is laid on his dining-room table as though it were as essential for eating purposes as a knife and fork. 'Take this down,' he bellows excitedly, just as I am toying with the season's first asparagus. Or 'I am going to use this in the *Daily Express*,' he says to a guest as he starts to scribble the news he has been hearing. If the guest objects then, that is the end of it; the scribble is destroyed. But he will grumble, 'People shouldn't tell me news if they don't want me to print it!'

We go walking in Hyde Park and on to Knightsbridge until we come to a flower shop. He orders roses to be sent to somebody and also selects a couple of dozen orchids all growing on one stem for my wife. This gives me time to get my notebook out in an endeavour to recall, not so much the words, but the mass of subjects we have discussed. But not for long.

'What's your address, Chris?'

'I'll write it on the envelope for you, sir.'

'No, you won't. Your wife will think you sent the flowers if you do. *I* want the credit.'

We walk home and suddenly he gets an attack of asthma. He has forgotten his nasal spray, and by the time we are back, he sounds as though he is playing 'The Marseillaise' on his bronchial tubes.

'Bring me a drink, a whisky,' he croaks to a manservant.

'It's very good for breaking up asthma,' I say sympathetically. 'I know, because it's very good for Michael Foot's.'

'If you wanta know,' says the old mischief-maker, quick-witted even in pain, 'it causes Michael's asthma.'

We spread all the morning newspapers on the carpet and tiptoe alongside them. 'Which d'ya like best of all today's front pages?' This I knew to be the signal that today's *Express* is not popular. There is a longish story about the weather, with which subject, being a Canadian, he cannot understand our British preoccupation. One of his old political cronies from 1918 has died and has not made even a 'brief' on the front page. Some of the 'filler' paragraphs at the foot of the column are on the trivial side. There is a murder case, which he likes, with over-prominent headlines, which he dislikes.

'Tellya what I'd have made your paper look like today' – he seizes a notepad and starts drawing column rules, and filling in headlines. Everything is in single-column form, and with the exception of the murder case, is news of importance: political, industrial and financial.

'What'ya think of that?'

'It wouldn't sell.'

'I agree.' And as he says it he kicks the *Daily Telegraph* right in its centre column.

This discussion of the merits of the other newspapers never ceases. 'Let's go for a motor-car ride; bring your notebook and a copy of the paper,' he said one day. From Stornoway House we travelled west until we pulled up outside a modest house in Kensington. Without any explanation he took me inside and there we were in the studio of Jacob Epstein.

Lord Beaverbrook took his place on a throne. Epstein took a wet cloth off a lump of clay. I sat at the foot of the throne on a wooden chair.

Said Epstein, with a sardonic grin broader if anything than Beaverbrook's: 'Your Lordship has had his hair cut since his last sitting.'

Beaverbrook: 'Ya-as I have, and I hope I did not do wrong. Christiansen, do you think "Beachcomber's" column is funny?'

Christiansen: 'It always makes me laugh.'

Beaverbrook: 'Then read it out loud and see if it makes me laugh.'

The Epstein head of Lord Beaverbrook was presented to him by Isidore Ostrer, head of the film family, and has been in the main hall of the *Daily Express* building in Fleet Street since 1934.

The unveiling of the head was the occasion of one of Lord Beaverbrook's rare visits to the office. Long before my time, he had given up living in a flat on the top floor, and now he came once a year at the most. His visits were supposed to catch the staff unawares, but the management's secret service was most efficient and the whole place was spruced up with the spit-and-polish that usually attracts hostile press publicity when an army barracks gets the full treatment before a royal visit.

Lord Beaverbrook hated untidiness in the office, although in his own home he litters the floor with newspaper cuttings, bits of paper and discarded manuscripts. On his occasional visits, he rooted around even in the waste-paper baskets. 'What's this?' he growled to the General Manager when he unearthed an empty beer bottle and a length of electric wiring. 'Drinking and waste in the office. It won't do, Robertson. Give me a report on it.'

He could be as penny-wise as a son of the manse and as pound-foolish as a winner of the treble chance in the football pools. When I visited the Glasgow office in 1957, the local Editor's secretary typed a memorandum for dispatch to Lord Beaverbrook in London. She took the view that nothing but the best was good enough for him and typed the message on double-thick cream-laid paper. 'This means trouble for us all,' I forecast to 'Sandy' Trotter, the Editor. 'Then let's have it typed again on cheaper paper,' Trotter suggested. 'No,' I said, for years soaked in the frugal approach. 'That would make a double waste; just let's see what happens.'

And sure enough, up came the rocket in the form of a message demanding to know (a) why this notepaper had been used; and (b) what stocks still existed, and what other uses they were put to.

Inter-office communications must not be sent in unused envelopes in the Beaverbrook organization; secretaries must collect old envelopes for this purpose. Nor must these communications be typed on embossed or even printed letter-head notepaper. When I told the proprietor of a local newspaper of these economy rules, he exploded that they were a waste of time. When I told Isidore Gluckstein, the benign chairman of J. Lyons & Company, an organization far bigger than Beaverbrook's, he said that vigilance in the use of envelopes led to care in bigger expenditure, and that it was not the saving of a few hundred pounds a year that mattered so much as the outlook. There must be something to this, for the gap between revenue and expenditure in the newspaper business is small.

Lord Beaverbrook never looked particularly excited, happy or even interested when I talked money, but he was a wonderful exponent of the policy of calculated extravagance. 'Show me your editorial salary list,' he said at least once a year (and sometimes, to be 'different', at intervals of only a month or two). 'We mustn't let that fellow Robertson make too much money.' With Robertson sitting there tight-lipped but resigned, the editorial payroll would be increased by £250 a week, spread among a dozen or so promising youngsters.

Ben Sonnenberg, the highly sophisticated American publicist, met Robertson some years before his retirement. 'He was a man who *looked* as though he worked for somebody big. You see that face all over the world,' said Sonnenberg. Robertson was the kindest and most generous man in his personal life, but in business he had to be hatchet-faced and to know how to wield the hatchet. He also had to be calm and understanding in face of the Beaver's rages in which no one was spared, including Robertson himself; yet the two men were on very intimate terms, and the Beaver relied on Robertson as his guide and comforter.

Beaverbrook's outbursts of extravagance seemed genuinely to upset Robertson, I suppose because he had to earn the money and present the balance sheet. Robertson once complained to me that it cost a couple of shillings to airmail a copy of the *Daily Express* to a foreign correspondent. 'Goddamn it, Chris, why can't the fellow wait for it to come by sea?' he asked, pulling his nose in a typical gesture. On the other hand, when in the thirties I urgently needed a bank guarantee for a loan of £3,000, Robertson went to Beaverbrook and caused the money to be given to me as a gift.

Within a few months of this act of generosity, I received a letter from Beaverbrook which said:

> The devotion that you give to your task as Editor of the *Daily Express* cannot be rewarded by money . . . You are already well paid and your salary increases have been many. At the same time I have no use for money in excess of my present supplies and on that account I must try to place my Editor in the same position.
>
> Robertson has been told on the eve of my departure for a long journey to give you another £1,000 in the New Year.

This kind of incident happened to many others as well as to myself, and at unexpected moments. 'Is Morley Richards a good man?' Beaverbrook asked me at a cocktail party he gave at a private room at the Savoy. I said he was a very good man, and my News Editor was sent for. 'How much money d'ya get, Richards?'

'Fifty pounds a week, sir.'

'Not enough. I've told Christiansen to give you another twenty.' It made no difference that Richards had been paid an extra £10 a week only three months previously.

Beaverbrook's parties to meet the staff were both fabulous and 'different'. Sometimes he invited a round hundred to 'tea', which was his way of inviting them for drinks, and began by serving tea. Sometimes he asked the entire editorial staffs of his three London papers to a sit-down dinner on three successive nights.

Once he gave a reception and dance at Stornoway House. It was a gay affair and the champagne flowed. Only one incident marred the occasion: in a corner there was a complete stranger who was obviously the worse for wear. 'Who's that?' asked Beaverbrook sharply. No one could identify the fellow so instructions were given to have the gatecrasher flung out. The party continued until 1.00 a.m., when the liquor supplies were turned off. After much hand-shaking, and the last guest had gone I was left with the boss. 'Godeson,' he said to his butler, 'how much did they drink?' Godeson gave the figures: sixty-three bottles of champagne, eight bottles of Scotch and so on.

'A remarkable bunch of people,' ruminated Beaverbrook. 'So much consumed, and only one drunk.'

'My staff are always in training,' I answered.

The next morning I received a letter of resignation from the one drunk. He was in fact a junior member of the financial staff who worked in Throgmorton Street, and had never been seen before by anyone in the Fleet Street head office. His letter also asked if he could have his overcoat back from the cloakroom in Stornoway House. Everyone, including Lord Beaverbrook, tried to get the young man to withdraw his resignation – we even held on to his overcoat for a day or two – but he was adamant and left the *Express* to join a firm of stockbrokers. He returned to journalism after the war, however, and is now a City Editor whom Beaverbrook Newspapers would be glad to employ.

Lord Beaverbrook was so encouraged by the behaviour of the *Daily Express* staff that he decided to repeat the success by inviting the *Sunday Express* staff to a reception and dance the following week. But the *Sunday Express* were not in such good training as my lot. For example, Bill Taylor, the News Editor, thought his taxi-cab home had stopped when it was still travelling, and ended up in hospital.

There is never a dull moment working for the Beaverbrook organization, whether your wounds are, like Bill Taylor's, self-inflicted, or whether they are the honourable scars of battle. Every day is a new and exciting experience, and it was the Beaver's habit to make sure that no two days were alike. If he could have made the sun rise in the west, it would have delighted him, because unlike the rest of us he would have been up to see it.

# Empire Crusader

Cartoons by Vicky, Low, Strube,
Cummings and others

Beaverbrook by Cummings

Vicky – 'Humility is Essential for Happiness'
(*New Statesman and Nation*, 29 May 1954)

Horner – 'The Beaver'

Tony Wysard – 'Lord Beaverbrook and the Hon. Max Aitken'
(*World's Press News*, 5 July 1934)

F. Autori – 'Political Lead'
(*Daily Express*, 21 October 1931)

Strube – 'Is this Cricket?'
(*Daily Express*, 17 May 1934)

Strube – 'Make It Snappy! (It is reported that a "No courtesy" movement
has started in America)'
(*Daily Express*, 14 July 1938)

Low – 'Dreamland'
(*Evening Standard*, 26 April 1935)

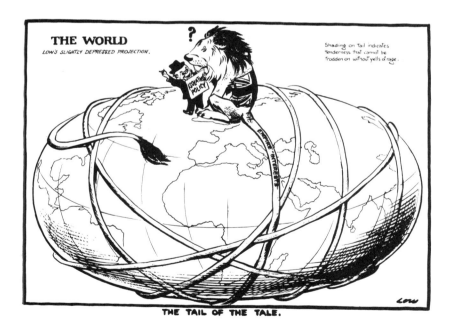

Low – 'The Tail of the Tale'
(*Evening Standard*, 22 June 1934)

Strube – 'Empire Overture'
(*Daily Express*, 2 May 1934)

Cummings – 'The Artist at Work'
(*Daily Express*, 29 October 1955)

"OH DEAR, THE BEAVER'S OFF AGAIN ON ONE OF HIS CRUSADES TO STRENGTHEN THE TIES OF THE COMMONWEALTH..."

Vicky – 'Empire Crusade'
(*Daily Mirror*, 5 July 1955)

Beaverbrook by (clockwise from top left)
Vicky, Low, Strube and Cummings

# The Man from the Miramichi
# Bernard McElwaine

The memory of the late Lord Beaverbrook may fade in some parts of the Empire he tried so hard to promote, but you would have to go very deep into the woods of heavily forested New Brunswick and live with hibernating black bears not to be reminded, somewhere in the inhabited regions, of his name.

In the city and port of Newcastle, where he grew up as the son of the manse, old men have passed on tales of his youth there. Young Max had an eye for a dollar. They remember stories from a father or a grandfather of working a paper round with Max. On examination it turns out to be 'for Max' not 'with Max'. Not for him the hard slog in the wintertime on snowshoes to get papers to homes. He organized the routes, drummed up the customers, and took the lion's share. At fifteen he had started a paper of his own – although it ran only for four issues.

In Newcastle, scholarships were later to be bestowed on pupils at his old school. Then postgraduate scholarships were added. Then special ones for teachers. And there was always a steady stream of neat quiet men with briefcases to arrange trust funds, and pensions to retired teachers, and their families who 'knew him when'. That included all his former classmates who may have needed something extra.

In the town there is the skating-rink, the town hall, the theatre, the library, the town square, all built with his money. His bronze bust on a cairn looks out from the town square across the Miramichi River – the most famous salmon river in North America. Locals reckon that, while he was still alive, he planned it all right down to the way it would face, because of the fact that from where the bust would face, someone's house blocked an otherwise uninterrupted view, till one of his quiet men with briefcases arrived in Newcastle and bought the house. A year passed and permission was requested from the town council to demolish it. Permission granted – naturally. So when the cairn was erected and the bust placed on it, his ashes were flown from England and set in the cairn. He got the view he wanted.

Locals told me that an attempt had been made to steal the ashes. I figured that some bested business rival (and there were hundreds) must have had the macabre idea of putting them in an egg-timer and making the Beaver work free for ever.

One of his pious biographers, a Newcastle local, reported that, by the time Max was thirty, he had made $30 million. And one oldtimer remarked 'And a dollar was a dollar in them days.'

In the face of so many benefactions, the explanations of where the millions came from tend to be brief and glib. 'He amalgamated companies.' Stockholders and directors of such companies felt after-wards as if they had stepped into a lift shaft when the doors opened – and the lift wasn't there.

But it wasn't all just signing cheques. He was visiting his home town one time – by special train complete with security guards – when an elderly coloured man turned up at the railway siding enquiring about Lord Beaverbrook. Coloured men are few on the ground in those parts (Scottish-Irish, with a substantial percentage of Arcadian-French speakers dominate) and he was told to 'beat it'. Then he called out: 'If Lord Beaverbrook knew that Stanley Duckins was out here, I wouldn't be sent away.'

The Beaver, who hadn't gone to bed, called out, 'Send him in at once.' The security men outside heard happy chat and laughter for some hours. Stanley Duckins had been a drummer in the Salvation Army, and a boyhood friend. After the Beaver left, another of the men with briefcases appeared, a lawyer this time from St John. A trust was set up and the last years of Stanley Duckins passed in comfort, worry-free. When he passed away, he was buried in the best casket the town could provide and someone said there were more wreaths than you could find on the Kentucky Derby winner – all with a simple card . . . 'Max'.

Around the province, in Fredericton, there is a much-expanded University of New Brunswick, halls of residence galore, skating-rink and an art gallery. He wanted Canadian snow scenes for it and Krieghof, who specialized in wintry scenes in Quebec rural comm-unities, came into vogue. Dealers said, 'If you can find a painting with a snowflake on it, the gallery will pant after it.' St John has a law library and the inevitable skating-rink, as has the city of Chatham to which he threw in a town hall for good measure. The rest of the province is festooned with church steeples, church organs, furniture, street lamps and other gifts.

He was the honorary colonel-in-chief of my regiment – the North Shore (New Brunswick) Regiment – and, unlike many holders of such offices, took a great interest in us. The officers had standing invitations to spend their leaves at his country home. But most of them didn't realize how rich he was. They looked at his *Daily Express* – wartime restrictions kept it to four pages – and said 'He can't have much money out of four pages – my paper back home [probably from some teeming metropolis like Nigadoo, Boctouche, Upsalquitch, Pokemouche, Burnt Church, and Kouchibouguac, maybe even Skoodoowabskookis, and what a title that would have given him] has twenty-four and the owner drives a pick-up truck.'

The North Shore (New Brunswick) Regiment sounds truly rural, but the men were hardy types – about one-third Arcadian-French speaking, lots of lumberjacks, trappers and fishermen – and highly trained as assault troops. Thus it was that on D-Day of the Normandy invasion, in all the resultant confusion when shouts went up, 'We're Lord Lovat Scouts, who the hell are you?' we were able to reply, 'We're Lord Beaverbrook's Battered Bastards.'

After the war someone asked him to come down to Aldershot and inspect us. He won over about 1,000 men when he replied, 'They must be sick of inspections, bring them up to London and I'll buy them a dinner.' In a post-war London short of everything!

He made a few calls to executives who I feel sure must have contemplated suicide or re-enlistment (far away, probably in the Foreign Legion). 'Need a special train, top-class banqueting-hall to seat a thousand, overnight accommodation and breakfast. And speak to the Commandant of the Military Police – don't want any of my men arrested that night.'

And so it was as if by magic we all assembled at the Connaught Rooms, and 'The Colonel' got up and opened the proceedings with the cry: 'Let the drink flow like the waters of the Miramichi.' And it did.

When I was in Canada this summer I noticed that certain old friends were combing bookstores for copies of one of his books, *A Man of Courage: the Story of Sir James Dunn*. The rumour had gone round the province that the second Lady Beaverbrook, Sir James Dunn's widow, was also looking for this book – though not to read, because she had already read it. The suggestion was that she didn't want anybody else to read it. No wonder perhaps? His dear friend Max said about him,

among other things: 'He was a shrewd and unyielding competitor . . .
tough and harsh . . . Often unjust – and frequently guilty of outrageous
conduct to his fellow men.' The Beaver also wrote of Sir James Dunn's
bitter proxy fights with the aluminium interests; deals in Hungarian
bonds; and other matters. Max also listed, almost breathing his
admiration into the text, details of Dunn's will. He left, among other
trifles, £67,991,000 (and the pound was a pound then). And as one
might add, 'And that's just what they could find in his pockets!'

Beaverbrook needed a Boswell but it is too late now. The distinguished novelist Brian Moore, who emigrated to Canada and made
his name, before writing novels, on Montreal newspapers, was offered
a tempting fee to be that biographer by Lady Beaverbrook. It was a most
attractive idea until Moore said he would start his research out in
Calgary, Alberta, where many hairy deals in railways, property, oil, gas
and stocks, real and imaginary, were features of business in the early
1900s. Her Ladyship insisted that Moore begin in the stock exchange
in Montreal. He wanted the story to be financial warts and all and
declined. Before she became Lady Dunn in 1942, and then Lady
Beaverbrook in 1961, she was Marcia Christoforides, a secretary to
financiers, and knew a secret or two herself.


To the casual enquirer/collector of 'Maxanecdotes': at the Lord
Beaverbrook Hotel (in New Brunswick), they say, 'We will always
remember him . . . he never left a tip.'

# Beelzebub
# Michael Foot

*My son if thou come to serve the Lord,*
*Prepare thy soul for temptation.*

Ecclesiasticus, quoted by Arnold Bennett,
'Books and Persons', *Evening Standard* (1930)

Legends are created, as every journalist knows, in cuttings libraries at the newspaper offices; no sooner are a man's or a woman's eccentricities established there than they become embalmed, and may be disinterred, in every plausible detail, until the last trump is sounded. But history, against the odds, must attempt some readjustments.

'You Bollinger Bolshevik, you ritzy Robespierre, you lounge-lizard Lenin,' Brendan Bracken is alleged to have roared, as he strode up and down the drawing-room of Lord Beaverbrook's Stornoway House, gesturing as he went somewhat in the manner of a domesticated orang-utan, and his victim was Aneurin Bevan. 'Look at you, swilling Max's champagne and calling yourself a socialist.' The assembled company, including Bevan, listened with delight. Or so the tale has been recounted by Brendan Bracken's latest biographer, but his recital is based on a first report, presumably from Bracken himself, as relayed by Randolph Churchill in a newspaper article dated 8 August 1958, and the emphasis must be examined. Certainly Bracken had a gift of invention, if not of the gab, but his conversational assaults were rarely delivered with such alliterative polish, and who can believe that Aneurin Bevan sat silent beneath the downpour? The story I was told by another eye-witness, Frank Owen, a qualified reporter, was that Aneurin Bevan claimed his right to like good wine, adding with the approval of the whole company: 'The best I ever had from you, by the way, Brendan, I'd call bottom lower-class Bolshevik Bollinger.' The mysterious Brendan was not in the habit of offering us working journalists liquor of any brand; he supplied instead a steady flow of fanciful news stories which had to be laboriously checked the morning after. For the rest, however, the scene is authentic: the assorted company, the polemical free-for-all, the deluge of drink and journalism and politics, the orang-utan manner, the absolute rule that no holds were barred; indeed, customarily, an incitement from the host that the more eminent his guests, the more ferocious should be the cross-examination or the raillery.

I made my timorous entry into this unimaginable world, thanks to a word to Beaverbrook from Aneurin Bevan. Here was the origin, or rather in the earlier social exchanges between Bevan and Beaverbrook was the origin, of all the tales of a sinister Bevanite–Beaverbrookian conspiracy which historians of the Nuffield school – notably Mr Philip Williams, the official biographer of Hugh Gaitskell – have now sought to erect into a major theme of vilification. I hope to show that there are more things in heaven and earth than the Nuffield school may include in its curriculum.

However, back to 1938: at the time Aneurin Bevan was on the board of the recently founded, but already financially ailing, weekly *Tribune* where I had worked as Assistant Editor and with whom I had quarrelled over the sacking of its first Editor, William Mellor. I was a journalist-innocent, innocent in most other ways too, having spent as a journalist only one year of semi-freelance penury on the *New Statesman* under Kingsley Martin's critical eye, a few odd months learning typography from the master, Allen Hutt of the *Daily Worker*, and nearly two years of elation and occasional dejection on *Tribune*. I was not exactly equipped with the suit of armour recommended for those summoned to Lord Beaverbrook's Stornoway House or his country house, Cherkley, but that was where I turned up one Saturday evening, after a first peremptory phone call.

I cannot recall too precisely what happened at the dinner table that night; I was tongue-tied by the general company and atmosphere but also by the apparition who sat at my side, an exquisitely beautiful girl who had some trouble with her English, but who seemed otherwise at ease, and who I took to be a Hungarian countess or something of that sort. Next day also she was floating through the house; her disturbing presence seemed to be everywhere. But immediately I had other matters pressing for attention. Beaverbrook came downstairs in his riding attire and asked whether I had read the newspapers. When I replied, 'Yes a few,' he insisted: 'Read them *all*. Albert, see that Mr Foot is supplied with all the papers in the library. I will return in an hour or two, Mr Foot, and perhaps you will be good enough to tell me what is in the newspapers.' When he did return, he made a bolt for the swimming-pool, calling for me to follow, and prepared to plunge, naked-ape-like, into the water. 'You've brought your notes with you, Mr Foot, now let me hear what is in all those newspapers.' But I had no notes, instead what might have just passed muster as a photographic memory. I had memorized the Sunday newspapers as no one, I trust, has felt required to do before or since.

'Come with me with no delay,' he said as the recital was concluded, and he led me where the assembled score of house guests, one of his usual congregations of the incongruous, were drinking their pre-lunch drinks on the spacious porch overlooking the Surrey woodlands.

'Mr Foot will now tell you what most of you no doubt have been too damned lazy to read for yourselves.'

I got the offer of a job and started immediately on the *Evening Standard*, at what was then the union minimum of £9 per week which however was exactly double my salary of £4 10s on *Tribune* (cut from the original figure of £5 to help meet the first of *Tribune's* series of financial crises).

For the next twenty-five years of my life I knew Beaverbrook as well, I believe, as almost any man did (not attempting for the moment to compete with the women), and for all that time, with occasional spasms of fury or hatred and one of four years of something worse, I loved him, not merely as a friend but as a second father, even though throughout I had, as I have often indicated, the most excellent of fathers of my own. Many friends found this friendship absurd, inexplicable, discreditable, scandalous, evil; for the simple, widely disseminated view of Beaverbrook was that he was a kind of Dracula, Svengali, Iago and Mephistopheles rolled into one. Anyone who crossed his threshold, anyone who took his shilling or the larger sums soon on offer (my £9 was increased to a munificent £12 within months, and much more later on) was jeopardizing his immortal soul.

'Well, how was it in the House of Rimmon?' my real father would ask when I returned to his chaste, puritan, teetotal hearth. He at least cheerfully accepted my discriminating reports.

When I first set eyes on the monster, he was sixty years old; everyone working at close quarters talked of the Old Man (no one called him the Beaver) but, apart from lapses into hypochondria, chiefly on account of his asthma, he showed no signs of age or decline in any of his faculties. Mind and body could move with an electric alertness. The first impression also was sharply different from that conveyed by the cartoonists, Low and Strube and Vicky, who, doubtless for their own good reasons, made him gnomelike, too squat, too much dominated by the big head and the big smile. He liked to dress with a careless elegance and was positively vain about the delicacy of his hands and the meticulously well-shod feet. His strong Canadian accent which he himself fostered and exploited, and which so many who came in contact with him found tempting to imitate, was more likely to surprise by its softness than the calculated bursts of power. And most remarkable of all, in this general physiognomy which was somehow shifted from the expected focus, were his ears, and the purposes to which he put them. He *listened*. He took in everything said to him, everything he overheard. No use giving *him* false scents, misleading hints, half-baked suggestions; he could always remember. Nothing but candour could survive his sensitive powers of cross-examination and recollection. Yet on this same level of personal exchange there was no cant, no personal pretension, no side, no snobbery, not the smallest tincture of it. I soon discovered I could say anything to him. No sacred topics, political or otherwise, had to be skirted. Indeed many of the public crusades which he espoused could be quite safely derided in private, and he had quite unexpected sympathies in personal dealings and a political imagination which could be convulsively stirred. The private Old Man I met in the autumn of 1938 remained for me ever afterwards a figure of bewitching interest. Nothing the public man did could kill it, and truly the public Beaverbrook, I believe, has not received his due honour.

One partial explanation of the devotion he could excite in the most unlikely quarters derived from the nature and scale of his emotional radicalism. Observers whose first or lasting impression of him was imprinted by the *Daily Express* of the thirties ('No war this year or next') or even by that journal in its last great decade of the fifties may rub their eyes in bewilderment at any such claim, but there was always this one clue to the mystery, evident to anyone who saw the man himself, instead of the varying portraits which, for whatever recondite purpose, he sought to present to the outside world. When he had arrived in London in 1910, he had at once become embroiled in the dismal politics of the Conservative Party, and the rest of his life might be construed as a prolonged exertion to break loose. He was a rampaging individualist – no one could ever question that – and he always favoured the rumbustious, marauding private enterprise system which had enabled him to become a multi-, or as he would call it, a Maxi-millionaire.

But he brought with him too, in those pre-1914 days, inherited from his Covenanting Scottish ancestors or blown across to him in the continent of his birth from the tradition of American populism, a detestation for the stuffiness and stupidities and snobberies of the English Establishment. He was an instinctive radical in the true sense in that he had an urge to get to the roots of the question and the will to wrench them up with both hands. This is what he did at his greatest moments, in 1916 and 1940, and at several dates less famous in our history. His paradox-loving biographer, A. J. P. Taylor, has even gone so far as to see Beaverbrook as a reincarnation of another radical hero, Richard Cobden, but that cap will never fit on this unique skull. For Beaverbrook was interested in political moods and intrigues, not theories or principles, and Cobden, unlike Beaverbrook, was a born and dedicated leader and organizer. None the less Beaverbrook's radicalism was deep and abiding and would break out when least expected, and was often active behind the scenes, it appeared to me, in his approach to journalism and indeed to politics too.

He loved good talkers, good reporters, keeping a strict ration on the monologuists, even if the offender happened to be Winston Churchill. Beaverbrook was a good talker himself; Arnold Bennett, no mean judge surely, called him the best dramatic raconteur he ever heard. Exaggerated or not, he certainly knew what good talk was, and had assembled around him no conventional crew. Viscount Castlerosse could talk; no one who ever heard him doubted that he was one of the real wits. But the difficulty of proving the claim is that he relied very little on his considerable powers as a storyteller; his forte was the sudden audacious blow between the wind and the water which could convulse the whole company and send his victim – usually one who richly deserved it – reeling through the ropes. Everything depended on his exquisite timing, or rather the timing plus the presence; it was incomprehensible how this grotesque elephant of a man could deliver his thrusts with such feline precision. As a ne'er-do-well Irish Catholic peer, dependent on the Calvinist Beaverbrook to keep him in cigars and mistresses, he might have cut a pitiful as well as a ridiculous figure, but by sheer nerve and talk, he carried off the whole performance. 'And how is the old bucket shop today?' he was reputed to have asked as he entered the banking sanctum of his Baring Brothers relation, Lord Revelstoke, who had tried to find him a niche in the City. That stroke helped to end his career as a financier, and he was soon back at Beaverbrook's for board and bed.

Robert Bruce-Lockhart was another in the company, the dashing, handsome author of the *Memoirs of a British Agent*, once the friend of

Trotsky and the suitor of the 'big-minded, big-hearted', wise and beautiful Moura Budberg who had understood him so well and some others too, from Maxim Gorky to H. G. Wells. 'Moura says,' Bruce faithfully reported, 'I am a little strong but not strong enough, a little clever, but not clever enough, and a little weak but not weak enough.' Moura knew. And Moura also was there on one of the very first weekends I spent at the house of ill-fame, not with Bruce or Gorky or even Budberg, but with her later lover, H. G. Wells, and I heard H. G. in person protesting against the playing of the national anthem 'and all that Hanoverian stuff' in a fine republican squeak which the near-republican Beaverbrook was happy to applaud.

H. G. Wells had the distinction of being invited back again though he had committed the unforgivable solecism of satirizing in a book 'one of those crude plutocrats with whom men of commanding intelligence, if they have the slightest ambition to be more than lookers-on at the spectacle of life, are obliged to associate nowadays'. Of course, the villain of *The Autocracy of Mr Parham*, Sir Blasted Bussy Bussy Buy-up-the-Universe Woodcock, was a composite figure.

He's the sort of man who buys up everything. Shops and houses and factories. Estates and pot houses. Quarries. Whole trades. Buys things on the way to you. Fiddles about with them a bit before you get 'em. You can't eat a pat of butter now in London before he's bought and sold it. Railways he buys, hotels, cinemas and suburbs, men and women, soul and body. Mind he doesn't buy you.

Beaverbrook was not quite engaged in that scale of business, but there was the popular suspicion, and Sir Bussy was also 'a short ruddy man' with 'a mouth like a careless gash', and, more precisely incriminating still, the book also contained a cartoon by David Low in which the Cherkley luncheon party was indelibly portrayed. There, in the corner, was Castlerosse, flirting with two flappers of the thirties, and 'hangers-on and parasites of the worst description', calling Sir Bussy Woodcock, 'Bussy dear'. The whole scene could have ensured that neither H. G. Wells himself nor David Low nor even the still radiantly composed Moura Budberg would ever darken his doors again. But there they all were, graciously invited back for more; the magnet was irresistible.

H. G. Wells was one of the heroes of my youth. I had devoured *Kipps* and *Mr Polly* and *Marriage* and all the rest and, when it came to *Tono-Bungay*, had rationed the reading to twenty pages a day so that paradise would not come to an end too abruptly. Beaverbrook had devoured those same pages, too, twenty years before, not quite in the same spirit of socialist excitement, but with all his own discernment. So he managed his ménage not quite in the manner of Sir Bussy Woodcock after all. Souls and bodies might be in peril in his household, but the atmosphere was subtler than any caricature.

The morning after my own Cherkley hiring, I was instructed to report to Frank Owen, Editor of the *Evening Standard*. We became from that moment bosom companions, night and day, if such terms may be used without giving any misleading notion about one so spectacularly heterosexual. During those next months, indeed the next year or so, he gave me an intensive pressure-course introduction to the world, the flesh, the devil, and his notion of Beaverbrook, not troubling always to draw too sharp a distinction between the last two on the list. He was himself a superlative journalist and editor, being capable of enlisting an incomparable allegiance from those who worked for him. But the man was even more appealing than the journalist. His high spirits had a Godlike quality. His physical capacity was such that he could drink all night, everything and anything set before him, and be hard at work at his desk, after a couple of Coca-Colas, at seven o'clock next morning. So he continued for some twenty years, with suitable recuperations at weekends, until tragically that physical apparatus suddenly snapped, never to be restored to full working order again. Women fell for him in droves, at a glance; no one else I ever saw was ever in the same competition. Yet he did not treat the matter offensively or vain-gloriously but rather as if this triumphant promiscuity had been the natural lot of man (and woman) since Adam or soon after. More than any other human specimen I have ever known, he was utterly absorbed by the pressing moment. He could forget everything except the article he was writing, the next edition to catch, the next round of drinks, the girl in hand. He had a first-rate mind, according to the tests they make at Cambridge University, and would sit up all night devouring some new book when not otherwise occupied. He liked to call himself a Trotskyite, partly because he was steeped in Trotsky's writing and partly also to disown the current Stalinite vogue which he abhorred. He was then (as he had been as the youngest MP in the 1929–31 Parliament) a Lloyd George Liberal, and he remained such till his dying day.

He had already experienced eight years of Beaverbrook, and had touched the heights and the depths. When in the first year or so of their acquaintance, Frank's lover had literally died in his arms, it was

Beaverbrook who knew best how to help him at the moment of human crisis, and when six years later he went off in pursuit of Grace, who became his wife, it was the possessive Beaverbrook who – along with several others – felt himself to be mistakenly abandoned. Frank viewed Beaverbrook with a finely balanced scepticism and admiration, a kind of adoring fury which lasted for nearly two decades.

Not so long after my arrival at the *Standard*, I was whisked away on a travel jaunt with Beaverbrook himself, alone, apart from valets and secretaries, on the Blue Train to Cannes, to Monte Carlo and back to the Ritz in Paris. I could hardly have been more surprised if Aladdin had turned up with his lamp and put me on a magic carpet to Baghdad. The idea was, apart from telling him what was in the newspapers, that I should be instructed in the business or art of writing a column. I was told to study the modern American masters of the craft: Arthur Brisbane, Heywood Broun and Westbrook Pegler. Soon some specimens were being despatched back to the *Standard* office and the row which one of them provoked started to endear my new master to me even more than the introduction to the delights of Heywood Broun. In pursuit of our belated aim of transforming the *Standard*, one idea was to provide a real *London* paper, and our leader column was to be freshly directed to that purpose. 'Pull Down the Railings' was the headline I had produced for a column and the proposed text began:

> Henry VIII built a fence round Hyde Park. The fence was changed to a wall and the wall to railings. And there those railings stand today, ugly iron monuments to the tyranny of a rapacious monarch. Someone ought to pull them down.

But in the sedate Shoe Lane of those times, this smacked of the tumbrils. Captain Wardell, a constant attender at Cherkley, a passionate Munichite, and a scarcely less passionate philanderer, an admirer even of 'Tom' Mosley, a stern protector of the *Standard*'s élitist appeal but no equally successful protector of its finances, was shocked, deeply shocked. He knew, and also took the precaution to check, the long-standing objection of the police to the removal of Hyde Park railings; it was hard enough to guard against the spread of vice in any case, but, with the railings down, the task would become hopeless. However, Beaverbrook would have none of it, and his message was conveyed to the pious and passionate captain in his presence, and in a manner not calculated to advance my popularity in the office: 'No more of it, Captain Wardell. You have beautiful beds in Claridges and all over London where you can do your fucking. What about the rest of us?' The column was printed without amendment – and indeed with a mischievous reference to the expected protests from the moralists – on 2 March 1939.

Within a year or so, I had become, I suppose, one of the family, a favoured son, and the real sons and daughter showed not a twinge of enmity or jealousy. Max and Janet and Peter all had strong streaks of the Beaverbrook charm but none of them possessed their father's devotion to politics and journalism, the two inextricably mixed together in one tempestuous passion. Each had other pursuits: apart from romantic explorations, Max was off flying passenger planes in America or delivering war planes to Republican Spain and acquiring the exceptional experience which made him the best-equipped pilot in the world when the catastrophe finally came. He was as handsome as Apollo, as swiftly moving as Mercury, but newspapers would have to wait for his attention until after he had helped win the Second World War. Janet had a streak, too, of the old man's guile to add to the charm, but she was still no politician. Only one member of the family, so far, has inherited the golden journalistic talent. She was Jean Campbell, daughter of Janet, and when I first went to Cherkley she and her brother were seven and five years old respectively, and I played with them round the porch where I had once recapitulated the contents of the Sunday newspapers. Her Beaverbrook smile was already the most bewitching of the lot. (Read the Jean Campbell reports from Chippaquidick, 1969, if you want to know how a true Beaverbrook can report.)

The word *charm* keeps intruding, and may seem quite out of place in the light, say, of the H. G. Wells caricature and many others besides. But, as with Charles James Fox, it is his charm that lives even if the debased word is insufficient for the purpose. Beaverbrook's charm was more like the secret potions used in *A Midsummer Night's Dream*, and he could apply them, seemingly at will, to men and women alike. So, sharply contrasting with the harsh or even crude appearance which readers of his newspapers might deduce, he fitted regularly into no definable category, political or personal. He was wary, high-spirited, erratic, cunning, calculating, passionate, sentimental, restless, impulsive; he could be mean and magnanimous; he had the most perfect manners, and he could turn savage. If intuition is a feminine characteristic he was at least half-feminine. It was the perpetual interplay of temperament and character all around him, in politics, in Fleet Street, and in his own circle, which fascinated him and which doubtless gave rise to the notion that he was engaged in some vast Faustian conspiracy against the human race. But most of his critics knew barely one per cent of the story, and the nearer one approaches the whole truth, the more necessary it is to speak in nuances and to search for qualified judgements. He could combine – almost in the same deed, on the same day – the most staggering misjudgements and the most piercing insights. He had many of the visions or far-seeing appreciations of greatness but he could also feel his way round the furniture of the English political workshop like a blind man.

Apart from his own prodigious reading in the first years after his arrival in Britain, it was Arnold Bennett who guided or kept pace with his enthusiasms either in person or in the *Evening Standard* 'Books and Persons' column. Always thereafter Beaverbrook wanted to recapture the exhilaration of that book column, the best that ever was, and always he would be berating his barbarian editors who failed to comprehend that all wisdom could be found in books, and that at that precise moment all over the planet, authors in their solitude were producing the stories which each intelligent editor should seek to purvey first to his readers. Arnold Bennett said that his own curiosity about new books was unappeasable and divine; Beaverbrook's was not quite in that class, but almost. His own library, like those of other rich men, had been partly bought for show, but some writings, apart from the Psalmist, he knew intimately and could summon to his aid at will.

The interaction between his mind and Arnold Bennett's offers sidelights into both. Beaverbrook's first interest had been excited by the author before he ever met him, not by any Five Towns saga, but by the much slighter and lesser-known *The Pretty Lady* which no doubt started with the advantage, for Beaverbrook, of its semi-salacious appeal. But no doubt is possible about their shared instincts and cast of mind. They had the same down-to-earthness, the same taste for champagne and the sybaritic life, and the same lack of cant in avowing it, and above all, the same faith in life itself sometimes, and in books *always*; the same sacred gift of enthusiasm, Hazlitt's gusto. It was Beaverbrook who prompted, cajoled, bribed Arnold Bennett into writing that famous book column in the *Evening Standard* – just another proof of his inspiration as an editor. The whole collection (not republished, amazingly, until 1974) shows what a bursting storehouse of literary intelligence, knowledge, generosity and discrimination Arnold Bennett's mind truly was. Without Beaverbrook, this last particular display of Bennett's genius would never have happened. Without Beaverbrook, the forthcoming Bennett revival would have to wait a few more decades. Once Rebecca West wrote a piece in which she referred to the four 'uncles' of her youth – Shaw, Bennett, Galsworthy and Wells – the iconoclastic Rebecca being capable of worshipping four literary uncles in place of gods. Three of those four were my uncles too, as they were for the whole of our socialist generation, and here, lo and behold, before my eyes was a fellow who actually knew Arnold Bennett, knew him indeed as few others ever knew him.

So I soon discovered that, along with the political-cum-journalistic obsession, I shared with Beaverbrook other oddities or interests: a firm biblical grounding, if a lapsed Methodist may make the generous concession to a lapsed Presbyterian; a taste for films and pop music perpetually on tap; an asthma affliction, both real and exploitable; and an eye for the same girl – but more of that in a moment. When I had a bout of asthma, Dan Davies (not yet Sir Daniel and physician to the Queen, but already Aneurin Bevan's friend) was despatched to my bedside. He brought no cure at all but those mitigation potions, without which asthma can be hellish, and to which Beaverbrook was perpetually resorting. My brand of the disease, I believed, was at that time more chronic than his but the claim was not pressed too hard. As for the pop music, the place shunted when I first went there to the rhythm of 'A tisket, A tasket, my little yellow basket', and since that was my current favourite too, I took it as an augury. His favourite of all time was 'See what the boys in the backroom will have, and tell 'em I'm having the same', sung by Marlene Dietrich as she danced along the bar counter in *Destry Rides Again*.

A topic never to be mentioned was Orson Welles's *Citizen Kane*. No one could deny it: there was just an element of Citizen Kane in him, and he could be furious with any reference which exposed it. The speech in the classic film, for instance, did give a flash of Beaverbrook on the hustings, and there are other glimpses too. It was deeply sad that he never appreciated Orson Welles who could worthily have taken a place alongside his Edward G. Robinson. However there was never any danger, as enemies suggested, that Beaverbrook might lapse into the paranoiac condition of a Hearst or a Northcliffe. His sense of humour remained his lifeline to sanity.

He was saved, moreover, by the war which he had said would not or should not come. Deeply shaken as doubtless he should have been by the collapse of the appeasement policy, he scarcely emerged, in the first few months of the so-called 'phoney war', from the worst bout of surliness which he – and we – ever experienced. But the release and rejuvenation when they came were all the more spectacular. Long before the Norway fiasco, he and we and most of the nation besides (there was nothing perspicacious in the observation) had been coming to recognize that a dramatic change in the constitution of the British government would have to be engineered. Who better to conduct the conspiracy than the arch-conspirator of 1916? As it happened, his hand was not required for that purpose, but he was emotionally prepared to play his decisive role in the greatest crisis in British history, the moment when we could have become the victims of a Nazi conquest and when we saved ourselves by our exertions, Beaverbrook's among them.

Yes, he truly played his part in our finest hour, preparing for it and at the moment itself, and in the *Evening Standard* office we naturally watched the performance with some pride. In those first weeks we had another interest too. Right up till the moment when Hitler's tanks smashed through the Ardennes, Beaverbrook had continued to exercise his perpetual, erratic, inescapable surveillance over the newspaper; he was the editor-in-chief and everyone inside the office knew it. Then, one fine memorable morning, peace descended. The Blitz was just about to burst upon us in all its fury. All Beaverbrook's improvising energies were devoted to his task, night after night, for weeks on end. So, led by Frank Owen, we on the *Evening Standard* went about our task all the more zestfully, producing the best paper sold on the streets of our beleaguered city. Day after day, I dare say, our tone became more exhilarated and revolutionary – that was the mood of the time. And one morning I embroidered a leading article with a quotation from Cromwell on the eve of the Battle of Dunbar: 'We are upon an Engagement very difficult . . . But the only wise God knows what is best. All shall work for Good . . .' – that and more. Within a few hours – it seemed more like minutes – of that paper reaching our street-sellers, the Blitz-laden peace of the previous weeks was broken by a thunderclap. It was Beaverbrook back on the telephone: 'How dare you, Mr Foot, how dare you use the columns of the *Evening Standard* to attack the Presbyterians. The tale is spread in Westminster and Whitehall that Beaverbrook no longer takes an interest in his newspapers. I would have you understand, Mr Foot, that his newly developed good nature does not extend to some damned dispensation permitting attacks on Presbyterians. And Cromwell at Dunbar, I would have you know, had no title to pray to the God of battles to destroy his Presbyterians . . .'

So the tirade continued and I had no courage left at the end to remark that Cromwell's prayers at Dunbar were in fact answered. Still it was good to know that our most regular reader was still perusing the newspaper.

Like Beaverbrook himself I could not live by politics alone, and
Cherkley for me in those years had one special irrepressible attraction.
Making a pass, however shyly or ineffectually, at the boss's girl may
not normally be recommended as the road to fortune, but I never lived
to repent it and I never quite knew how he viewed the matter. I had had
my first glimpse of Lili Ernst on the very first night I had arrived a
Cherkley in the autumn of 1938. It was a stunning glimpse too, but
then she vanished before I knew who or what she was. She was the
Hungarian countess who in reality was neither Hungarian nor a
countess but a much more exciting combination.

Many months later, after the war had started, I wrote an article
about the civilized treatment which should be offered to refugees from
Hitler's Europe, and she wrote to me. I met her again, and she told me
part of her story, and no one in his senses could fail to be captivated.
She was a Yugoslav Jewess, a ballerina, beautiful and delicate and
fragile, attached to a famous Viennese opera company. Beaverbrook
had met her when she was dancing in Cannes, and had told her to
communicate with him if she were ever in trouble. Thanks to his
intervention, she was smuggled out of Vienna a few weeks after
Hitler's troops had occupied the city; thanks to his assistance she had
what proved to be a last, fleeting glimpse of her parents on a holiday in
Switzerland.

Beaverbrook had fallen for her, no possible doubt about that, and
one day, just about the time when I was having trouble with Captain
Wardell, I wrote, on Beaverbrook's incitement, a full-length leading
article in the *Daily Express*, not the *Evening Standard*, on the Jewish
Feast of Purim, on how Haman was hanged in place of Mordecai, on
how the Nazis would never be able to execute their monstrous
programme for the final extermination of the Jews. Readers of the
*Express* must have rubbed their eyes in some amazement; never before
had the paper shown itself so passionately pro-Jewish. Readers of the
Bible must have rubbed their eyes too, for although the story was
retold well enough and reverently in the space available, I trust, it was
the story of Haman and Mordecai without Esther – a serious, and most
unconscionable omission. When Beaverbrook had recited to each of
us, Lili and myself, that Bible story, Esther had certainly not been
overlooked; she is, and was, and always will be, the heroine. However
the leading article did serve its purpose. Lili was pleased, and he was
pleased, and the readers of the *Express* could lump it. Thereafter, I took
leaves, whole chapters, from his book, and wrote in the *Evening
Standard* on Jewish themes and Yugoslav themes and sometimes the
two together (we became, at a somewhat later date, enthusiastic

supporters of Tito) at every available opportunity and thereby helped
to win her friendship but not her heart.

Then came graver, terrible complications. What happened to Lili's
family and friends in Yugoslavia when it was overrun by the Nazis no
one could know; the assumption was that they had been hauled off to
Auschwitz. Her home in Yugoslavia was gone, never to be revisited.
She loved Beaverbrook and he loved her, but doubtless he could be
hard and demanding as well as sensitive, possessive and wayward by
turns, as he was in politics. Her health broke down and the doctors,
including the expert Dan Davies, diagnosed the disease as incurable.
She moved from hospital to hospital, from doctor to doctor, and then
finally devised her own cure. She made her escape from him and lived
(and still lives) happily ever after. She was lovely, zestful, affectionate,
independent, inquisitive; a passionate Maccabean upholder of the
rights of the Jewish people, just like Esther. And the best thing I ever
knew about Max Beaverbrook was that Lili Ernst had truly loved him.

To set the chronology straight, I left him about three years before
she did, and I took what I thought was the proper course of doing it
without a row. For two years, from the departure of Frank Owen for the
forces, I had had the enthralling job of editing the paper which he,
above all others, had created: the wartime *Evening Standard*, the
*Standard* in its very greatest days, I naturally contend, although it has
had some other great ones since.

But back to Beaverbrook: during the next few years my association
with the Old Man became bruised almost beyond recognition or
repair. Beaverbrook in the distance looked a very much less enchanting
figure than he had done at close quarters. All through the period
towards the ending of the war, the election of 1945, the overthrow of
Churchill, the instalment of the Labour government, my own election
in Devonport, every public issue seemed likely to inflict fresh wounds
on any private feeling which remained. Perhaps there were jangled
jealousies left over from the Lili Ernst days. Many who had worked for
Beaverbrook would devote a considerable part of the rest of their days
to his vilification, and perhaps I had started down the same path when
I said in a Commons debate on the Royal Commission on the Press,
instituted by the Labour government, that the occupational disease
among newspaper proprietors was megalomania. Many a true word is
spoken in venom, and yet for me to have wasted much time on that
theme in dealing with Beaverbrook would have been dust and ashes.

Providentially, an occasion occurred which set matters aright.
Someone invited me to a dinner to celebrate Beaverbrook's seventieth
birthday at the Savoy Hotel on 28 April 1948, and the chairman asked

me to speak. It was natural to recall the finest hour when he had waited each night for his son, Max, to return from the skies where London was saved and when he himself had seemed to be translated into another being. I quoted Milton:

> . . . With grave
> Aspect he rose, and in his rising seem'd
> A pillar of state; deep on his front engraven
> Deliberation set and public care;
> And princely counsel in his face yet shone,
> Majestic though in ruin; sage he stood,
> With Atlantean shoulders, fit to bear
> The weight of mightiest monarchies; his look
> Drew audience and attention still as night
> Or summer's noontide air.

The diners were properly hushed and impressed, and then I had to remind the ignorant bunch that they were just that. Of course, those famous lines had been written about Beelzebub. It was a trick purloined straight from my father but I doubt whether he had ever had a more apposite occasion for working it. Beaverbrook was overcome. He sent me next day an emotional and touching letter scrawled in his barely legible hand. Our friendship was renewed, and never collapsed thereafter. Destry rode again.

I think I was as well placed as anyone to see what Beaverbrook did for all of us in those supreme years, and I am prepared to repeat the testimony anywhere and at any time, including the Day of Judgement, where possibly, now the thought occurs, I may have a chance of giving evidence before he does. But at that higher tribunal, I suppose, one would have to be careful about quoting Milton with effect: there it may not so readily be appreciated that Beelzebub had a better side to his nature.

Two other improbable friendships contributed to mine with Beaverbrook. First and foremost, Jill, my wife, knew how to deal with him from their very first meeting, how to awaken and sustain his curiosity, how to keep his eyes on today and tomorrow and not the past, how to appreciate all those human sides of him which the outside world believed not to exist. Mostly Beaverbrook was on uneasy terms with the wives of the journalists who worked for him; he wanted exclusive rights. Many quarrelled with him because of their wives, and some of the wives he preferred were already on bad terms with their husbands. But Jill was one of the very few who knew best how to deal with him in every mood and extremity. And it was with her blessing that I went off one morning to get £3,000 from him when *Tribune* was faced with extinction in 1951. Without it we would not have survived and I felt I could argue that the *Express* newspapers had not paid me a penny when I left in June 1944. However, that was really beside the point. At the time, no one except Jill knew where the money had come from, but when Alan Taylor was writing Beaverbrook's biography, he wrote me a personal letter on 6 May 1970:

> Here is a little query to take your mind off greater things. You told me that Max gave *Tribune* £3,000 in 1951. I decided to forget it. Now I find from the letters that Max told Robertson to charge this to the *Daily Express* and added: 'What would we do for recruits without *Tribune*?' My rule is include everything about Max good or bad. Like all rules it has an exception which I know Max would have approved of: nothing to hurt Mike. So if you ask me to forget it again, I will do. Otherwise I'll put it in. It is for you to decide. A Yes or a No on a postcard is all I want.

I said, and Jill said: 'Put it in,' and quite right too.

Alan Taylor's friendship was the other unlikely one which shaped and enlivened Beaverbrook's life in the last decade, and it all started because Alan read Beaverbrook's books with fresh eyes. His style, in any case, had a kinship with Alan Taylor's own; the taste of the two men for brevity, clarity and mischief was similar. But Alan also set aside the preconceived assumption that Beaverbrook must be a second-rate journalist writing for the hour or the day or for the immediate sensation. He wrote a review in the *Observer* in which, incredibly in the light of all previous academic judgements, he compared Beaverbrook with Tacitus. I was present in the room when Beaverbrook read that review, and his life took on a new exhilaration. He had truly always been most modest about his own writings, never expecting to be regarded as anything more than a chronicler, the good teller of a tale which he knew himself to be a fair assessment. As for the comparison with Tacitus, utterly flattering as he believed it was, it meant a new world and a new friendship had opened before him. Alan Taylor became his intimate confidant on all these questions, his biographer and his friend indeed. Certainly the public judgement on Beaverbrook as a writer was revolutionized by that single verdict. Not all his writings, of course, are in any sense in the same class. Most of them were sheer journalism, good or bad. But the three or four main books on politics *are* masterpieces of political writing and it took Alan

Taylor's discernment to make the discovery in full measure. Moreover, as with Taylor's own style, there are no adventitious aids to conceal the quality. Dubieties are made as hard as diamonds. The high, bold, bald claims can be put to the test; he is never seeking to dodge or prevaricate. Beaverbrook, the historian, is always giving the evidence, if it is there, against his own preconception, against his own party, even against his own heroes. Who could ever have believed that he of all people would have assumed the mantle of historian? Yet it is true and, in the case of his Conservative Party, he played the part with a special relish and glee.

It is there, to his humour, we must always return. 'If Max gets to heaven,' wrote H. G. Wells, 'he won't last long. He'll be chucked out for trying to pull off a merger between heaven and hell . . . after having secured a controlling interest in key subsidiary companies in both places, of course.' But the merger had already taken place under his roof. A mixture of heaven and hell was what it could be like but, after some moments of Miltonic doubt about the outcome, it was usually heaven which triumphed in that combat, and a heaven which no Calvinist could recognize, one which was always liable to dissolve in laughter. Even at the gravest moment the chance of such a beneficient explosion would reappear, and the House of Rimmon might resound to the healing strains of 'The Red Flag', led, say, by another companion treasured for his company alone, Stanley Morrison of *The Times*, ex-jailbird, ex-pacifist, militant Catholic and, as far as I can recall, a light baritone. 'Stanley,' said Beaverbrook, 'does not make the mistake of pouring old wine in new bottles. If the wine is old and really good, he has another use for it.'

Truly, it was his humour which had a special all-encompassing dimension. This was even more part of him, I believe, than the ceaseless energy with which he could whip everyone in sight; the furious yet fitful zeal for the great causes and the others, strange and terrible, in which he believed. Not all the paroxysms of anger, of urgency, of frustration could shake those walls as the laughter did, and there was in it no vein of pretence or hysteria but rather a rich comic view of the human species. It could be called Dickensian or Chaplinesque were it not for the fact that Dickens and Chaplin, along with the Co-op or Covent Garden or the British Council, were listed among his *bêtes noires*, and were it not that he lacked the last full measure of compassion which only the greatest comedians have. Anyhow, Beaverbrook's was a volcano of laughter which went on erupting till the end. No one who ever lodged for a while beneath that Vesuvius will ever forget.

# The Better Side
# Jill Craigie

As I am predisposed in favour of anyone who is fond of my husband, my relationship with Max Beaverbrook was most congenial. I saw, on the whole, the better side of his nature, his charm, sense of humour, capacity for affection, perennial curiosity and, more surprisingly, his understanding of points of view opposed to his own.

At one memorable dinner the guests included a number of American businessmen and Mr Luce, the owner of *Life* magazine. The evening threatened to be deadly, until Max proceeded to give an account of the Cold War as seen by the Soviets. He told how the West, without sufficient justification, began to instal military bases on Soviet frontiers. Brilliantly, he gave the exact dates and locations for the establishment of the bases, from the Arctic to Turkey, maintaining that these apparent threats to Soviet security could only provoke counter-threats. When he had concluded, an American turned to me and asked to my amusement: 'Is this fellow a Commie?'

Dazzled by the performance, I burst out with: 'Oh Max, how marvellous it would be if down a whole page of the *Daily Express* you would show on one side, with maps, the Cold War as seen by the Russians, and on the other side the Cold War as seen by the West. Why don't you do that? It would be so original; it might even do some good.' He merely smiled, then the company exploded, voicing their objections vociferously. The Beaverbrook press seemed to support the conventional view of Soviet Union aggressive intentions. I have wondered since whether that was what Max really believed.

Judging by the few millionaires I have met, they seem to be better than most of us at turning the blind eye to circumstances which might turn out to be inconvenient to themselves. One such incident arose when, for a while, Michael and I were homeless. We had rented a flat on a strictly temporary basis, but when the time came to leave, we had still found nowhere to live. I was working in films at the time and had to drive to the studios every day, so we ran two cars. Having filled them both with an assortment of baggage, some of it tied up with string, also loads of books, kitchen utensils, the odd broom, bedding and laundry wrapped up in a sheet, we returned to the flat to make sure that we had left it in proper order. While we were considering where to go, the telephone rang. Max invited us to dinner.

These invitations were in the nature of command performances. No one was expected to refuse. Michael explained that we could not come as we had to look for accommodation. 'You can have my housekeeper's place,' said Max. 'Come here at five o'clock.' We assumed that the housekeeper must have gone away for the weekend. We arrived at Cherkley, his estate, on time, looking like refugees, to find Max awaiting us in the drive sitting in his limousine, the make of which I never knew, but was far too grand to be called a car. He got out, opened the gate of a field, returned to the steering wheel and, averting his eyes from our unseemly assortment of chattels, told us to follow him.

In solemn procession the three cars weaved their way between a herd of cows, approaching what seemed from a distance to be an old shack. A closer view revealed a timber-boarded bungalow, patchily creosoted, set amid a huge thicket of flourishing nettles. Wielding a stick, Max beat down the nettles, which nevertheless penetrated my stockings, unlocked the front door and stepping inside announced proudly: 'Here it is.' We gazed in astonishment. It was completely empty, damp, derelict, without electricity or gas. 'I've got another one,' said Max cheerfully. 'You can take your choice.' We bumped across a still larger field towards a more promising-looking cottage, but that too was empty and derelict.

We saw four altogether in various parts of the estate, each in appalling condition. They had remained unoccupied since the outbreak of war. By then it was almost time for dinner; there was no escape. We expected to be invited to stay the night, but Max seemed unaware of our predicament. Later, in the darkness, Michael pulled up at the nearest telephone booth and threw himself on the mercy of his friend, the late Curly Mallalieu, MP. We had only hoped to stay the night, but thanks to Rita, Curly's wife, we remained with them for several weeks until, at last, we moved into a new London home.

Three or four times during the subsequent six months, Max wrote to enquire, not *if* we would like to take one of the cottages, but which one we had chosen and when we would be moving in. It had not occurred to us to take the offer seriously, but in his last letter Max showed signs of feeling aggrieved. I was wondering how to reply when it suddenly struck me that there might, after all, be something to be said in favour of accepting the offer. Michael was out of Parliament at the time and wanted to write a serious book about Jonathan Swift. To be free from any disturbance, what better, thought I, than to spend our summers residing in a bungalow surrounded by cows where even the postman would baulk at deliveries. At the same time, I doubted the wisdom of occupying a grace-and-favour residence owned by a Conservative press-lord. Max had already made it clear that the question of rent did not arise. Michael showed not the least interest in the matter; he prefers to leave household arrangements to me. I consulted Nye Bevan. 'It's not what you take, it's what you *give* that matters,' said Nye. Far from reassured, I then consulted my father-in-law, Isaac Foot, the wisest man I have ever known.

He wanted to know how much it would cost to make the bungalow habitable. For the inside I reckoned the sum would amount to between three and four hundred pounds, but the outside would have to be painted, it would need a terrace, preferably in York stone, and I would certainly need outside help to create a lawn and a bit of a garden. So long as we spent as much on making the place habitable as could fairly be charged in rent, my father-in-law thought the arrangement equitable for both parties, and that would not put us under an obligation. Max and young Max, as we called the son, were so delighted with the restoration that they soon set the builders to work on their other cottages.

During the time we spent on the estate, we saw a lot of Max. We were on the spot for dinners and he sometimes called during his walks. He and Michael had much in common. They both suffered from asthma, of which Michael has since been cured. They liked to talk of the liberal administrations of Lloyd George and Bonar Law; of literature, especially of H. G. Wells, Arnold Bennett and Kipling, whom Max had known well. They talked too about newspapers and journalism. Ever on the search for new talent, Max never failed to make a note of Michael's recommendations. Several journalists, unbeknown to themselves, owed their promotion to him; a few others were saved from dismissal. Irrespective of his private opinions, Michael always stuck up for those who had fallen out of favour.

It was a father-and-son relationship, which did not inhibit Michael from attacking the Beaverbrook press most ferociously in public. Only the corruptible can be corrupted. It was a measure of Max's affection and his bigness that he took no offence. We were also on excellent terms with Max's relatives, including later his new wife, Christofer, who treated us with great kindness and gave me a taste for pink champagne. She sent me a generous supply when I was recovering from our car-crash.

Yet, of all the good times we spent together, the most trivial incidents recur most often in my memory – the way, for instance, with Alan Taylor and others, Max liked us to sing 'The Red Flag' after dinners. I also recall most vividly an occasion when Max invited me to accompany him on a walk. He had brought his dog, a dignified rather world-weary-looking chow. When we approached the drive, Max announced his intention of playing rabbits. The rabbit, I soon learned, was to be the limousine. He had got in at the back leaving the chow outside. I sat beside the chauffeur. Looking out of the back window, Max gave the order to drive very fast. The chow came pelting after us with a speed which seemed entirely out of character. Then, without giving the chauffeur the chance to change gear, Max issued in rapid succession a series of confusing, contradictory orders which ran something like this: 'Fast, *faster*, FAST, I said FAST. STOP. Good boy, come on, boy. Fast, *faster*, tease him, TEASE HIM, slow, slowly, good boy, fast, slow, stop. I said STOP. Very slowly, very fast . . .' So it went on, up and down the long magnificent drive, seemingly interminably. The flustered chauffeur turned so unhealthy a shade of purple right down to the bottom of his neck that I feared he might have a heart attack. Max and the dog enjoyed themselves immensely.

He could be a difficult employer, but generous to his employees in retirement, helpful to journalists in trouble. Many socialists regarded Lord Beaverbrook as the embodiment of evil. His was a multi-faceted nature, infinitely complex, contradictory, whimsical, a nature of which the last word can never be said. Besides, he, his children and grandchildren, young Max, Janet, Jean and the others, seem to have been endowed with such a super-abundance of charm that it sometimes required an effort to remind myself that none of them could truthfully be described as angels.

# 'A Shoulder to Cry On'
# Percy Hoskins

When a man lives a very, very long time, his obituaries tend to be written many times over. Most people have read the story of the remarkable Beaverbrook – the son of the manse who made a fortune in Canada and stormed across to England to become an all-powerful newspaper magnate. Some biographers claim he used the power ruthlessly and in a Machiavellian way to influence politicians and public alike. They may be right, but there was another side to Beaverbrook which is scarcely ever mentioned – his sympathy for and understanding of the problems of the reporter. Two examples stand out in the memory of my forty years' association with him.

An MP had reported me to the Speaker of the House of Commons, alleging that I had broken an embargo on the contents of a White Paper. (Actually it was an accurate forecast from an entirely independent source, but at the time, it was one of those 'you must disclose your own source' situations.) Almost immediately the Beaver was on the telephone saying, 'Percy, I hear you are in trouble. Always remember there's a shoulder here for you to cry on.'

On another occasion I was alone in protesting a man's innocence of murder. Ted Pickering – who was then the Editor – has since told me that the Beaver was a little uneasy about my positive stand. The jury took only twenty minutes to agree with my conclusions. Within a matter of minutes there was another telephone call and the voice with the rasping Canadian accent said, 'Two men have been acquitted today, the prisoner and Percy Hoskins.' That was the Beaver's way of letting you know that the power was behind you in storm and in calm.

Probably the most bizarre investigation I ever undertook for the Lord – as he was known in the office – concerned Brendan Bracken. The origin of Brendan Bracken (later to become wartime Minister of Information, head of the *Financial Times* group, and finally a peer who never took his seat in the House of Lords) were clothed in a mystery mostly of his own making, which he embellished from time to time with the most incredible inventions.

His name did not appear in any reference books. To some he said that his parents had perished in an Australian bush fire; in others he encouraged the belief that he was an illegitimate son of Winston Churchill. Reference was made to this last claim in a recent television series in which Lady Churchill tackled the former Prime Minister on the question only to receive, not the expected denial, but just the noncommittal query, 'In what year did you say he was born? Yes, I suppose it could be.' So intimate to the family did Bracken become that Randolph Churchill is said to have made frequent references to 'my bastard brother'.

In 1935 the Beaver and Bracken quarrelled bitterly and the former became determined to clear up the mystery. I was called to Stornoway House and taken off all other work until I had definitely established the origins of this remarkable man. Lord Castlerosse, who was in the room, gave me one valuable hint: 'You should start in Dublin,' he said.

But in the Irish city I quickly discovered that even if you knew the approximate date of birth, the search for a certificate could take anything up to three weeks and Beaverbrook was not the sort of man to wait that long.

The only friend I had in Dublin was Oliver St John Gogarty, the novelist, and a member of the London Press Club. I contacted him and was promptly invited to dinner. One of the other guests that night was W. B. Yeats who was curious to know about my mission to Dublin so I casually remarked, 'I am here to do a profile of Brendan Bracken.'

'In that case,' replied Yeats, 'you should take a trip to Templemore, but be careful, you may not find the natives very co-operative.'

The reference books revealed that Templemore was a small town near Tipperary. On its outskirts was a hikers' retreat known as the Devil's Mountain because the tip was shaped as if it had been bitten off. I purchased a hiker's outfit, got off the train at a station before Templemore, ran some of the way and then – a little breathlessly – called on the oldest doctor in the place. I complained about not feeling too well and after taking my pulse and blood-pressure the doctor commented, 'A man of your weight should not be climbing mountains.'

As he sat down to write a prescription, I remarked, 'It is strange that I should be taken ill here for I believe this is where my MP for North Paddington comes from.'

'You mean Brendan Bracken?' enquired the doctor. 'I brought him into the world.' In the next few minutes he poured out the whole family history. Brendan's father had been the local stonemason. 'In fact,' said the doctor, 'there is a Bracken carrying on the business and he is up the road now carving a tombstone for one of my patients, and Brendan's sister is still living in Dublin.'

A quick search of the parish records and I was back in Dublin interviewing the sister and dispatching a detailed report to Stornoway House. Now, Beaverbrook never used that information, although he admired the way in which it had been obtained. At some later period the two men patched up their quarrel and Bracken remained Beaverbrook's protégé and constant companion.

Fifteen years elapsed, and one Sunday morning I was awakened by a telephone call from the Lord who said, 'I want you and Jeannie to come to dinner at Cherkley tonight' – a command not to be ignored. At the Leatherhead mansion we found an assorted number of other guests: Beverley Baxter MP; a former Editor of the *Daily Express*; Sir Dan Davies, the Harley Street specialist; Frank Owen; a few ladies and Brendan Bracken. The conversation over dinner yielded no clue as to why I had been invited, but as the meal ended and the company rose to move into the private cinema to see the press lord's favourite film *Destry Rides Again*, Beaverbrook laid a restraining hand upon my arm and said, 'Percy, I'll look after Jeannie but I want you to stay and have a chat with Brendan. Aneurin Bevan says he is going to resign from the government and it may mean a general election. Should the Tories win, Brendan will be the new Home Secretary and I want you to put him wise to all the current problems of the police and crime.'

And so for the next hour or so I played guide and counsellor to the man who, years before, I had been sent to Ireland to expose. Events were to prove my advice unnecessary but it taught me the lesson that a politician's worst enemy today may be his greatest friend tomorrow.

Bracken's first admission of his origin came when he received a life peerage just before his death at the age of fifty-seven. The title he selected was Lord Bracken of Templemore.

# 'Robin Badfellow'
# Tom Driberg

The head is too big for the boots. It is a powerful head, broad, rather flat-topped, bulging – almost as if its contents were pressing the bone structure outwards. The brow is deeply furrowed, there is a skirting of wispy grey hair.

The face is dark in hue, a mottled tan, permanently sunburned. The mouth is just as in every cartoon of him by Low or Vicky, a satchel-mouth, bisecting the face in an enormous grin; when something is said which appeals to his sardonic humour, the mouth suddenly gapes in a harsh thunderclap of laughter. Sometimes, when he laughs, he throws his head back and the eyes are as wide open as the mouth, staring as if in astonishment, white glaring above iris. When he is pensive or angry, the eyes narrow nearly to slits. They are 'piercing' eyes – perhaps through deliberation, as an element in the tycoon mask. In friendly or in formidable mood, it is a magnetic face. The Sutherland painting and the Karsh photographs show that he likes to be portrayed, like Cromwell, 'warts and all'.

Long years of public life in England have not modified at all the Canadian resonance of his voice. Sometimes it is loud, grim, and rasping; sometimes it sinks to a melancholy or a coaxing purr. There often seem to be echoes of its intonations in the voices of those who have worked much with him; and they affectionately imitate him in conversation with each other.

When he is dressed (in unobtrusive dark-blue suit, with plain white shirt and plain sombre tie, rather like a humble dissenting minister in the days before Methodists wore Roman collars), the rest of his appearance is an anticlimax. He is five feet seven inches in height, slight of build, with a suspicion of a paunch. The short legs taper to small, neatly shod feet.

He takes no interest in men's clothes, his own or other people's. He likes to see the women at his dinner table elegantly gowned; he does not notice if the men are in evening dress or not. Mostly they are not, for many of those whose company he enjoys prefer not to put on dinner jackets or white ties, and they are often bidden to dinner at short notice – Frank Owen, for instance, unkempt, snarlingly argumentative, red tie flying.

Dinner is the social climax of Beaverbrook's day, and almost its only period of purely social relaxation. There are rarely fewer than seven or eight guests. He is a good and a genial, if a dominant, host. When he is at his house in Cherkley, he does not sit, as most hosts do, at one end of the long table: he sits in the middle of one side, and can thus take part in all the talk and control its theme. He will take pains to make a new, young, shy guest feel at home, to draw him, or her, out. Some say this is like being taught how to swim by being thrown into the deep end of a bath, for Beaverbrook has no 'small talk' and his idea of a conversational opening is to fire direct, searching, often intimately personal questions at novice and expert alike. The impulse is genuinely hospitable; the technique also digs out fodder for the insatiable, wide-ranging curiosity which has helped to make Beaverbrook the most successful newspaper publisher of the century. The process may be a test of character, too, more severe than those to which candidates for posts in the Foreign Service or commissions in the army are subjected: a young man who keeps his head, answers concisely and vigorously, and says when he disagrees with his host, and why, may pass with honours and be invited again; the flounderer or the stooge may be rewarded with a grunt of disgust or a surprisingly violent tirade against some person or institution with which he has to do. Most acceptable of all are those who can contribute some item of hard news to the discussion, though they may be startled to see their host leave the table when they have spoken and scribble a note on a writing-pad on the sideboard – a particularly disconcerting procedure if the story has been embroidered for effect.

The food is of the finest quality – the most delicately flavoured Scotch salmon, a saddle of the most tender lamb, Demeter's cornucopia of young fresh vegetables, a pudding that would have won gold medals at any of the most grandiose gastronomic tournaments of the nineteenth century – and it is prepared by a chef who can have few, if any, equals in the private houses of England today. Yet Beaverbrook eats little himself, and must reject some of his chef's most lyrical offerings.

The wine matches the food. Many bottles are collectors' pieces. All are scrupulously catalogued in a massive cellar-book. From this cellar, on many a Sunday during the Second World War, two bottles of Niersteiner Auslese 1935 would be sent to the War Cabinet offices, where Beaverbrook used to lunch with Winston Churchill, and put on ice for them.

In this respect at least, he is not merely a rich man who has bought the best of everything. He has a true appreciation of wine. Duff Cooper once said: 'If anything could reconcile Max to Belloc' – to whose Catholic and European culture he had a congenital, irrational, bristling antipathy, no doubt richly and hilariously reciprocated – 'it would be Belloc's "Heroic Poem in Praise of Wine".' He knows that carefully cellared champagne, like the company of some women, can be enjoyed at a more mature age than is popularly supposed. Most rich men of seventy-five leave it to their butlers to open and pour wine: there are three manservants waiting, yet he himself gets up from the table, uncorks bottles and replenishes glasses. If it is a bottle of champagne, he will stand up in his place, grip the bottle by its base and point it at each glass in turn round the table, pouring accurately in each: no mean feat. An epicure, if ungratefully critical, might say that he fills the glasses rather too often and fast for wines of such quality: few guests are known to object.

He himself also mixes the cocktail before dinner. It is usually a daiquiri – the West Indian cocktail of rum and cracked ice. He mixes it in a machine which makes a noise like twenty electric razors. He has one of those machines in each of his houses.

It is only in the evening that he himself takes wine, or any alcohol. Even then, he takes it in moderation, though he has one of those apparently iron-clad insides which can absorb champagne and whisky in alternate doses. In the spring of 1954 he gave up alcohol altogether for a time – to the distress of his associates, who found that, without it, he was able to relax even more rarely than before.

His constitution seems to have grown stronger, and his health to have improved in the past decade. At one time he was spoken of as a hypochondriac, and there was some truth in the assessment. He did worry a good deal about his health, and the worry in itself may have aggravated the asthma which has been his chronic complaint. It was partly cured by a stay in the dry, desert climate of Arizona, but his and his valet's day is still punctuated by frequent inhalations and applications of drops and douches.

If, however, hypochondria means completely baseless worry about completely imaginary ills, it was an exaggeration to apply the term to Beaverbrook. He had solid grounds for anxiety, especially about any complaint affecting his throat. Few of his personal friends or employees knew that, in 1918 and 1919, he was ill with a rare, often fatal, fungoid infection of the throat, actinomycosis. For a time cancer was suspected; the rumour ran round that he was dying of it. His bitterest enemies began to forgive him; even Mrs Asquith, whose husband's downfall he had helped to engineer, wrote to say that she regretted some of her more tart epithets.

Mr Wilfred Trotter, an eminent cancer specialist, operated twice. The operations were not successful; the fungoid growth returned. Beaverbrook was advised to see a Portuguese doctor, Gomes by name. His treatment, as Beaverbrook recalls it, was simple, drastic and agonizing: he poured four hundred drops of iodine down Beaverbrook's throat daily. Then there was another, minor operation. The throat healed. Beaverbrook did not die. Long afterwards he said: 'It had not been my intention to die.' A secondary pleasure of his recovery may well have been the knowledge that his enemies would now be cancelling their forgiveness and Mrs Asquith regretting her remorse.

He used to worry about his eyesight, too. It seems to serve him adequately now, though he does not like to waste it, or his time, on long letters or long articles. 'Keep it short' is a maxim of his, and short articles are therefore preferred to long in his newspapers.

From his 'hypochondriac' period dates a general instruction to news and feature editors that stories of disease and medicine, of strange plagues and new cures, should be given prominence. 'People like reading about them,' he would say. If his editors were able without too much difficulty to identify the 'people' in his dictum, they were not so foolish as to question it. It may well, in any case, be true. At least when asthma obliged him to give up smoking, there is no evidence that the newspapers were ever instigated to an anti-tobacco crusade. Had they been, there is little doubt that the efficient men who run the business side of them would have pointed out, as it would have been their duty to, that much of the advertising revenue was derived from the sale of space to cigarette manufacturers.

There is little or no smoking after dinner at Cherkley – not because Beaverbrook, like some fanatical non-smokers, dislikes it in his presence, but because, as soon as dinner is over, he steers his guest firmly into his comfortable private cinema, in which smoking is forbidden by the safety regulations. Most of the good films of the day are shown here; it is one of the incidental, though not one of the least important, duties of one of his film critics to select films likely to entertain him. The films are gladly lent by the companies making or distributing them. It is one of Beaverbrook's idiosyncrasies that, just as children's presents are supposed to be a 'surprise', he prefers not to tell his guests in advance what films he is going to show them. An attempt seems sometimes to have been made to choose films likely to please particular guests. Beaverbrook's own taste includes a penchant for good westerns. His favourite film is *Destry Rides Again*; he owns a copy of it, and is said to have seen it sixteen times.

When the film is over, he may sit for a while in the drawing-room with his guests and the old chow dog, probably in order to tidy up items of work with those of them who are also his employees. The hours in the cinema may have been, in a sense, an escape from the conversational obligations that normally follow a dinner party. Merely social chatter, or balanced discussion of general principles, bores him: light gossip is beneath him (unless it is personal and of political or business significance); abstract, philosophic, artistic or antiquarian argument is beyond his competence; his passionate obsession is with the concrete, the 'human', the financial, the topical. He may play a few records on the gramophone (the latest batch from New York, or calypsos from the West Indies); or telephone to a night editor his comments on any important late news, of which he will have been notified; or dictate a few memoranda into the Dictaphone near the grand piano, one of many such machines in the various rooms of his various houses. Mr Percy Cudlipp once said that Beaverbrook's two favourite musical instruments were the gramophone and the telephone; he might have added the Dictaphone, possibly the dominant instrument in this machine-age trio.

If the dinner party has not been a formal one, and he is in a convivial mood with a few cronies, he can sometimes be persuaded to sing: songs of the Canadian lumbermen and the Scottish metrical paraphrases of the Psalms are his favourites, and of the latter he likes best 'The Lord's My Shepherd, I'll Not Want' to the tune of Crimond.

Soon, however, he will be off to bed, gravely offering his guests the full-arm's-length handshake characteristic of him. A vigilant servant will have seen to it that the lift is down in the hall for him. It is an unusual lift. Because it was installed long after the house was built, it has no shaft: it descends, silently, straight from the open hall. If an unobservant guest is standing underneath it, he may be alarmed but he is in no danger; some magic device causes it to hover and stop an inch above his head.

The lift carries its master slowly up to his bedroom. He is asleep by midnight or one o'clock. For he wakes early, and he has a busy day.

It starts between five and seven in the morning, whenever he happens to wake. He reads voraciously, but fragmentarily, the books, magazines, and newspaper clippings which are piled on and around his enormous bed. As he glances at the cuttings, he throws nine out of ten to the floor; they are done with. The tenth he puts aside: there may be an idea for an editorial in it, or something he wants to check.

Soon the carpet looks like the scene of a paperchase. The same phenomenon attends Beaverbrook wherever he is, if he is on his own ground (and he stirs from it, nowadays, as little as possible): whether he is at Cherkley, or at his penthouse in Arlington Street, Piccadilly, or at his farmhouse in Somerset, or at his villa, La Capponcina, at Cap d'Ail in the south of France, or at one of his three Caribbean houses. ('He has seven houses,' a friend has said of him, with a not-altogether note of pity, 'and no home ... Every one of them is a glorified office.') The same phenomenon occurs when he is in his car: cuttings, cuttings, Kleenex tissues, memoranda, cuttings, reports. Most of them go on the floor, some to his secretary, sitting in front by the driver: 'Here y'are Miss Rosenberg, here y'are ...'; and every minute or two, again, 'Here y'are.' The same phenomenon occurred, too, in the caravan – specially built on a bus chassis, and now sold – in which he used sometimes to travel to his West Country farms, entertaining his guests en route to luncheon. Paper is Beaverbrook's element. It is almost as necessary to him as air. His campaigns against the restriction of newsprint supplies correspond psychologically with his own limitless appetite for his essential raw material, as they do economically with the interests of his newspapers. For his own private letters and memoranda, he often uses the thinnest, cheapest flimsy, innocent of engraved or printed address, and of the pretentious coronet with which less powerful peers adorn their notepaper.

At about eight o'clock, after he has done his deep-breathing exercises, he rings. Breakfast is brought to him, with all the morning newspapers – the direct cue, of course, for a new orgy of paper-tearing and paper-discarding, for the dictating into his bedside machine of several dozen messages to his staff.

By ten he is on the telephone fairly continuously, collecting news, exchanging views with business and political cronies, giving instructions to stockbrokers and secretaries and editors, issuing sharp summonses ('Will you come and see me at 11.30 ... Goodbye to you.') Similar activities occur in the early evening, or indeed at almost any time during the day or night: he has under his control, after all, newspapers published every weekday morning, every weekday evening, and every Sunday. There is never a moment when some column is not being compiled; some editorial onslaught is always brewing. There are always relays of people available to see him: he dislikes being alone. Transport is provided for visitors as a matter of course, however far they are coming – an elderly taxi from Leatherhead Station or an air fare from London to Nice. He paid the transatlantic fares, by air or sea, of guests who came from Canada to his seventy-fifth birthday party in May 1954. His friends are useful to him as sources of news, but it is not primarily because they are useful that he cultivates them: his feelings of friendship are genuine. He is, however, hypersensitive: a slight mistake, or a joke that he does not care for, will sometimes antagonize him disproportionately. He is also naturally, and cannily, combative. 'When a man hits me,' he once said, 'I wait until he's not looking and hit him twice.'

When some political or personal quarrel ends or interrupts a friendship, or when a close acquaintance, for some reason, cools off and ceases to seek his company, he is not the man to shrug his shoulders and forget about it; he is apt to feel, passionately, that he has been bereaved, or even betrayed. His reactions to such experiences, however, are neither simple nor uniform. In some cases he will inveigh against the lost friend sonorously and cumulatively, with the sombre fury of an Old Testament prophet castigating human wickedness: 'Ah . . . what a scoundrel! Did you ever know such a scoundrel? Never was there such a rascal . . .' and so on. In such cases it is unlikely that the erring friend will receive favourable publicity in Beaverbrook's newspapers.

In other cases, the parting is an occasion of sorrow rather than of anger. Rudyard Kipling was for many years an intimate of Beaverbrook's: their ardent imperialism was a link; they were congenial companions. Kipling's name (with those of Tim Healy and Bonar Law) is on the first page of the visitor's book at Cherkley, dated 13–14 July 1912. This book was a gift from Kipling, and he inscribed in it verses composed by himself:

> This is the prayer the Cave Man prayed
> When first his household fire he lit
> And saw the solemn stars o'erhead
> Contemptuously look down on it –
> The sweep and silence of the night,
> The brooding dark on every side
> Oppressed his simple mind with fright
> And, 'Heaven send me friends!' he cried . . .
>
> And that is why I send this tome
> Of virgin pages fifty wrought
> To hold the names of all who come

Beneath your roof at Cherkley Court.
O long, long may the record run,
And you enjoy until it ends
The Four Best Gifts beneath the Sun:
Love, Peace, and Health, and Honest Friends.

These agreeable verses were certainly written without ironic intention;
yet it may be doubted whether so generous a share of the 'four best
gifts' has fallen to the man to whom the verses were addressed as falls
to the average citizen of modest means. The record has run long
indeed, but Kipling himself was not to see it to its end. Some years
before his death he was estranged from Beaverbrook – because, oddly
enough, in one respect, Beaverbrook was a less thorough-going
imperialist than he: Beaverbrook favoured home rule for Ireland at a
time when this issue provided a sharp test of Tory loyalty, and Kipling
never forgave him for it. Years after the quarrel, Beaverbrook sought
reconciliation. Kipling answered him coolly. Those who knew both
men throughout those years cannot recall any occasion on which
Beaverbrook spoke harshly of Kipling.

By about eleven o'clock the main work of Beaverbrook's morning is
over. In his bathroom an open fire is burning. After his bath – reclining
in which he has, on occasions, dictated editorials and interviewed
employees – he dresses quickly and goes downstairs (passing on the
way, if he is at Cherkley, Eric Kennington's vivid portrait of his son
Max Aitken in RAF uniform). He is still a keen walker: every morning,
and sometimes in the afternoon as well, he will walk for several miles,
talking all the time to some congenial companion. In London he walks
in Green Park; at Cherkley a car takes him up to the top of a hill and
meets him three-quarters of an hour or an hour later at the other end of
a path – the Long Gallop – that runs along a fine, open, well-wooded
ridge, part of a property that he gave some years ago to the National
Trust. (He regrets having done so, for he now disapproves of the
National Trust and has often denounced it as a device for enabling
hereditary aristocrats to live in houses that they cannot afford to
maintain, and rich men to avoid spending as much as they should –
citing especially the case of one of the socially exalted families with
whom he is always feuding, the Astors.)

Wherever he is, Beaverbrook goes for his walks. Most of all he likes
to have someone with him to whom the scene is new: in the country or
in town, he is an enthusiastic and informative guide, pausing
frequently to draw attention to the excellence of the trees in this
plantation or of the houses in that street. A friend walking with him

once in Toronto was puzzled by the vehemence with which Beaverbrook exclaimed again and again, pointing along street after street of
ornate but characterless skyscrapers – 'Look at that! Isn't that
beautiful? There now ... Beautiful, beautiful!' – until it dawned on him
that, beauty being in the eye (or mind) of the beholder, the special
beauty of these busy modern streets lay in the fact that Toronto was
the most prosperous city in Canada. Prosperity, to Beaverbrook, is not
merely an indispensable material condition: it has a positively
aesthetic appeal. It is no accident that his own best-selling book was
called *Success*; and that its main theme is success in making money.
When he is reminiscing about his boyhood, and the games of marbles
which he used to play with the other boys, he boasts: 'I knew the value
of every marble in the place.' To him 'value' is synonymous with 'price'.
He is profoundly cynical about human character and its weaknesses:
in this respect he conforms with the classic definition of a cynic – 'a
man who knows the price of everything and the value of nothing'. He is
almost a pure materialist, in the Western, non-dialectical sense of the
word – yet only 'almost', for his materialism and his hard-boiled
cynicism are relieved by impulses of generosity and personal loyalty.
He will go to some pains to buy good presents for every boy and girl
invited to a children's party; he keeps on his payroll many old
employees who are long past useful work; there are a few old intimates
in public life – outstandingly, Winston Churchill – whom he will
never attack in print or speech even if he disagrees with their policies.

Many rich men indulge in public benefactions, and it is never easy
to be sure of the integrity of their motives in doing so: Beaverbrook has
been a lavish public benefactor, but he also maintains so many private
pensioners that it is difficult to acquit him of some genuine kindness
of heart, or at least of a vestigial Calvinistic conscience. If taxed with
such a weakness, he will offset it by recounting some instance of
uncharitable conduct on his part. Or he will tell a joke against himself
– recalling, for instance, the case of an elderly Scottish woman, in poor
circumstances, who came to him one day and gave him a Bible that had
been used by his father before he emigrated to Canada. In the emotion
of the moment, and thinking to ease the remaining year or two of her
life, he gave her an annuity of £2,000 a year. 'Hah!' he snorts in mock
disgust. 'She lived to ninety-eight!'

If the weather is hot, he may walk in the garden at Cherkley. Near
the windows of the house he grows stroninium: from this flower is
extracted a drug supposed to relieve asthma. There are many blue and
purple flowers. Bees, he has observed, prefer these; they will get nectar
from catsnip and lavender, but 'never, never', he insists, 'from the

honeysuckle vine – never at all'. A guest was tactless enough one day to discover what looked like a honey-bee actively exploring the honeysuckle. 'It must be a bumble bee,' said Beaverbrook, slightly put out, 'a small bumble bee.'

He is less interested than most millionaires in the standard millionaire pleasures. He had a yacht (named, whimsically, *John Calvin*); but he owns no racehorses. For a time he did go in for racing and had a house at Newmarket (called Calvin House); but he soon fell out with the moguls of the Jockey Club. He was annoyed by what seemed to him the hypocrisy of rules, such as the rule against pulling horses, which were constantly broken with impunity. He found the company of racing people tedious. 'They know nothing about politics,' he grumbled, 'and nothing about newspapers. They know nothing about anything but racing.' So he took to arriving at race meetings after the first race and leaving before the last – and, pretty soon, he sold out. He had won a few races – none of them big. The experience had cost him some £200,000. Since then the leading figures of the turf, such as Lord Rosebery, have not been among his closest friends. His newspapers have also campaigned consistently against the exclusion of divorcees from the Royal Enclosure at Ascot.

He no longer bothers to maintain a private aircraft: it is simpler to hire or borrow one, or even, sometimes, to fly by the ordinary public service. (From flying, he got the idea of the safety seatbelt, which he has fitted in his cars.)

The toys of wealth may, indeed, seem less worth bothering about when literally everything can be bought that money can buy. Nobody, not even he, can compute precisely Beaverbrook's wealth; but he is certainly one of the richest men in the world. He has always, moreover, retained his Canadian domicile, and thus has an ample dollar as well as sterling resources. In February 1953, it was estimated by a Canadian magazine that he owned British and Canadian properties worth $70 million. His personal dividend from London Express Newspapers Ltd, for the financial year that ended on 30 June 1953, was some £85,000.

One of the axioms by which Beaverbrook's life has been guided is that money plus brains equals power. He has, it will be agreed, enough money; he has enough of the sort of brains that ought to be needed to secure the sort of power in which alone he is interested. Why, then, is the prevailing impression derived from a few hours or days spent in his company one of driving restlessness, of an absolute want of serenity, of a machine that must continue to operate after its function is exhausted?

Partly this may be because, after a boyhood little of which was devoted to formal education, the single-minded pursuit of worldly power has left him no time to turn aside and develop wider intellectual resources and cultural interests. Therefore, if he stopped doing the only things he knows how to do, his life and his mind would be a vacuum. (By contrast, his friend Churchill, though his academic performance in boyhood was undistinguished, read widely and deeply in early manhood and has in later life cultivated the art of painting.)

A main cause of this chronic restlessness, however, may be that the axiom itself has proved fallacious. He has the money, he has the brains: where is the power? It has escaped him. He has achieved high office, but not the highest. Most men have their price, but not every man. He has failed signally to influence public opinion, among those high in the state or among ordinary citizens. The former mostly regard him as a menace; the latter buy his newspapers in millions for their entertainment value, consistently disregard their editorial advice, and think of him politically, not without the bantering affection proper to a national institution, as a comic 'character'.

It is hard to find anyone who has had much to do with Beaverbrook who will praise him without qualification. Many, especially among Conservatives of the more feudal sort, regard him with remarkably intense disapproval. To the public he is 'The Beaver' – a zoological symbol of tireless industry. Some Roman Catholic intellectuals of the school of Belloc and Chesterton lampooned him as 'Caliban'; this did not increase his affection for Roman Catholic intellectuals generally – though Mr Stanley Morison, who might be so described, is a good friend of his and Mr J. B. Morton, Belloc's devoted biographer, has been employed by him for many years as 'Beachcomber'. The late Hugh Kingsmill, more wittily, called him 'Robin Badfellow' – a malign cousin of the good goblin of ancient folklore. One of his closest friends has said: 'Everything that everyone says about Max is true – the best things and the worst things.'

# The Terror
## James Cameron

I worked for Lord Beaverbrook for many years; I left him in circumstances of great and mutual disaffection. In later years I came to know him again, and found in him as a man all the qualities that were not in the tycoon.

I do not think anyone got to know Beaverbrook by working for him. Between him and the Beaver boys hung the impenetrable barrier of a common purpose. He did not believe anyone could possibly disagree with him and still be sane. Not when you took his money. When you stopped, then you found the charm. How he could charm!

His obituaries varied from the adulatory to the waspish. This is reasonable; it was virtually impossible to come to terms with Lord Beaverbrook in any sort of medium emotion. He was genuinely hated by some, and genuinely loved by some.

Others can adjudicate on his life and works as a politician. I can only consider him as a newspaperman, and at that he was a terror. He loved being a terror. He loved stimulating his gifted flock by keeping them forever on the edge of phobia, showering them with bounty and abuse, scaring them to death and giving lavish parties for them.

It is true that he bought men's souls. It was not always done with money. The man who could charm a bird off a bough could certainly charm left-wing journalists into the fold, sometimes before they knew what had hit them. What had hit them was the most galvanic personality in the business – a business that is that much shorter of the quality today.

But journalism to Beaverbrook was merely an extension of politics. He did not hide it; he proclaimed it. He told the Press Commission: 'I run my newspapers solely for the purposes of propaganda.' The business of garbing that propaganda in the most highly professional of expertise he left to his technicians. He pressed the buttons.

The paradox (which he wryly appreciated) was that the means came off and the ends didn't. He finished with a brilliant and prosperous newspaper empire and a trail of lost causes. 'I keep telling 'em,' he once said, 'and they pay no heed, but continue on their way like brands to the burning. Still, I hammer 'em.'

On his eighty-fifth birthday two weeks before he died, he made a speech, vitally articulate for a man so frail, and that was his theme. He had accomplished everything, and nothing.

He had made a million pounds, or maybe several, and that was all. No Empire Free Trade – nor, for that matter, any Empire. None of the causes for which he had laboured so long, or invoked so much talent, including Holy Writ itself. All he had left was a scintillating example of daily journalism – and, he proclaimed, a sense of humour.

All his life, especially as he grew old and exhausted, he thought back wistfully to the days when he had been a small-shot tycoon but a big-shot politician – the brave days of king-making in 1916, when the Beaverbrook homes at Cherkley and the Hyde Park Hotel were the hub of the splendid machinations to get Asquith out and Lloyd George in. It is pretty sure that he loved the machinations more than the objective. 'I laid my web,' he would say with relish. 'How they needed me!'

If he could be less than honest with those he disliked, he was completely candid about his own character. It seemed there was nothing he enjoyed better than explaining how he was tricked into his peerage. He had anticipated its bestowal, and when he wanted to reject it, he couldn't, to save his face. 'Thus was vanity my downfall, or up-fall,' he would say with pleasure. But he genuinely regretted being shunted upstairs, far from the splendid scheming of the Commons.

In that last speech – which was a farewell – he explained how first New Brunswick had become too small for him, then London too small for him. 'They say,' he mused, 'that I may well find the same trouble with hell.'

That we shall never know.

# Son of the Manse
# Logan Gourlay

A few minutes after the handshake, he gave me a daiquiri. The latter, I noticed, was decidedly stronger than the former. It was my first meeting with Lord Beaverbrook at his country house, Cherkley Court near Leatherhead, shortly after I had been summoned from Glasgow, my birthplace and training ground in journalism, to work for one of his newspapers in Fleet Street.

His detractors like Malcolm Muggeridge, who place him among the most evil men they have ever met (and in Muggeridge's case, that is quite a condemnation), have often accused him of trying to corrupt his young employees by encouraging their weaknesses for wine and women – and, in the case of Tom Driberg, for young men. However, Muggeridge has never gone so far as to blame Beaverbrook for the period, prior to his salvation by Jesus and the Pope, when he was a conspicuous consumer of wine and an ardent pursuer of women. And I trust that the Christian clarity of vision his conversion has brought him allows him to see in retrospect that, rather than encourage the highly talented, but hopelessly twisted, Driberg in his homosexuality, Beaverbrook did all he could to protect him from its legal consequences. To suggest, as Muggeridge has done, that by protecting Driberg Beaverbrook was 'luring him on' is surely a Machiavellian interpretation of a good Samaritan deed.

In my own case, although that first daiquiri from Beaverbrook was followed by many more, proudly prepared in his electric mixer (which was as much a part of his personal gadgetry as his Dictaphone), and by a considerable amount of champagne and other assorted beverages, and although I share to a limited extent Muggeridge's two main pre-conversion weaknesses, he will be disappointed to know that Beaverbrook never encouraged, or fostered, them, except in the sense that, while I worked for him, he made it possible for me to pay for them.

On the contrary, there was more than one occasion when, taking the part of the stern Calvinist uncle or Presbyterian dominie, as he sometimes did with me, he rebuked me for my excesses, and warned me that hell-fire and damnation might await me unless I mended my ways. If it suited his purpose, he liked to point out that, although I wasn't a son of the manse as he was, I should be grateful for my fairly strict Presbyterian upbringing in Glasgow.

My journalistic apprenticeship had started on the *Glasgow Herald* and continued on Beaverbrook's Scottish *Daily* and *Sunday Express*, for which I had worked as a reporter and sub-editor before a summons to Fleet Street to try my hand at writing a new column for the *Sunday Express*. The Editor, John Gordon, had decided the column should be launched under the heading 'Show Business', and it was to be a film and theatre gossip column, replacing the more sedately titled 'A Seat in the Stalls'. This had been a column of theatre and film reviews which Stephen Watts, another Glaswegian graduate incidentally, had decided to vacate after writing it stylishly and knowledgeably for several years.

In later years, when Beaverbrook cast an appreciative eye on my column, he would claim sometimes that he had decided on the title after hearing Ethel Merman singing 'There's No Business Like Show Business' in the Irving Berlin musical *Annie Get Your Gun*. If he were exceptionally appreciative he would also claim he had decided to summon me to Fleet Street after reading something I had written in the Scottish *Sunday Express*, to which, between spells of reporting and sub-editing, I had contributed a few film and theatre reviews and pieces of gossip. On other occasions, when I earned Editor John Gordon's approval, he would indicate that *he* had decided to bring me down the high road from Glasgow to London after he had been impressed by a piece I had written in the Scottish edition. It would have been a mistake to disagree with either of my overlords, and I was more than happy to accept, when required, one or other of the little myths, but the truth, I'm afraid, was less flattering.

After trying out a number of journalists eager to do the show-business column, and failing to find one to produce what he had in mind, Gordon turned to his Deputy Editor, Reg Payne, for suggestions. They tried a few more London-based journalists, and then Payne, who had served for a spell in Glasgow as Scottish Editor, looked north, partly in desperation but also in the knowledge that Gordon, and of course Beaverbrook, with their ancestral backgrounds, wouldn't disapprove of a recruit from over the border.

The name Jack Gourlay could hardly have stuck in Reg Payne's mind because of the brilliance of my contributions under that by-line

when he was Scottish Editor; and indeed on occasion he had spiked
them. But at least he associated the by-line with show-business
journalism, and the choices were narrowing. Anyway, one afternoon
he tracked me down by telephone to a Glasgow coffee bar, and I was on
the overnight sleeper to London. The arrangement was that I was to
write, or try to write, the new show-business column for two weeks. If
my efforts didn't reach the required standards, I could regard it as a
fortnight's paid holiday, and use my return ticket. It was never used. I
was launched on a new column with a new by-line.

One of Beaverbrook's decrees was that names like Tom, Dick, Harry
and Jack were not impressive enough to be used as by-lines in his
newspapers. My attitude at that stage was that I didn't greatly care
which by-line was used, provided I was adequately paid, so I agreed
that my full name, John Logan Gourlay, would probably impress the
readers more than just Jack. But when it was pointed out that it might
be a bit long for use in a single column, the 'John' was dropped.

Once again, depending on their opinion of my columnar efforts, the
credit for my Sunday rechristening would be taken on occasions by
Beaverbrook or by John Gordon, much to the annoyance of Reg Payne,
who never failed to say it was his choice, even though there were also
times when he thought, partly because of my lack of gratitude to him,
that I should be fired.

I might well have been fired at the outset because of the wine which
followed that pre-dinner daiquiri at Cherkley. I had been driven down
from Fleet Street by John Gordon, and he had warned me in an
avuncular way to be prepared for a Beaverbrookian baptism of fire.
Gordon said: 'The Old Man will probably try to catch you out in some
way. But you've got a good Scots head on your shoulders. You'll be all
right.'

'A good Scots head' was one of his favourite terms of approbation,
and he indicated that the possessor of one would not be too overawed
by the impressive array of guests I was likely to meet at the dinner
party; he spared me any overworked clichés from our national poetic
heritage like 'we're a' Jock Tamson's bairns'. It went without saying
that 'a good Scots head' was also one that could withstand a fair intake
of Scotch. I noticed incidentally, as I coped with the daiquiri that
Beaverbrook had thrust into my hand without asking if I wanted it or
not, that Gordon was so much at home at Cherkley that he was able to
go straight to a sideboard and help himself to a drink from a bottle of
Scotch.

The other guests looked impressive and they included one or two
Establishment figures whom I'd never seen outside the pages of a

newspaper, but before I could be introduced to anyone, dinner was announced. As the guests filed into the dining-room, Beaverbrook, who was standing at the door, told them where to sit. When my turn came, he surveyed me with a gnomish smile which spread from ear to ear, and which I was to learn to recognize as a warning signal. He said: 'Ah, you're my youngest guest and this is your first visit to my home. You must have a place of honour at the head of the table.' Leading me there, he added: 'I hope you're not one of those young radicals who wants to abolish the House of Lords.' I assured him I wasn't (and as far as I know, Michael Foot, who was among the guests, was not in favour of total abolition at that time either).

'In that case,' Beaverbrook went on, 'you won't object if I put a member of the House of Lords on your right. And on your left I'll put another journalist so you'll feel at ease. He's quite well-known.'

The passing years have erased the name of the peer but the 'quite well-known' journalist was Arthur Christiansen, Editor of the *Daily Express* and a famous Fleet Street figure. He obviously recognized Beaverbrook's mischievous mood and shared it as much as his own temperament would allow, but he was also doing his avuncular best to help me to cope with the situation. He whispered to me: 'The Old Man's trying to trip you up. Don't let him do it. Attack's always the best defence. What you should do is send the wine back. Say it's corked or something.'

The butler had just poured some wine and at that moment I was taking a sip to lubricate my dry nervous throat, but Christiansen's suggestion was so startling that I spluttered. Beaverbrook, who was sitting at the centre of the table, the real position of command, looked towards me as I spluttered and choked on his fine white Burgundy. His voice with that unmistakable Canadian accent, which until then had been as soft as maple syrup, hardened slightly: 'Is there something wrong with the wine, Mr Gourlay? Does it offend your palate?'

Before I could stop spluttering and answer, Christiansen said: 'I believe he thinks it's corked.' Turning to me, he asked: 'Isn't that right?' I answered with a nod that I hoped was non-committal.

The assembled company fell silent and stared at me. It was one of those moments of agonizing embarrassment for whoever is the centre of attention, best captured, without words, by a cartoonist. For a second, Beaverbrook looked as though he would like to crown me with one of the bottles from his cellar, of which he was justifiably proud. But then, perhaps realizing that Christiansen was sharing some of his mischievousness, the smile spread from ear to ear and he said: 'Now isn't that amazing? Here is young Gourlay just down from Scotland to work for me. He was probably weaned on whisky but we find he has a palate for fine wine. A young connoisseur from the Gorbals. Wonders will never cease. A young connoisseur from the Gorbals.'

Like all good propagandists he knew that repetition was effective and that strict adherence to the truth not always essential. I had been born and brought up in Govan, a slightly less deprived and depressed area of Glasgow than the Gorbals, but he could justify the remark because the *Express* office building in Glasgow, a replica of the gleaming black edifice in London, was located on the edge of the Gorbals where it looked particularly alien – like a structure dropped from another planet.

When the laughter, which had greeted his sally, died down, Beaverbrook, obviously savouring a situation like this, of which he was something of a connoisseur, ordered the butler to change the wine. The butler, knowing his master's moods and humours, may simply have pretended to go through the motions; I was too confused to watch carefully, but new glasses were brought and more wine poured. Beaverbrook signalled that the verdict of the Gorbals connoisseur was impatiently awaited. I sipped hurriedly and nodded approval: the meal proceeded. Beaverbrook barely gave me time to recover before he launched an attack on another front to test my reactions.

When there was a slight lull in the conversation round the table, Beaverbrook boomed: 'You must tell us what your politics are, Mr Gourlay. Some of my guests are politicians. They'd be fascinated to know what makes all you young fellas vote Labour. I suppose you do. Or maybe a young connoisseur from the Gorbals votes Communist, eh?'

Before I could answer, Michael Foot, showing as always that sympathy for the underdog (which may have occasionally been a handicap when he was Labour Party leader), leapt to my rescue: 'I'm sure we'd all be much more interested in hearing what your politics are, Lord Beaverbrook. It's difficult to know from day to day.'

The attention was immediately diverted from me, and Beaverbrook didn't return to the attack that evening. It ended with the showing, which had almost become a ritual, of his favourite film *Destry Rides Again*, in his private cinema. It would be some time later, after several visits to that cinema, before I mastered the art of dozing with my head at the correct upright angle to simulate wakefulness. On occasions, Beaverbrook must have taken a nap himself and the film shows were partly intended, I'm sure, to give his guests, young and old, a chance to relax before the conversational jousting that could follow over the final whiskies and sodas in the sitting-room.

At the stage when I started to work for him in London, we were well into what could be called the 'bronze age' of his Fleet Street reign, meaning that the staff saw no more of him in EC4, where he had once slaved and slept in a flat above the printing presses, than the Epstein bust which stood in the entrance hall. He controlled his newspaper empire from Cherkley, his flat at Arlington House overlooking Green Park, his villa, La Capponcina, at Cap d'Ail on the Riviera, and his house in Jamaica; and he kept in touch by such regular and persistent use of the telephone, the Dictaphone, and the postal and cable services that you, as a member of the editorial staff, felt at times that he was stalking the corridors of the office, peering over your shoulder as you tapped out the words on the typewriter, and reproaching you with bronze eyes as you crossed the entrance hall on your way to Poppins, the office pub, for a quick drink when you should have been at your desk.

After the dinner at Cherkley, my next meeting with him was at his flat in Arlington House when he finalized my contractual obligations to him – and completed his initiation tests. He had a firm rule that, if he conferred the honour on you of allowing you to write under your own by-line in one of his papers, you must not peddle your words elsewhere in other papers, magazines, books – or even on the air – without his consent, and he made it clear that I would be no exception. It would be several years later before I would risk the bantering question: 'Can I have your permission to write to my old mother?' At this stage, I was willing to agree to sell him, if not my soul, my entire word output and exclusive professional services, but he said: 'I believe you're a director of a rival publishing company. We can't have that. You'll have to resign.'

I told him, as he must have known, that it was a small, private limited company with authorized capital of £100, which I had formed with a colleague in Glasgow, and by no stretch of the imagination could it be considered a rival publishing company to his. Our publications were diverse in subject matter but, I pointed out, they were limited in influence and revenue. They were a monthly magazine about the film world, and a quarterly Scottish angling magazine, the revenue from which just about subsidized occasional slim volumes of poetry (some in Lallans with glossaries longer than the poems), linked to the Scottish literary renaissance, which at that time was taking place about every other year.

Nevertheless Beaverbrook ruled I would have to resign from the company: he couldn't allow me to devote any of my professional time and efforts to non-Beaverbrook publications, worthy though some of them might be. I suggested naïvely that he might like to take over my company. He indicated patiently that hardly a day passed without publishing companies of much greater scope and potential being offered to him at give-away prices.

The demand for my resignation from the Scottish company was repeated emphatically. I had a choice: a contract with him to write a weekly column that might lead to greater editorial eminence and Fleet Street glory, or a directorship in a small publishing company in Glasgow. (For the previous twelve or eighteen months, I had been working for his Scottish papers on a freelance basis.)

I tried to point out again that it was surely a mistake to compare my tiny company with his vast empire and to regard my tuppence-ha'penny publications as in any way competitors of his powerful papers. I said that it didn't seem to me I was being given a fair choice, and that in all conscience I couldn't just resign, particularly because it would leave my Scottish partner in the lurch. Fixing me with a bronze-hard look, he asked: 'Is that your last word?' I nodded: if I looked confident, I didn't feel it. The smile that followed was sudden and startling, as wide as usual, but the space between the ears was filled this time with more warmth than mischief. He strode from behind the lectern, one of his cherished props from which he had been looking down on me as I sat on a chair, like a Presbyterian preacher from a righteously elevated pulpit. He clapped me on the shoulder and said: 'Ah, you're a loyal fella. You made a good choice. I like that. Y-aas. A precious thing, loyalty. I think I'll arrange to pay you a bit more. Not much. Mustn't spoil you. But a bit.'

Over the next fifteen years, until I resigned from the *Express* group, he never mentioned my small company again. However, I had now become, whenever the mischievous mood took him, the young capitalist and company director from the Gorbals, as well as the wine connoisseur.

Then he discovered, in the course of the inquisition that usually took place when you were selected as the member of the staff to accompany him on one of his morning walks through Green Park, or up Bond Street, that in my youth I had been associated with the Communist Party in Glasgow. It was fuel for his mischievousness. He stopped and pointed his stick at me accusingly: 'My God, here I am in the middle of Green Park with a Red.' He chuckled: 'Ah might've known it. The Gorbals breeds Reds. But what a mixture. Capitalist, connoisseur, communist . . .' He was savouring the alliterative mixture. 'Communist, connoisseur, capitalist . . .'

I told him that I had never been a member of the party and that my links with communism were partly romantic: in my last year at school in Glasgow, I had met the girl I would marry in later years; she was then a member of the Young Communist League who, with the idealistic fervour of youth, wanted to chalk slogans on walls at dark street corners while I had equally fervent but less ideological aims, and whose father was a dedicated, indeed noble, Marxist, who sharpened my young fifth-form mind in long discussions about dialectical materialism. Beaverbrook's comment following this explanation was characteristic: 'So you're a Red by marriage.'

After he had met my wife at a staff party and discovered that her hair was red by natural Celtic heredity, and after I had been labelled a 'miserable coward' by an irate reader for attacking actors and actresses who couldn't answer back, Beaverbrook said smilingly: 'Any man who marries a girl with red hair as well as red politics can't be a coward.'

I didn't tell him that because of her fiery temperament, my pet name for her was 'Squibs', but he found out by chance from a colleague and, chuckling over the somewhat childish joke he occasionally enjoyed, he said: 'You should take out extra fire insurance on that house of yours.'

It was often difficult to decide how Beaverbrook regarded the marital ties of his staff and their domestic commitments and responsibilities. At times of family crisis – an illness, a death, a financial problem – no one could be more helpful and supportive. But at other times he could appear to be inconsiderate and even jealous if, in his view, one of his journalists was devoting too much time, energy and attention to a spouse, and not enough to the newspaper. Once, when I was taking leave of him at a late hour, I said: 'I'd better get back to my wife.' He asked with one of his quizzical looks: 'Which one? Don't forget you're married to the paper as well. Like me, you're married to that bitch goddess – journalism – there's no divorce.'

Though his church allowed it, the strict Calvinist core of Beaverbrook disapproved of divorce of any kind. This, despite the fact that, in his complex, contradictory way, he revelled in gossip about divorce, privately and in print, and indeed it could be said that he did little to lower the divorce rate, for his affairs were not always with unmarried women. One of his favourite after-dinner stories was about adultery, and featured the boisterous Viscount Castlerosse who, in the *Sunday Express* of the 1920s, originated the society gossip that has reached its nadir today in the work of Lady Olga Maitland.

It is a story that belongs to the world of that television serial, 'Upstairs Downstairs' but, if ever broadcast, would shorten the life of Mrs Mary Whitehouse. On his nocturnal prowl from one Mayfair party to another, the viscount's ever-roving eye was caught by a young street-walker. He decided he could afford to be half an hour late for the next party, and on the way to the bedroom she used for business, he enquired, as journalists and viscounts are wont to do, how such a nice young girl had got into such a sordid business. She explained sweetly that she was only a part-timer, moonlighting as it were, and that she was really a maid at the residence of Viscount Castlerosse. She had never met the viscount because she was a downstairs maid, and anyway the 'silly old bugger' was always out chasing the ladies. When the viscount, bottling his anger, asked why the viscountess allowed her out in the evenings to ply her trade in the streets, he was told: 'The old cow's always upstairs in bed with her bookmaker boyfriend.' The viscount rushed home to find, as Beaverbrook used to say, that 'the part-time prostitute was an honest reporter'.

Beaverbrook was less tolerant towards his own son, Max, who had inherited a great deal of the charm his father could turn on at will as well as little, or none, of his father's journalistic talents; a generous measure of his mother's good looks; some of his father's money, of course; and, as he had shown during the war, flying for the RAF, a large portion of his father's reckless courage. It would have been against nature if his lifestyle had been primly ascetic, and it would have been against his father's character if he had not criticized it strongly on occasions. At times some of this criticism was expressed in front of comparative strangers and members of the staff. This could be acutely embarrassing, particularly if Max himself was present.

Of course there is often a wide gap between the moral code that a father demands, or at least hopes, that the children will live by, and the one that he applies to the rest of the world, including himself. But in Beaverbrook's case, the gap was unusually wide – widened by the effects of his narrow upbringing in New Brunswick in the shadow of the Presbyterian church where his father preached, and his rebellion against it in the excessive, sometimes licentious, style of many other sons of the manse. In a sense he went on rebelling throughout his life and this must have been one of the main reasons (a Freudian analyst would no doubt have many more) for the sharp contrasts in his character, the confusing splits in his personality.

According to Harold Macmillan, who served under Beaverbrook in government, and knew him throughout his life, he 'seemed almost a Jekyll and Hyde'. In Macmillan's experience, however, he was always a considerate Dr Jekyll dispensing 'nothing but kindness'. There were others who also escaped Mr Hyde most, if not all, of the time, including his biographer Alan Taylor, Hugh Cudlipp, Michael Foot, and on a more modest level, myself. Perhaps, as Macmillan said, we were 'fortunate' and perhaps a minority. To many, he was a Beelzebub, seldom a benefactor, a sinner more often than a saint. If, as a friend once pointed out, everything about him is true, 'the best and the worst', many people had come to believe the worst. They included the people on his so-called blacklist which, as far as I knew, existed only in his mind, and he was always careful to keep it tucked away there. But everyone on the editorial staff knew of course, or should have known, that because of personal feuds that had obscure political or social origins, there were certain names that were better avoided, and if their newsworthiness made it essential to mention them in print, it was safer to stop short of eulogy. One of these was Noël Coward who, in his wartime naval film *In Which We Serve*, had shown the front page of the *Daily Express* with the bold headline, 'There Will Be No War' floating among the debris next to one of the war's first naval wrecks.

I wasn't unaware of the Coward–Beaverbrook feud when I first joined the paper in London and started writing the show-business column, but I was young and somewhat brash, and when the opportunity to interview the celebrated Coward presented itself, I took it. I was also a little naïve, and indeed Coward told me later when I got to know him better, that I had given him the impression at our meeting that I 'still had the heather growing out of my ears'.

Coward could be just as puckish, if not more so, than Beaverbrook, and he decided to set the heather on fire, as it were, knowing that the smoke would get back to Beaverbrook. It was done in his inimitable, boldly histrionic, way. The appointed hour for the interview was 6.00 p.m. When I arrived at the door of his Pimlico house, I was greeted by Leslie Cole ('Colie' to his friends and 'Old Queen Cole' to his enemies), who told me that the Master, as Coward was called by everyone in his domestic and professional circles, was awaiting me upstairs in the bedroom. Why, I wondered apprehensively, as Cole led me inside, was the Master waiting in the bedroom at 6.00 p.m.?

We were in a long, high-ceilinged room with a baby grand piano at either end and a minstrels' gallery on the wall outside the first-floor bedroom. It was, I thought, more of a stage set than the interior of a home, and I wouldn't have been surprised to see the Master standing in the gallery in a silk dressing-gown waving a long cigarette holder, his stereotyped image brought to life. But he was in bed, living up to the image in another more restful way, sitting up after a siesta looking smooth and dapper in pale yellow pyjamas that matched the sheets and pillows.

He motioned for me to sit down on the side of the bed. I did so cautiously, but the Coward charm was turned on and, after a few minutes, I started to feel more at ease, although I had the impression that I was on stage in a play and in a part for which I was miscast. When it was announced that the Master's bath was drawn, he leapt out of bed revealing that he was not wearing his pyjama trousers, and reinforced my impression that I was in a play – an elegant farce, but still a farce. The bathroom was *en suite*, and Coward carried on the conversation as he bathed. He had just come back from Jamaica, and he talked about the house he had there and the private beach where he could sunbathe in the nude. He was in that state when he came back into the bedroom and he commenced to make a somewhat exhibitionist ritual of drying himself. This was a scene for which I was hopelessly miscast. I tried to avert my eyes from the suntanned body which he was displaying with gay abandon, but he declared: 'Mr Gourlay, you're not looking at me.' Pause. 'I want you to observe something.' Longer pause. 'I want you to observe that I'm the only man in England who is suntanned to the tip .. . of . . . his . . .cock.' The timing was impeccable and the last four words were enunciated with that clipped precision for which he was celebrated.

It was an irreverent, phallic gesture aimed indirectly at Beaverbrook rather than a homosexual invitation to his columnist. I collapsed in embarrassed laughter. Coward laughed too, without embarrassment. Then he shouted to Cole: 'Bring me my drawers. We're making Mr Gourlay's Scottish senses reel.' Turning to me he said: 'Stay while I get dressed. You can advise me what tie and what after-shave to wear. I have to dine with another heterosexual, a really boring heterosexual – the American ambassador.'

Over the next few years, I established a friendly relationship with Coward – as friendly and close as it could be, allowing for the wide differences in our sexual proclivities, ages and, of course, professional talents. (I formed the highest respect for his talents, which was reinforced in later years when, as script editor of an American television series in which he was to star, I received some sharp lessons in scriptwriting from the Master.)

There was more than an indication of respect for his professional talents in the first piece I wrote about him after that memorable meeting, but of course no mention of the full extent of his Jamaican suntan. The article appeared without comment or alteration by the Editor, but when Beaverbrook sent for me shortly after, I expected a reprimand for writing about someone reputed to be on his blacklist. However he merely said: 'So you've been meeting Noël Coward. And you obviously think highly of that fella. I want to hear all about it.'

I gave Beaverbrook the unabridged version of the encounter. For a second he frowned, then slapped his thigh and burst out laughing; he looked more like a schoolboy enjoying a joke about his elders than a septuagenarian. 'A-ah, that's funny. But you can tell Mr Coward I don't want to see him on my beach in Jamaica. And you can also tell him that he wouldn't have risked that if I'd sent Tom Driberg to interview him.'

An encounter with one of Beaverbrook's oldest friends and colleagues, Winston Churchill, provided material for another dining-out story: it could also have been, for me, a bowing-out story.

It starts in Rome. I'm there for the best part of a week to report on the filming of *Quo Vadis* in which Peter Ustinov is playing Nero. I have spent a good deal of time with Ustinov and that means, of course, that I have also been in the company of the wide-ranging cast of characters he mimics so brilliantly. It includes not only all the other leading actors and actresses in the film, and every film he has appeared in, but also prominent statesmen like Winston Churchill.

At this stage, some background details are essential. It is 1951, and Churchill, as Opposition Leader without direct access to the news he was accustomed to making as Prime Minister, has formed the habit, on Saturday evenings after dinner, of phoning John Gordon, the *Sunday Express* Editor, who can tell him as he puts the paper to bed what's making the headlines.

For reasons not unconnected with Ustinov's expansive hospitality in Rome, I am late in returning to Fleet Street. Instead of arriving on Friday morning to write up my *Quo Vadis* piece so that my column can be locked away well in advance of the eve-of-publication rush on Saturday, I don't reach London till Friday evening. I creep into the office from the airport about 11.00 p.m. At that hour the *Sunday Express* editorial floor, the fifth, is deserted. I settle down at my typewriter and try to work. But the words do not flow easily: part of my mind is still on the Via Veneto. The phone rings. When I pick it up, a voice asks me to take a call from Winston Churchill. I assume I am listening again to Peter Ustinov, phoning perhaps to apologize for delaying me in Rome, but unable to resist an opportunity to mimic. When what sounds like the voice of Winston Churchill flows over the line, I say unhesitatingly: 'Why don't you fuck off and let me get on with my work? You know I should have been back here sooner . . .'

There is a loud rumbling at the other end of the phone, and a gruff demand for an explanation that is unmistakably Churchillian. The enormity of my mistake leaves me dumb for a moment, but when I recover the power of speech and offer profuse apologies, he accepts them with remarkably good grace in the circumstances, and says he has obviously been put on to the wrong Scotsman: he wants to speak to John Gordon as he usually does on Saturday nights. I say somewhat tentatively that I think it is Friday night, and I'm terribly sorry but I'm afraid that at this hour John Gordon will have gone home. A pause, then Churchill declares: 'It is Saturday night. Get me Gordon.'

His voice has now taken on a harsh, commanding edge. I apologize again, and tell him I will find Gordon without delay. I must have got back from Rome even later than I thought. If Winston Churchill says it is Saturday night, it *is* Saturday night: it's indisputable. But when I rush round the corner of the office to Gordon's room, it is dark. Then I remember that since it's Saturday night he will be on the main editorial floor, the second, overseeing the production of the paper. As I start to dash down I bump into a night watchman and I ask him for confirmation. Convinced no doubt that I've just staggered in from the Press Club, he looks at me pityingly, and states categorically that it is Friday night. To prove it, he waves a copy of Saturday morning's *Daily Express*, hot off the presses. I hurry back to my desk, wondering desperately after my four-letter insult if there's a diplomatic way of telling Winston Churchill he doesn't know what day it is. But when I get to the phone, Churchill has hung up. And returned to Friday.

Early next morning I am summoned to Beaverbrook's presence in Arlington House. He says: 'I believe you had an interesting conversation on the phone with Winston Churchill?' I nod and he goes on: 'D'you agree with me that he is the greatest living Englishman?' I nod again. 'And that he will be back as Prime Minister?' Another nod. 'Now you wouldn't like it to be known that the greatest living Englishman, and our future Prime Minister, didn't know what day it was.' I nod yet again. 'He's got so much on his mind, it's easy even for a great man like him to make a small mistake like that – even if he hasn't had a bit too much brandy after dinner. It must be our state secret. Just between you and me. And Winston. You must give me your solemn promise that you will never dine out on this story.'

I solemnly promise. I see him looking towards the Bible which is usually within reach. But he decides not to ask me to solemnize my promise with a biblical oath and I am dismissed with the customary 'Goodbye t'ya.' But, as I am leaving, his puckish smile spreads from ear to ear, and his parting words are: 'Don't tell the story more than once a week.'

It was an example of Beaverbrook at his most beguiling. It was also a minor, but memorable, indication of how well he understood human nature and its frailties in contrast to the occasions when, by his actions and attitudes to people and events, he appeared to be insensitive, ruthless, even cruel. It has often been said by journalists who worked for him that they had a love–hate relationship with him. Michael Foot writes that he loved Beaverbrook like a father. I felt less filial, but I came to have the affection for him I would have had for a worldly, somewhat wicked and indulgent uncle, or a wily old grandfather who gave me the benefit of some of the wisdom age had brought him, and allowed me at other times to share some of the fun of his second childhood. Affection is perhaps too weak a word for the feelings the brilliant old rascal inspired. Love *is* the word, though it's one he usually refused to take seriously.

One of his most lovable qualities was his self-deflating sense of humour. Churchill had it too. On one occasion when I met him in the company of Beaverbrook after the unfortunate telephone conversation, Churchill said: 'Ah, yes, Gourlay. I remember you. Tell me what day is it?'

A lesser man could never have said that. Only the really great have the God-given capacity to laugh at themselves occasionally. It saves them from the galloping megalomania which afflicts those men who have power but not even a glimmer of self-deflating humour.

Next to Beaverbrook the most powerful man in the organization at that time was another Canadian, E. J. Robertson, the General Manager. He was not in my experience blessed with a strong sense of humour, and it seemed to me that his understanding of the problems and snares of a journalist's life was limited. In my case it was so limited that he fired me.

I have now forgotten the exact details of the cause of the firing, but they involved a stormy row about expenses I had charged for entertaining at the Savoy Hotel, during which I told Robertson he was insulting me by suggesting I was a liar, and he told me I was insulting him by suggesting he was a fool.

Beaverbrook was in Jamaica at the time, and when he returned after several weeks during which I worked as a freelance for other papers, he summoned me to Arlington House and asked for details of my clash with Robertson, although it was fairly obvious he already knew most of them. He listened, and then said: 'I want you to know that Mr Robertson is a superb businessman and general manager. You're a first-class journalist. A very different breed. That's my problem. I need both breeds to keep my newspapers going. I don't suppose you're willing to apologize to him. And he's certainly not about to apologize to you. But I'll do it on your behalf to him and to you on his behalf. Now it's Thursday, isn't it? You haven't got much time to get a column ready for Sunday's paper.'

This time the customary 'Goodbye t'ya' was a welcome back to the fold. As I left he was giving instructions to his Dictaphone about my reinstatement to the staff of Beaverbrook Newspapers. Though it was on a comparatively petty level, he was obviously enjoying himself as the go-between, the mediator and honest broker – the role he had played profitably in business when he was acquiring his first millions in Canada and successfully in politics after he came to Britain, notably with Asquith, Lloyd George, Bonar Law and Churchill.

His overriding concerns were political, but his interest in show business, particularly the film industry, was always lively and well-informed. During the early period of his business career in this country, he had invested heavily and profitably in the film industry, and he knew many of the leading producers in Britain and Hollywood, some of whom had been his business associates. This could create awkward situations for anyone like myself writing in his papers about films.

When I wrote a three-part biography of Sir Alexander Korda, probably the most gifted, and certainly the most colourful, of Britain's film producers at that time, Beaverbrook provided some background material. He told me: 'Now this is an opportunity to deal with the rumour that's been hanging around for years, that Alex got his knighthood from Winston Churchill because he bought the film rights of a book of Winston's that is unfilmable. It's a wicked rumour about a man who's contributed so much to the British film industry. It's time to kill it. And you should say so.'

I did. But of course Korda, who had started his career as a journalist in Hungary, was well acquainted with the technique of spreading a rumour by purporting to kill it in print. He phoned me to say: 'Tell that old bastard Max that I'd buy the rights to make a film based on his life – *if* I made horror films.' He said it, however, with a Hungarian chuckle.

About this time, the major Hollywood companies, including MGM and, in particular, Columbia, decided that I should be sacked, along with Milton Shulman of the *Evening Standard*. They claimed that what we were writing about their films and stars went beyond the bounds of fair comment and criticism. According to a clerihew penned by an unknown Wardour Street hand at the time, I was the major culprit:

> I do not love thee Milton Shulman,
> I think thou art a very cruel man.
> But this I say and say most truly
> I love thee more than Logan Gourlay.

The Publicity Director of Columbia Pictures declared: 'We spend fortunes building up the right images for our stars and then that bastard Gourlay takes the piss out of them.'

Beaverbrook's comment was: 'He couldn't do that if they weren't suitable subjects for the process.' He scorned any suggestions that what Shulman and I wrote should be toned down in any way. In defiant mood, he told the film-company executives: 'They are employed by me to write what they think, not what *you* think they should write. They are journalists, not advertisement copywriters.'

Completely underestimating and misunderstanding their adversary, the film executives threatened to withdraw all their advertising from Beaverbrook newspapers. He told them to go ahead. They did, but they were surprised by his attitude: he was delighted by their surprise . . . Destry was riding again.

After a few weeks, with Beaverbrook, as always, happy in conflict and the film executives unhappily realizing he couldn't be blackmailed, they sued for peace and rebooked their advertisements.

Although the frank and irreverent style of journalism, encouraged and fostered by Beaverbrook, in the columns of his newspapers could lead to problems with thin-skinned impresarios and hypersensitive stars, who had implicit belief in their own publicity, and who sometimes refused to talk to the press, particularly 'the scurrilous Beaverbrook press', I usually found that his name and reputation opened more doors than it closed. This was perhaps because the readership of his papers was huge and, as Beaverbrook once said to me in cynical mood, 'They'd deny it, of course, but, if they were honest, most actors – and particularly the ones who call themselves politicians – would go along with the old showman's slogan "It doesn't matter what you say about me as long as you spell my name right." See that you always spell their names right.'

There was one time in Hollywood when his name was particularly useful. It helped me to get an exclusive interview with the principal character in what could be described as a real-life (or as real as life ever is in Hollywood) rehearsal for a melodramatic episode of one of those television soap operas like 'Dallas' or 'Dynasty'.

The principal character was Walter Wanger, who had started his career as a cinema manager in London (when he had got to know Beaverbrook), and who became one of Hollywood's leading independent producers, with many notable films to his credit including *Queen Christina, Stagecoach, Foreign Correspondent* and *Cleopatra* .

Wanger was a man of strong passions. When he discovered that his wife, Joan Bennett – at that time one of Hollywood's foremost stars and beauties – was having an affair with her agent, Jennings Lang, Wanger plotted a cuckold's grim revenge. The private eye he had hired supplied the information that the adulterous couple were meeting in an apartment lent by a friend in a skyscraper block, for what Joan Bennett, who had a European background, liked to call *cinq à sept*. Early one evening Wanger waited in the parking lot of the apartment block, and when Jennings Lang appeared to collect his car *après cinq à sept*, Wanger took careful aim with a gun and fired. Wanger was an accurate shot. His selected target was Lang's genital area. Lang survived but, it was alleged, with impaired interest in amorous assignations. Groucho Marx, who could never resist a cruel crack, told the audience at a night club the following night: 'Jennings Lang was not shot in the parking lot. He was shot in the amusement centre.'

The morning after the shooting, the newspaper headlines were as high as the type would stretch. By the evening I had received, at the Beverly Hills Hotel where I was staying, a cable from the London office telling me that Lord Beaverbrook wanted me to interview his old friend, Walter Wanger. I composed a reply pointing out that, since Wanger was locked up in the local jail, it would be difficult, if not impossible, to interview him even as a representative of his old friend, Lord Beaverbrook.

When I went to the front desk of the hotel to send off my cable there were two men standing next to me. One was issuing instructions that his client must not be disturbed, particularly by the press, when he got to the private bungalow in the hotel grounds he would be occupying for a few days. I looked with interest at his client standing next to me, hiding behind dark glasses. He looked like Walter Wanger.

Hesitantly, I said: 'Excuse me, but aren't you Walter Wanger? I work for one of Lord Beaverbrook's papers in London . . .'

He took off his dark glasses, glanced at me and said: 'Yes, I am. I've just come out of jail. My attorney here arranged bail . . .' The attorney tried to interrupt but Wanger to my astonishment added: 'You're just the man I'm looking for. Didn't I meet you with Max Beaverbrook in London? I want to be sure the true version of what happened gets into the papers. But not the American papers. They'd distort everything. I'd like to see my story in a good English paper like the *Express*. I'm staying here for a few days as Mr Smith to avoid the American press. Come to my bungalow.'

I tore up my cable to London and followed Mr Smith to his bungalow, delighted that he considered the *Express* a good paper compared to the American sheets, and praying that we wouldn't encounter any of their reporters lurking in the hotel grounds. Safely in the bungalow, Wanger ordered drinks and told his story with amazing composure and detachment, as though it were the script of his latest film. This made it easier for me to ask the awkward question about the vital target area he had selected, already reported gleefully by the Hollywood gossip columnists. 'Ah, yes,' he said, maintaining his detached composure and trying to show, I suppose, that he was an anglophile who knew how to choose the right phrase for a good English paper. 'I had to make sure he wouldn't bat again, hadn't I?'

The story appeared in the paper, without the cricketing metaphor of course, and the details of the vital target area, but for once it merited the overused label 'world exclusive'. As so often applies, it was due more to luck than to any journalistic enterprise or skill. And, in fact, before I had bumped into Wanger in the hotel, there there had been another encounter that was also strangely fortuitous.

About a week before the shooting in the parking lot, on a day when she didn't have a *cinq à sept* assignation, Joan Bennett had been invited for afternoon tea by Mr and Mrs James Mason, who liked to keep up English habits at their home in Beverly Hills. I had been one of the other guests. After tea, Miss Bennett had kindly offered to give me a lift in her car back to my hotel. On the way, we had passed her own house, a palatial establishment worthy of Mr and Mrs Walter Wanger's Hollywood eminence, and I had accepted her invitation to 'stop for a drink and meet Walter'. He had still been at the studios, however, but when she had shown me over the house I had noticed a volume of Shakespeare on the desk in his study. It was open at *Othello*. She had said: 'No, I don't think Walter's going to make a movie of *Othello*. But then I never know for sure what he's planning . . .'

I suspect that even a 'Dallas' or 'Dynasty' soap-opera writer would hesitate before including something as bathetic as that in the script.

The bonus which I received for the Wanger world exclusive was accompanied by a message from Beaverbrook, whose bouquets could sometimes be as blunt as his brickbats: 'With journalists like you working for us, we can say balls to the rest of the world's press!'


About the same period in Hollywood, I had an interview with Marilyn Monroe which aroused Beaverbrook's interest. At that early stage in her career, when the wider range of her talents and attributes was still undiscovered, she felt that too much attention was being focused on the hip-swinging, buttock-bouncing walk which had propelled her provocatively to fame; and she resented the suggestion, made by some newspapers, that she did it merely to attract head-swivelling attention.

She claimed that, for her, it was a perfectly natural movement, and she offered to give me a demonstration. It was an offer no man could refuse.

Although fame had descended on her, the studios, which had her under a tight contract, were withholding fortune, and the setting for the demonstration was the narrow lounge of her modest apartment off Sunset Boulevard. Apart from space restrictions, the demonstration was further complicated by the fact that she had injured one of her lovely legs in a minor accident on the film set and its symmetry was marred by a plaster cast. However it was on the calf below the knee and, although it made her limp slightly, it did not in any way restrict the movement of her hips and buttocks, which were enclosed in a tight skirt. As she sashayed up and down the room, she declared: 'Look, I can't walk any other way – even when I'm lame. It's just the way Mother Nature made me walk. It's anatomical. That's what it is – anatomical. I don't do it for effect. See what I mean?'

I withheld judgement until she repeated the demonstration. I was judging from a seat on a sofa, and holding a glass of Bristol cream sherry, a bottle of which she had ordered thinking it would be a suitable drink for a visitor from London, England. It was a thoughtful, sweet (if not over-sweet) gesture that had to be respected, and though I would have preferred Scotch, I was finding that, on this occasion, sherry had acquired aphrodisiac qualities.

She was sipping a glass, too, held daintily in her hand as she demonstrated her walk. She had the earnestness about her which often afflicts American intellectuals and makes them difficult to bear, but in her case, it had an engaging, almost childlike quality. It was very much in evidence when I mentioned the books on a shelf in the room, which I had noticed included two or three volumes of the work of Oscar Wilde. She displayed an interest in him, which was, to say the least, surprising, but it was untutored for, after I had trotted out one or two trivial facts about his tragic life, she seemed to regard me as an authority on him and his work.

An hour or so later, at the end of the interview, when we had talked about many things apart from Oscar Wilde, his unnatural habits, and her natural walk, she suddenly stood up and recited a line or two of verse. Then she said: 'D'you know what poem that's from?' I didn't. Clapping her hands like a gleeful schoolgirl, she trilled: 'It's from the "Ballad of Reading Gaol" by Oscar Wilde.'

Only a churl would have pointed out that her pronunciation of 'Reading' was wrong and that the English, in their perverse way, pronounce it as though it were 'redding'.

It was difficult, if not impossible, to convey the full flavour of an interview like that in the *Sunday Express* in the unpermissive 1950s when Beaverbrook and, to a greater extent, his Editor, John Gordon (who could be even more narrowly Calvinistic), insisted that nothing in its chaste columns could offend any members of the family on the Sabbath. However Beaverbrook got the unprintable details from me, and at a later date, he remarked: 'John Gordon's getting worried about you. Very worried.' He waited till I asked why.

'Waal, he thinks you might be getting corrupted by Noël Coward and all those queens in show business. There you were alone in an apartment in Hollywood with Marilyn Monroe. She's swingin' her hips at you, and all you can talk about is Oscar Wilde. I'm worried about you, too. I expected more from a red-blooded young Red from the Gorbals.'

John Gordon may have been genuinely, though mistakenly, worried, for as regular readers of the 'Current Events' column knew, he nursed a strong prejudice against homosexuals, or what his successor, the equally prejudiced Sir John Junor, calls 'poofters'. It was obvious, however, that Beaverbrook's worry was feigned, and that he was yet again in an impish mood, for he had just emerged from the shower, and as he spoke, he was standing before me displaying the fact that, although his suntan was a rich deep brown, it was not as extensive as Noël Coward's.

Beaverbrook was in the habit of carrying on conversations with friends and employees while he was in the nude and just out of a bath or a shower, without showing a trace of self-consciousness or embarrassment. Unlike many men, he didn't seem to lose any dignity or authority when divested of clothes. This may have had something to do with the fact that the clothes were not chosen to make an impression or cut a dash. He wore an inconspicuous daytime uniform of dark-blue suit, matching loosely knotted tie, white shirt, black hat and brown shoes, which were in breach of sartorial rules. Out of uniform, he was still inconspicuous, not endowed by nature for male modelling, yet neither too fat nor too thin, too tall or too short. His head was a bit larger than normal and his neck shorter, giving the impression that he wasn't as tall as in fact he was.

On this out-of-uniform occasion, we were in the bedroom of his villa in La Capponcina on the Riviera. When I had arrived earlier in the afternoon, I had been told by the butler that he was having a swim in the Mediterranean at the bottom of his garden, and he had left instructions for me to join him. I made my way slowly down through the garden to the rocky water's edge, hoping that I would not be asked to strip and leap into the water with him. But when he saw me, he waved, came out of the water, gave me a handshake that was literally dripping with courtesy, and leapt in again. I was now slightly disappointed that I was not being asked to follow him for his attractive French mistress was having a dip with him. I was left standing awkwardly on the rocks, answering a few shouted questions while they bobbed around in the sea like a couple of sporting dolphins. I felt somewhat out of place and about as welcome as a keeper in a dolphinarium who has no fish to throw.

When they emerged from the water, he got on to a sort of converted golf cart which she drove up the steep garden path to the villa. He sat in the back seat glistening in the sun like an Eastern potentate, and surveying me as I toiled behind, getting more and more out of breath with each step.

'Ah,' he commented, 'you're out of condition. A young fella like you should be able to run up the garden. You must be smoking too much. How many cigarettes a day d'ya smoke?'

I made a cowardly cut in my daily consumption, bringing it down from about thirty-five to fifteen but he said: 'That's too many. Altogether too many.' Turning to his mistress, he said: 'Tell him it's too many.' She dutifully told me in her charming French accent, but I was left with the sad impression that she would not have been greatly concerned if I had dropped dead on the spot from nicotine over-indulgence.

The state of his own health was a subject of constant concern for Beaverbrook but, like many hypochondriacs, he must have been fitter and tougher than he thought. Asthma, to which he was a martyr for years, is, according to some medical authorities, mainly a psychosomatic ailment, and he often suffered attacks (which his detractors called convenient) when he found himself facing exceptionally difficult problems. The attacks may have been convenient psychologically and tactically, but they were undoubtedly highly uncomfortable physically as well, and he had an impressive array of inhalants and medical apparatus to alleviate breathless asthmatic misery.

There were one or two fellow sufferers among his employees, with whom he could discuss symptoms and exchange medications. They included Michael Foot, who had suffered from asthma before he had ever encountered Beaverbrook. But there was another journalist with a similar left-wing background to Michael's who, as far as I know, had been sound (in body at least) before he came to work for Beaverbrook. Within a short space of time, however, he lost his left-wing political convictions and developed asthmatic symptoms. Such was the speed of the conversion that his colleagues cruelly, but inevitably, described it as breathtaking.

Admittedly there were times when Beaverbrook's unpredictable reactions and demands left many of his journalists more than a bit short of breath, but most of us were able to soldier on without developing acute asthma. Despite my addiction to strong French cigarettes, I survived for more than fifteen years on his staff in a reasonably healthy state; the fact that I was able to overcome my addiction to cigarettes after I left him may, or may not, be psychologically significant.

At one stage when I was trying to overcome the addiction, I decided to try hypnotherapy as practised by a Harley Street doctor, who had written books on the subject and was free of any suspicion of quackery. I enjoyed no more than a short spell of hypnotized abstinence, but when Beaverbrook heard that the doctor had brought relief and, in some cases, cures to asthmatics by hypnotherapy, he decided to try it. A consultation was arranged but it was a complete failure. The doctor admitted later: 'He nearly hypnotized me.'

Despite this failure, Beaverbrook investigated other branches of alternative medicine, not only because he was seeking a cure for asthma, but because, although he may not have realized it, he was satisfying his curiosity. The Beaverbrook curiosity was a striking characteristic, and it was one that contributed greatly to making him the only press lord, apart from Northcliffe, who was also a talented journalist – indeed a more talented journalist than any he employed. He once told the Press Commission, 'I run my newspapers solely for the purposes of propaganda,' but that was one of his misleading, provocative remarks; he should have added, if he were being totally honest about himself, that he also ran them to satisfy his curiosity. It was insatiable – boundless and, although it focused on the big issues of the day, it also laid him open to the charge that he was over-concerned with the trivial. Beaverbrook wanted to know every detail of a story – realizing that the smallest can turn out to be among the most significant – and of course he always wanted to know the details that could not be printed because they might break the libel laws or offend public taste.

When Ingrid Bergman confessed to me in an interview that she had been rude to Cardinal Spellman, when he had flown from New York to see her in Italy at the time when she was being condemned throughout America because of her runaway romance with Roberto Rossellini, I was unable to tell the readers of the *Sunday Express* exactly what she had said to the cardinal. But I was able to tell the enquiring Beaverbrook that, when the cardinal had advised her to leave her twins, just born out of wedlock, in the custody of the nunnery and return to America to ask 'Mr and Mrs America for forgiveness' in a coast-to-coast broadcast, Miss Bergman had given the cardinal a straight Scandinavian look and said: 'Go to hell, Your Eminence.'

When I took Marlene Dietrich, the star of his favourite film *Destry Rides Again* to supper after her performance at London's Café de Paris where she was appearing in cabaret, Beaverbrook wanted to know exactly what she had eaten and drunk. He seemed a shade disenchanted when he heard that, like many ladies blessed by the gods with a metabolism that keeps them naturally slim, she could eat like a horse, and that after three hearty courses, she taxed the resources of 'the boys in the back room' of the Mayfair night club where we had supper by demanding bread and honey plus a glass of milk.

Over the period that I wrote the show-business column for the *Sunday Express*, there were many other stories which aroused the omnivorous Beaverbrook curiosity and which could not be printed in full. Even in today's more permissive climate, I would be reluctant to rush into print with some of them, but now that Laurence Olivier, for example, after years of almost Victorian reticence has written his autobiography *Confessions of an Actor* in which he removes his corset and chucks away his cod piece to reveal the least flattering aspects of his career and his marriage to Vivien Leigh, I see no reason why I should not disclose a minor incident involving them.

It was during the period when, protected by libel laws and Fleet Street writers who, with one or two exceptions, were dutifully sycophantic, the Oliviers reigned as monarchs of the English-speaking acting world (he, of course, as a triumphantly successful Shakespearian monarch and she somewhat less so). I was at a backstage party following the first night of one of his Festival of Britain productions at the old St James's Theatre where he was installed as actor-manager. I was standing next to Vivien Leigh while her husband was making a long rambling speech to his cast and his guests. Pointing to her empty glass and to a champagne bottle on a table next to us, Vivien Leigh whispered to me: 'Open the bottle.' I demurred, saying in a low voice that the pop would ruin her husband's peroration. Without moving what looked like an adoring gaze from him, she said softly: 'That's the idea. He's such a fucking bore. Always is when he's using his own words.' She looked angelic as she always did when she was using barrack-room language.

It may seem, when I recall some of my experiences as a show-business columnist, that there were few boring moments. Certainly there were stars like Orson Welles, Humphrey Bogart, Robert Mitchum,

Trevor Howard, Laurence Harvey, Bette Davis and Vivien Leigh who, unlike Olivier, could be just as electrifying (sometimes more so) off stage as they were on stage, as stimulating using their own words as they were when a writer supplied them, but after writing the column for nearly a decade, I was only too aware that they were the minority, and that too many of their colleagues could be desperately dull off, as well as on stage. If I had been solely concerned, as a critic, with what they did on stage, or in front of the cameras, the job would have been easier to sustain. But if I found myself interviewing an actor or actress, who had little or nothing to say, I couldn't put words into his or her mouth, and I couldn't bore the readers by telling them that so-and-so gave such a lacklustre performance in the Savoy Grill at lunch that the smoked salmon curled up on the plate and the champagne went flat.

One grey day in May at the Cannes Film Festival I decided firmly that I'd had enough. Regular attenders at these flesh-peddling affairs will know that they can provide the right conditions for grey disenchantment. It seemed to me that there was no one there who could dispel it, with the possible exception of Melina Mercouri. She had shot to international fame in the film *Never on Sunday*, and she was beginning to show signs of the political ambitions which have now made her Greece's Minister of Culture. Throughout a long evening of festivities, a Wardour Street film producer kept inviting her to step aboard his large yacht which was moored in the harbour, obviously hoping that she would share the double bed in his stateroom. He did it with as much finesse and gallantry as a drunk sailor chatting up a prostitute. She tried patiently to change the subject to current affairs and to films, pointing out that her career as a prostitute had started – and ended – in *Never on Sunday*. But the producer was maddeningly persistent. Finally about 3.00 a.m. in the night club, she turned to him, smiled seductively, and said: 'OK, I give in. I'm yours. I'll sleep with you on your yacht – if you give me one thing.'

His cigar glowed. 'Anything you want. Anything.'

'It's a big thing.'

'I mean it. The yacht. Anything. Just name it.'

She paused for a moment before delivering her punchline: 'Just give me the Elgin Marbles.'

Beaverbrook, who knew (and disliked) the producer, was amused by the story, which I told him the next day when I was summoned to his villa along the coast at Cap d'Ail. He seemed less amused when he asked for the rest of the news about the Cannes Festival, and I told him about my growing disenchantment with films and festivals and show business generally. He growled: 'What d'you want to do?'

I told him I'd like to write a general column about some of the other players on the world stage, including politicians, some of whom, as I'd heard him say, were better actors than many of those I had been meeting. He said: 'It's a wise actor who knows when to make his exit.' He gave me a reproving look. We were standing beside the villa's swimming-pool, and I wondered for a moment if he was going to push me in – a parting gesture from a press lord to an ungrateful columnist. Then the characteristic smile spread suddenly from ear to ear: he had been indulging in a little acting. 'We can't let you get stale. If you get bored you'll bore the readers. We can't have that, can we?' One of his most impressive attributes was his ability to make quick decisions and implement them without delay. Within a week I was transferred to the *Daily Express* and given the best part of a page to fill every Friday with a general column; and of course if I stumbled across a story during the week that wouldn't hold, it was given the space it merited on any other day.

Among the leading politicians in the Westminster cast, whom I got to know after a spell on the daily paper, were George Brown and Harold Wilson. I interviewed them when they were candidates in an election for the deputy leadership of the Labour Party, and in the piece I wrote, I risked the prediction that Wilson would beat Brown. I was wrong. In that election, not long before Wilson became the party leader following Hugh Gaitskell's death, Brown was the victor. Beaverbrook said: 'Waal, you picked the wrong man. But Wilson's the better actor. No doubt about that. Take it from me, it's not easy to pick party leaders – even deputy ones. I should know.'

There were times at the outset, following my transfer to the daily paper, when I felt like an actor trying to escape typecasting after a long run in a television series. When any of the stars, particularly visitors from Hollywood, came into the news, the Deputy Editor Harold Keeble, a brilliant manipulator of type, headlines, pictures – and people – expected me to draw on my experience and write a piece. So did Beaverbrook on occasion. When I got a message that he wanted me to go to Rome to see the pontiff, I thought at first it must have been scrambled as sometimes happened in transcribing from his Dictaphone, and that he meant the film producer, Carlo Ponti.

I knew that, following the marriage of Ponti to Sophia Loren, Beaverbrook was extremely curious about how a beautiful nubile young woman could be attracted to an older ugly man. On my way to see him, I reminded myself that, even if I could think of a light-hearted, witty way of doing so, it would be fatal to try to draw any comparison between Signor Ponti's attractions for Signora Loren (whatever they might be apart from his power and wealth), and Lord Beaverbrook's for a younger mistress. When I arrived, however, it was immediately clear that his mind was on more elevated matters. There had been no mistake in the passing on of the message: he did in fact want me to go to Rome to see the *pontiff*.

It had been announced that the Moderator of the Church of Scotland was going to Rome to meet the Pope, and Beaverbrook, as a staunch Presbyterian, disapproved: he was suspicious of any ecumenical moves, and he wanted another Presbyterian, even a lapsed one like myself, to go to Rome to find out what was going on. An audience with the Pope was being arranged. Ill-equipped though I was for the assignment, I was intrigued by it, and besides I had learned over the years to tread warily when Beaverbrook was in a Bible-thumping mood.

I had received my first lesson in this shortly after I had started writing the show-business column for the *Sunday Express*. Bob Hope had opened at the Prince of Wales Theatre not long after Danny Kaye, making his first appearance at the London Palladium, had been apotheosized by critics, the public and members of the royal family, notably Princess Margaret.

Referring to this, and resurrecting an old joke, Hope had told his audience that the next time Danny Kaye came over to London, he would not be flying, he would be walking over the water. With his immaculate timing, Hope had made the old joke sound newer, and I had quoted him in my column on Sunday. At eight that morning my bedside phone rang: Beaverbrook was on the line, as wrathful as an Old Testament prophet.

'You're a disgrace . . . blasphemer. You've made fun of the Scriptures in the columns of my newspaper . . . made a joke about Jesus and His miracles. How dare you . . .' When I was able to interrupt the blast, I pointed out meekly that the joke was Bob Hope's, not mine. 'That's no excuse. If a barbarian comes over here from Hollywood spreading blasphemy, we keep it out of my newspapers. We do not make fun of *any* religion in my newspapers. You'd better remember that. I'm deeply disappointed in you. You were brought up in the right church. You should have known better. Now you will get out of bed. I know that's where you are, you lazy young sinner. And you will go to church to ask forgiveness. That's what you'll do. Give me your word that you will do that this very morning.'

I mumbled that I wasn't sure where the nearest Church of Scotland church was. It was a weak, stupid remark, and it set him off again. 'D'ya mean to say you've never been to church since you came down here?' I wasn't brave enough to interrupt to ask him when he had last been to church. 'That makes it even worse. I'll have to talk to the Moderator about you. Maybe you're beyond redemption . . . beyond redemption.'

He hung up. As he did so his 'Goodbye t'ya' sounded like a funeral knell, consigning me to the eternal fires. I was then living in Strawberry Hill in Middlesex, and the wrathful voice had come down the line through an exchange called Pope's Grove which was named after the poet, not the pontiff. There was, however, a nearby Catholic church (with a deviant priest, who would have interested Graham Greene), but there was no Church of Scotland church in the vicinity.

But the hands of John Knox, the Moderator and Beaverbrook stretched out from the next county. Within a week I had a visit from the minister of a Church of Scotland church just over the border in Surrey, who told me he had received instructions from the Moderator to visit me to recall me to the flock. He failed in his mission, but not completely, for although I never visited his church, he came back to see me more than once when we discussed – and sought – the meaning of life over glasses of usquebaugh, which is, of course, the water of life.

A few years later I had another, somewhat different, religious experience at Beaverbrook's home in Cap d'Ail. I was in Monte Carlo on a story and he invited me to dinner at the villa. The other guests, including his mistress, were all French. Unexpectedly at the coffee and cognac stage, he said in his most impishly provocative manner: 'Logan, do you realize we're the only Presbyterians here? We're surrounded by Papists.' He gave the last word a pejorative hiss, and when his mistress raised a chiding eyebrow, he proceeded to bait her about what he called 'the fallibility of the Pope' and her church. She countered by saying that he would think differently if he ever met the Pope (who was then Pius XII).

'A-ah,' said Beaverbrook, 'but I have had a meeting with the Pope. I'll never forget it.'

'There you are,' she said, 'meeting the Pope is an unforgettable experience. What made it so unforgettable for you?'

'His smile,' said Beaverbrook. His own smile was now distinctly devilish.

'I know exactly what you mean,' said the lady, walking into his trap. 'His smile is . . . heavenly . . . belongs to another world . . . makes you realize he is close to God.'

'No, it wasn't that exactly.' The devilish smile widened as he added

with devastating timing, 'I'll never forget the Pope's smile . . .' Pause.
'Y-aas, never forget it . . .' Pause. 'Because I've never seen so many shiny
gold teeth. But maybe you're right – they shine just like the golden
gates.'

While she was recovering he turned to me and said: 'Logan, I think
we should sing a verse or two of the Twenty-third Psalm for our guests.'
As his guests sat transfixed, our voices (his loud and resonant, mine
much less so) floated out through the open windows into the balmy
night. Even on the Côte D'Azur, where all kinds of nocturnal noises
have been heard, I doubt if anything quite so bizarre, and inappropriate,
had disturbed the darkness.

Beaverbrook's 'Amen' at the end of the Riviera psalm recital was
echoing in my ears years later when he was briefing me for my visit to
Rome to see the Pope, who was then John XXIII. But when the
appointed date came round I was delayed in London, not, I'm sure, by
divine intervention, for the cause of the delay indicated a satanic
sense of humour. It was in fact a libel case brought by a Mr John Gaul
against me and the paper. Several months earlier, during a visit by the
Prince and Princess of Monaco to London, Mr Gaul, who was seen
regularly in their company, had let it be known that he had been to the
same English public school as the prince, and had boasted that he was
one of the prince's oldest friends. He had also informed me, when I had
phoned him, that he was a property developer, and the owner of several
properties in Soho, including a pub called, appropriately enough, the
Coronet.

I had conveyed this not very vital information to the readers of my
*Daily Express* column in a short paragraph which had infuriated Mr
Gaul who had alleged that I had libelled him by implying that he was a
social climber, a mere pub owner pretending to be a prince's best
friend. Our lawyers offered him an apology in print and even, if I
remember correctly, a payment out of court which would have more
than covered the cost of a holiday in Monaco, where he could bask in
the warmth of the sunshine and the friendship of a prince. But Mr Gaul
would not be appeased: he was determined to go to court to seek full
retribution for the slur on his honour and reputation. He briefed one of
the leading silks of the day, Sir Patrick Beyfus, to present his case, and
the equally eminent, and expensive, silk Gerald (now Lord) Gardiner
agreed to defend me and the paper. The date of the hearing was fixed,
and then a few days before, word came through from the Vatican that I
was expected in Rome on the same day for my audience with Pope
John.

What was to be done? Obviously the date for the court hearing could not be changed at the last moment, and neither could my appointment at the Vatican. I saw no solution. But Beaverbrook did not hesitate for a moment. The temporal took precedence over the spiritual. I never discovered how he did it, and it may be that, with his anti-popery prejudice, he enjoyed himself, though he could hardly have risked a blunt, undiplomatic message to the effect that the Pope would have to wait while his reporter appeared in court in a libel case. But whatever influence he brought to bear, whichever powerful strings he pulled, I was told that my presence at the Vatican would not be required for a week, and that I was to go to court the next day.

The crowning irony was that, when I turned up in court, I was informed by Gardiner that I need not have troubled, and that he wouldn't be calling me as a witness, because, in his view, journalists made a bad impression on juries. Gardiner also let it be known that he thought we had little chance of winning the case, because most juries – with or without journalists as witnesses – tended to reach verdicts that were unfavourable to millionaire press lords and powerful national newspapers.

Fortunately, however, the jury in this case was even less impressed by the plaintiff, Mr Gaul, than they might have been by a journalist. Gardiner, by skilful cross-examination, led Mr Gaul into the boast that he was probably as rich, if not richer, than Lord Beaverbrook. That did it. The Beaverbrook fortune had shrunk in the jury's eyes and I became, by comparison with Gaul, just a poor scribbler. We won the case, and Gaul, the self-styled millionaire, property owner and friend of a prince, had to pay the staggeringly high costs.

Beaverbrook was delighted. Minor legal and journalistic history had been made, and I left for Rome with a note of undeserved, punning praise from Beaverbrook: 'After conquering Gaul you should take the Vatican by storm.'

I arrived in Rome just as the epic, ill-fated endeavour to film *Cleopatra* with Elizabeth Taylor, Richard Burton and Rex Harrison was beginning. The hotels were full, but with Vatican influence I found myself installed in a suite in the Grand Hotel next to the one occupied by Caesar himself, Rex Harrison.

Mr Harrison's voice, though high-pitched, is penetrating, and he learned as a young actor with the Liverpool repertory company, and elsewhere, how to project it, so I could not help but overhear him rehearsing his lines as I waited next door for the summons to meet the Pope, whose advisers, not surprisingly in the circumstances, had found reasons to postpone the appointment for a few days.

At that time, the late lamented Rachel Roberts, who subsequently married Harrison, was what the gossip columnists used to call his constant companion. One evening when Harrison was rehearsing some of Caesar's lines, which were penetrating the walls to my ears next door, I heard her interrupt him to say: 'Rex darling you're not in *Fair Lady* any more. You're meant to be Caesar – but you still sound like Professor bloody Higgins . . .'

Harrison exploded. The walls almost shook as he screeched: 'What do you know about acting, you Welsh . . . bitch. Just bloody well shut up.'

Miss Roberts, always a spirited lady, responded with Welsh eloquence: 'And what do *you* know about acting? D'you know what you are? You're nothing but a jumped-up, fucking Liverpool rep actor.'

The next day the papal summons finally came, and as I was leaving the hotel, I bumped into Harrison. I nodded in greeting, but Harrison, whose relations with the press, particularly the Beaverbrook press, had never been friendly, gave me one of his most patronizing looks and said: 'God, is there no escape from the Beaverbrook press even in Rome?'

It was an irresistible cue. Trying to make my tone as patronizing as possible, I said: 'Lord Beaverbrook has sent me to Rome to have an audience with the Pope – not to interview a jumped-up, fucking Liverpool rep actor.'

The arrogant Rex was routed: mighty Caesar silenced.

I was still gloating over my victory when I got to the Vatican, but in its hallowed atmosphere, I began to realize that, though I had to confess that I had thoroughly enjoyed myself, it had been a decidedly petty and unchristian act. However when I met him, the Pope quickly eased the burden of any sins I carried, particularly professional ones.

To my surprise, he told me that Lord Beaverbrook and I belonged to a highly honourable profession. The gospels, he pointed out, were reports of great events, and the disciples could be called reporters. It could be said that they had followed the same calling as Lord Beaverbrook and myself. If only, I thought, Beaverbrook had been present. Even he, when he got over his surprise, would have been disarmed and impressed.

Unlike the present incumbent, Pope John was no polyglot, and my Italian was scanty, so we conversed through an interpreter, but the Pope's personality was so warm, his gestures and facial expessions so eloquent, that I felt I understood every word he said. Showing that he had been well briefed by someone in the Vatican intelligence service, who must have taken a look at my full name on my passport, the Pope went on to remind me flatteringly that my Christian name was the same as one of the biblical reporters. With a papal wave of the arm, he told me that I must pay particular attention to the ninth commandment and always observe it. Did I know it? Even without my regular childhood attendance at a Presbyterian Sunday school, it would not have been difficult to guess that it must be 'Thou shalt not bear false witness' . . .

I received a nod of approval, and I was tempted to ask if strict observance of the ninth would earn me a papal dispensation exempting me from one or two of the other nine commandments. But I resisted the temptation: it would have been altogether too irreverent a request, even from a lapsed Presbyterian like myself representing a born-again one like Beaverbrook.

When he came to the subject of the Moderator's visit to Rome, the Pope was a model of ecumenical tact. He looked forward to a period of greater understanding between the two churches and between all Christians. With what could now be called prophetic vision, he said that the day would come when the Pope would make the journey to Scotland to meet the Moderator of the Church of Scotland. Had he lived, Pope John might have preceded Pope John Paul II by a few years on an ecumenical journey to these shores.

From Beaverbrook's point of view my interview with the Pope was hardly a triumph, and he probably would have been better pleased if I had come back with a story about a wicked, deep-laid plot to convert the Moderator, if not to Catholicism, at least to celibacy for himself and all ministers of the Church of Scotland – even unto sons of the manse.

However there was no suppression, or editing of the piece that I wrote, although I made no attempt to conceal the fact that, while I did not accept the Pope as a direct representative of God on earth, I felt I had been in the presence of an extraordinary man who possessed much more than the normal measure of virtue allocated to humans. The piece appeared with a cheeky sub-heading, which must have been suggested by Beaverbrook: 'A Presbyterian Meets the Pope'. Beaverbrook's comment was: 'I was worried that it might have to be changed to "A Convert Meets the Pope" . . .'

He had a long memory. Some time afterwards when I was in New York and he was installed in his suite in the Waldorf Towers on one of his seasonal visits, he sent for me and said: 'I think you should go down to Havana, Cuba, and interview Mr Fidel Castro. You're just the man for the job. He won't have to convert you – as the Pope nearly did. After all, you were brought up more or less as a Red, weren't you? Same faith as Fidel.'

That insatiable curiosity of his was always particularly aroused by anything, or anyone, labelled revolutionary red, and up to a point, his sympathy was aroused, too, for although his own political label was a different hue, it was never true-blue Conservative. He was a dissenter, a rebel with too many causes (not all of them misguided), and with too much individualism ever to belong, wholeheartedly and exclusively, to any one political party.

Paradoxically enough, Stalin, whom he met when Churchill sent him on a mission to Moscow in 1941, was probably more of a small 'c' conservative and less of a revolutionary than Beaverbrook. At any rate, although there were disagreements and misunderstandings between the British mission and their hosts about the conduct of the war and the replacement of the heavy Russian losses in armaments, Beaverbrook got on like a house on fire with Stalin or, as I once heard him say when reminiscing about these grim times, 'like a tank on fire'. Alan Wood wrote in *The True History of Beaverbrook*:

Why was it that Beaverbrook admired Stalin so much? The answer, I think, is quite simple: in essentials Beaverbrook was always a Marxist himself. After all, there must be two sides to any class war; and though Beaverbrook would generally be considered on the opposite side to Stalin, this was a trivial detail compared with the common philosophical background they shared. Beaverbrook was indoctrinated throughout with the Marxist concept of economic forces being the most important; it came out again and again; witness, for instance, his insistence that the greatness of the British Empire must be based on economic self-interest. Then Beaverbrook was a realist, a pragmatist: he shared Engels' view that 'before there was argumentation there was an action. The proof of the pudding is in the eating.' His actions, too, showed more than a touch of the Marxist idea that the end justifies the means. The doctrine of Calvinism and predetermination, as preached in the Presbyterian Church, had something in common with the deterministic element in Marxism. I do not think it is over-fanciful to find some points of resemblance between the characters of Beaverbrook and Marx himself. Consider, for instance, a description of Marx by Bertrand Russell in *Freedom and Organisation*: 'He had all his life a love of domination associated with a feeling of inferiority, which made him prickly with social superiors, ruthless with rivals, and kind to children.'

I doubt if Beaverbrook would have accepted that as a true, or fair, character assessment, and if he had lived to read the book, he might have been as angered as he was when, after reading the first draft of Tom Driberg's biography, he instructed the butler to tell Driberg, then his guest in Jamaica, to pack his bags and leave – never to darken the doorstep again. At the same time, Beaverbrook in his unpredictable way might have been highly amused by Alan Wood's categorization of him as a kindred spirit of Karl Marx, and in one of his impulsive, impish moods, he might have ordered flowers to be sent to the Marx grave in Highgate Cemetery.

What I do know is that, despite all the grim, post-war evidence that Uncle Joe was a ruthless monster, Beaverbrook continued to see him in the avuncular light as a tough but likeable old bear, who enjoyed a hard drink and a rough joke. So I wasn't surprised to be told, as he was briefing me before I set out for Havana to interview Castro, that I should ask him what he thought of Stalin – a fairly obvious question, but also one, I thought to myself, that Castro might not be anxious to answer with any degree of honesty.

Beaverbrook was obviously curious to know as much as possible about Castro, whose power would never equal Stalin's, but whose influence in North, Central and South America was increasing. Beaverbrook was always interested in men with power (political or financial), particularly those with more than he had himself. As it turned out I wasn't able to ask Castro a single question, and I was in fact fortunate not to be detained in Havana much longer than I had planned, answering questions from his secret police.

When I first arrived in Havana, the officials at the Ministry of Information greeted me with Cuban courtesy and told me predictably that mañana might bring some news about when I would have the honour of meeting their leader. The mañanas passed pleasantly and uneventfully, but it was difficult to venture far from the hotel lest by any chance I missed the summons from Castro which I was told by our local stringer was likely to be sudden.

After about a week, when I was having a siesta one afternoon in my hotel room and wondering what mañana would bring, two secret policeman arrived. As they came into the room, it was clear that their mission was decidedly unfriendly. First of all, they presented me with a cable from my foreign desk in London, which should never have been sent, and which had no doubt been copied and placed on Castro's desk. The cable informed me that there had been a lurid story in a New York tabloid about Castro's full and varied sex life, and asked me to investigate. The man who sent the cable did not remain much longer in Beaverbrook's employment, and I have since found it in my heart to forgive him. I might even have been able to explain away the cable by saying that we were doing research for a newspaper survey, in which their heroic leader would be compared with other great statesmen and world figures, such as Turkey's Kemal Ataturk and Britain's Lloyd George, whose sex lives had also been full and varied. But there was worse to come. Demonstrating that their international intelligence service was operating efficiently, one of them produced a photostat copy of the leader page of the *Daily Express* containing an article I had written about eighteen months before. It was an interview with Batista, former dictator of Cuba and associate of the American Mafia, who had fled when Castro staged his revolution. After hiding out in the Dominican Republic for a spell, Batista was offered sanctuary by his friend and fellow dictator, Salazar of Portugal. When I had encountered him in Lisbon, I had asked him the obvious question: what did he think of his revolutionary successor, Señor Castro? Batista had said: 'The man is a murderer.'

I had reminded him as diplomatically as I could that his own period of office had not been entirely bloodless.

'Ah,' he said, 'but if blood had to be spilled – if people had to be killed – I permitted it only because I had no other choice. I hated to do it but it was expedient. That is the difference between me and Castro. I did it because I had to. But he enjoys it. He bathes in blood. He is a psychopathic murderer.'

Now, many months later, one of Castro's secret policemen was pointing to the article and telling me that I had committed the offence of calling their great leader a 'psychopathic murderer'.

I tried to point out that it was Batista who had used the offending phrase, but I was told that if I used a dirty word like 'Batista' again in their presence, I might be forcibly shut up.

When I picked up the phone, thinking it might be wise to try to get through to the British embassy to ask for some help and advice, it was snatched out of my hand, and I was pushed down on the bed by one of them while the other blew cigar smoke in my face. Feeling decidedly unheroic, I made no attempt to interfere while they searched the room and my luggage. They must have hoped to find some evidence of espionage activity or even some pornographic material, linked to a full and varied sex life, for they went through everything. One of them even squeezed out toothpaste from the tube in the bathroom and the other slit the lining of a jacket in the wardrobe.

My wallet, which was lying on the dressing-table, was examined carefully. In addition to some travellers' cheques and Cuban pesos, it contained four US 100-dollar notes. One of them took out the notes slowly and put them in his pocket. I asked politely what he was doing and he said: 'It is a fine. You are being fined for insulting President Castro.'

I heard myself saying: 'Thank God, I had the right amount.' A minor example of spontaneous wit, and also an example of fear sharpening the mind, but not very wise. For a moment it looked as though the summary justice might be extended to a punch-up as well as a fine, but I was let off with a light oral whipping.

'You are a cheap lackey of the yellow, capitalist, gutter press.' This sounded stilted and strange spoken with an American (not a Russian) accent. They liked the sound of it, and they repeated it, leaving me to speculate about my fate as 'a cheap lackey' while they had a final check to ensure that I hadn't secreted any microfilm, pornographic pictures or US currency in my clothing or anywhere else. They looked disappointed when they found nothing, not even a single extra, green, capitalist dollar. Then the final sentence in the hotel courtroom of strange summary justice was passed: 'You have until tomorrow to leave Cuba. You are deported. If you are still here tomorrow at this time you will be arrested.'

They left. I was more than relieved, but I was also puzzled and suspicious. Did the *mañana* mentality extend to deportations and arrests? Were they playing a Cuban cat-and-mouse game and waiting to arrest me when I got to the airport?

I decided to pack up and leave as soon as possible, calling in at the British embassy on the way to the airport to seek some help and guidance. My travellers' cheques would cover the hotel bill and I had enough in Cuban pesos to pay for a taxi.

The embassy was closed and shuttered for siesta when I arrived, but I managed to arouse a servant after persistent bell-ringing, and discovered that the staff, like Noël Coward's mad dogs and Englishmen, were out in the afternoon sun playing tennis. I was in no mood to be told to return *mañana* and I convinced the servant that it was a matter of life and death: he went to fetch a diplomat.

With the passage of time, our memories fortunately erase the most painful details, so I have forgotten the name of the diplomat who came panting in reluctantly from the tennis court. All that I can remember is that he was a second secretary and a twit of the first water. If he is still alive, and serving Her Majesty in the diplomatic corps, I hope he has now sunk to third secretary. His advice was: 'Go, for God's sake, go. Get out of Cuba as soon as you can. Newspaper chaps like you are always turning up in places like this and causing trouble.'

I pointed out that newspaper chaps like me only turned up in places like this to report trouble caused by politicians, and often exacerbated by diplomats like him. His parting shot was memorable: 'If you don't mind, let the consul in Miami know if you get there safely. When we hear from him we'll know we won't have the boring job of looking round the jails for you here.' I cannot remember my parting words to him, but they were not diplomatic.

I had asked the taxi driver, a friendly Cuban who spoke fluent American, to wait, and I set off apprehensively for the airport. I knew that, like most taxi drivers on the island whose business had slumped since the revolution, he would not be a fervent supporter of Castro. I also knew that, like most taxi drivers throughout the world, he would probably be a source of useful local information not published in the official guide books, so I decided to tell him my plight: it was a wise decision. He listened sympathetically, and when I finished, he stopped the taxi and said: 'The airport is no place for you to go now. By the time we get there it will be night and they're tougher then. You'll have a better chance of getting out without any trouble early in the morning.' When I pointed out that I had only just enough money left to pay his fare, so it would be difficult to spend another night in Havana, he said, 'Don't worry. My sister will look after you.'

His sister was in charge of one of the few three-star brothels still open for post-revolutionary business; but business without the tourists was, of course, in sad decline, and she was even less of a supporter of Castro than her brother. When she heard what had happened to me, she greeted me not as a peso-less 'cheap lackey' but as an honoured guest, a victim like herself of an oppressive regime – even something of a hero. She was a walking, and hip-swinging, cliché, that stereotype of literature – the tart with a heart of gold. She herself had literary links and tastes. She told me proudly that, not only had she been in contact with the great Graham Greene when he was doing research in Cuba, but she had read the book *Our Man in Havana*. However this paragon among prostitutes was no literary snob and, though a mere newspaper hack, I could not have been given more professional care and skilful attention had I been that year's Nobel Prize-winner for literature. Yet all I could offer in return for my night of pneumatic shelter was a thank-you. An offer to send currency from America was rejected, and although I promised myself that I would send a leather-bound set of the collected works of Graham Greene for her establishment's library, I'm sorry to admit I never did.

Her brother's advice about the airport had been right, and when he drove me there early in the morning to catch the first plane to Miami, the officials and airport police were sleepily unconcerned about the departure of a deportee. Nevertheless, until I was aboard the plane, I expected the heavy hand to descend on my shoulder. I fastened the seatbelt and for once, as we took off, a plane's seatbelt made me feel secure.

That garish strip of hotels in Miami Beach looked almost friendly and welcoming when I arrived. It was convention time, and the lobby of the Fontainbleau Hotel when I checked in was full of men all wearing the same peaked caps and lapel identification badges. Ironically, they looked more regimented than any groups I had seen in Cuba. When I stepped into the elevator, I was asked why I wasn't wearing my cap and badge, and I knew I was back in the land where everyone is free – especially free to conform.

After I filed a story for the paper about my $400 fine in the Cuban court of summary justice, I was summoned to New York to explain it all to Beaverbrook. It was a story on which his relentless curiosity could feed, and when he had extracted the full unexpurgated version, he made characteristic comments: 'You should never travel with bank notes. They're too much of a temptation,' and 'If you had been paying, what would the rates have been in that high-class brothel?' and 'I've heard it said that Havana cigars have a special flavour because they are rolled by the local ladies on their thighs. But that's a myth, isn't it?' and 'Pity you didn't see Castro. I'd have liked to know more about him. I'll bet his beard smells of cigars. He looks intelligent – a cunning character. Like Stalin. Did you find out how much aid Castro gets from Russia?' and 'You're now an expert on what the girls in the fancy house think of Castro and the revolution. What does the man in the street think?' and 'Is the Catholic church still a power on the island?'

As always the questions were endless and in part unanswerable.


I had to face even more questions when I did succeed in interviewing the ruler of another country, another autocrat but one of a sharply different political hue – His Imperial Majesty, the Shah of Persia, the Shahinshah, the Shadow of God, proud occupant of the Peacock Throne. The interview came about in an unusual way. I had been on a visit to Kenya not long before that country became independent. Just before leaving I was invited to judge a jiving competition at a Saturday-night hop in a dance-hall on the outskirts of Nairobi. I agreed to do it, thinking it might provide some material for a light piece in contrast to the somewhat heavier stuff I had been writing about Jomo Kenyatta, the Mau-Mau and Uhuru. When I got to the dance-hall, I discovered that the two other judges hadn't turned up, and I was the only

European there. I also discovered that the popular belief that all Africans have an innate sense of rhythm is a myth. Indeed, some of the dancers had all the grace of a herd of hippotamuses, but as I eliminated a section of the herd from the competition, it became clear that they had supporters in the audience who saw them as gazelles, and who disagreed loudly with my judgements. The atmosphere became distinctly hostile, and I needed no reminding that some of the young dancers in the hall had probably been displaying their proficiency not so long before in Mau-Mau ritual dances in the bush.

I appealed to the master of ceremonies, a former student of the London School of Economics, for some support, and I suggested that he interrupt the proceedings to tell the crowd that the judge was doing his best to be fair and impartial, but that some competitors had to be eliminated. He decided that the best tactic was to impress them, first of all, with my importance by telling them that I represented Britain's biggest newspaper, and that I was one of its leading columnists. But he stumbled nervously over the last word, and when it boomed out over the distorting microphone, I became a leading 'communist'.

Immediately the atmosphere changed: my popularity rating rose. From then on my verdicts were accepted, even cheered in some cases; and I decided it would be foolhardy to defect from the party before the evening was safely over.

On my way back to London, I stopped for a few days in Rome, and at a dinner party given by a film producer, I told the story of my one-night conversion to communism in darkest Africa. One of the guests, a wealthy Iranian woman, said: 'The Shah would be very amused by that story.' It wasn't just one of those snobbish remarks that are name-dropped into the coffee cups at pretentious dinner parties in European capitals: she was a second, or third, cousin of the Shah, and her husband was a court official. Emboldened by a little of the host's cognac, I told her that I would be more than happy to relate the story to the Shah if an interview could be arranged.

I wasn't at all hopeful, but thinking I had nothing to lose, I repeated the offer by cable when I got back to London. To my surprise a reply came, telling me that if I presented myself in Tehran as soon as possible, the Shah would graciously grant me an interview. Beaverbrook's comment as I set out was: 'Better not tell the Shah the Africans weren't the first to make you a communist. He'll put you in jail.'

My first few days in Tehran were painless. The hospitality of the court official and his wife, but for whose chance remark at a dinner party in Rome I would never have been in Tehran, was lavish. However, after nearly a week with no summons from the Peacock

Throne, I was beginning to wonder if my flirtation with the party on Red Clydeside had been discovered by SAVAK, but then I was informed that the Shah had graciously consented to be interviewed by me on the following day.

I was given a final briefing by one of the court officials who told me I must preface every question with 'Your Imperial Majesty, may I ask...' The official was a stuffy, pompous bureaucrat, and he was not amused when I enquired if I would have to ask the questions from a kneeling position. But to my relief His Imperial Majesty, the Shahinshah, the Shadow of God, was much less pompous than his courtiers. (A similar comparison can be drawn, I believe, in many courts, including that of our own dear Queen.) After saying 'Your Imperial Majesty, may I ask...' a few times, the Shah, who spoke idiomatic English, said: 'Please stop calling me that. Why don't you sit over here in this chair. It's more comfortable. Now we can have a cigarette and a chat. There are a few questions I want to ask you.'

As an experienced interviewee he know how disarmingly valuable charm could be; obviously he had also learned the defensive stratagem of turning himself into the interviewer on occasion, and of course, as a monarch who was omnipotent on his own territory, he felt free to ask as many questions as he liked. I wasn't surprised that many of them were about the spread of communist influence throughout the world, for during my week's wait, I had heard the virulent anti-Shah propaganda which poured over the airwaves into Tehran from Moscow.

His briefing about me had been impressively thorough, including the details of my swift conversion to communism in that Nairobi dance-hall and also the fact that I had been in Berlin not long after the Wall was built, when Checkpoint Charlie was the focal point of tension with Soviet and American tanks lined up menacingly on either side of the barbed wire. He wanted to know if I thought the Americans were firm in their resolve to withstand Soviet pressure in that beleaguered city. It was a question I could not answer, but I was able to tell him an anecdote about the reaction of one American, which, like the Nairobi incident, fitted into the category of black (and Red) humour.

The American was a drag artist, whom I encountered in one of the night clubs that are to be found all over West Berlin. Some of them are like upholstered bomb craters, and the décor and entertainment they provide is usually crude and vulgar, but they are havens of civilization and culture compared to the ugliness and obscenity of the political landscape outside in the vicinity of the Wall and Checkpoint Charlie.

Unlike his compatriots in khaki, the American in his uniform of tight dress, high heels and blonde wig was there by choice, and not by military command. I asked him what he would do when, as the rumour-mongers were predicting, the Soviets rolled their tanks into West Berlin. He adjusted his blonde wig, and said in a lilting Southern accent as broad as the Mississippi: 'Darling, I'll wear a *red* dress.'

It occurred to me as I reached the end of the anecdote that the Shah might find it distasteful, but no court jester could have had a better response.

The rest of the interview continued on a serious note, and the Shah talked informally and informatively about his White Revolution, his plans for land reform, his efforts to curb corruption in all sections of the community, the resistance to change from the rich land-owning families and the mullahs, and in general the difficulties he faced trying to move a backward country with a high illiteracy rate into the second half of the twentieth century.

All in all, it was an impressive performance. But how much, you may ask, was it a performance? Did a haughty monarch decide that, for an hour or so for the benefit of the Western press, he would play the part of a gentle and reasonable ruler? Was I hoodwinked by the Shadow of God, deceived by a cynical despot?

Because of his grim record which was later revealed, it is impossible to look back now and offer any objective answers. All I can say after so many years is that if there were any incipient symptoms of the galloping megalomania which overtook him later with tragic consequences for himself and his country, I wasn't perceptive enough to note them.

I wrote a long piece based on the interview in which I quoted the Shah at length; it was given front-page prominence and hailed as another 'world exclusive'. According to the blurb, an '*Express*man' (a label which made journalists sound like train drivers and which I never liked) had done it again. What I had not done was give any indication that the powerful Pahlavi dynasty would come to a bitter and melodramatic end within a comparatively short period. But then neither did the world's leading statesmen and diplomats until the last ill-fated moments.

Beaverbrook's cross-examination when I came back was as exhaustive and exhausting as ever, taking in minor details as well as vital matters. Did the Shah smoke a lot? Had I counted the number of cigarettes he got through during the interview? How big was his army? Was it well equipped? How many planes in his air force? Were his palace guards smart and well drilled? Did he look healthy? Was he a womanizer? How did the Tehran hotel rate by international standards? What was the price of caviar over there? Was the British ambassador any good? Was the Shah really serious about giving land to the peasants? Was he a religious man? Did he pray several times a day like a good Muslim? Was he a teetotaler? Was he the complete boss, the autocrat – or did anyone else have real power in Iran? And so on . . .

Although the Beaverbrook curiosity showed little sign of flagging, although he still held autocratic control over his own newspaper empire – and although he was still declaring, as he had for years, that he never exercised that control – I was beginning to see some signs that his declarations might be beginning to bear some relation to the truth. The Old Man, as everyone on the staff had called him since he was middle-aged, *was* ageing a bit. He was then in his eighties, and although in his case these were by no means the exhausted eighties, he was, as he liked to point out, well over his allotted biblical span.

One of the signs that his grip was loosening was that his son Max was allowed to appoint an editor who didn't have Beaverbrook's full approval. He didn't have mine either, but I had no executive authority or influence, nor did I wish any. I did, however, have a long holiday due to me, and I decided to take it to work on a book of short stories I had started. I rented a villa in the south of Spain and managed to complete the first draft of about 70,000 words before my holiday ended. When I got back I felt less and less inclined to write any words for the *Daily Express*.

I thought that there was a considerable lack of flair and judgement in the managerial and editorial hierarchy of the *Express* at that time; an arrogant and ill-conceived judgement on my part, perhaps, but other writers on the paper shared it, and in our view it applied particularly to the chairman, or young Max, as Beaverbrook's son was known to everyone on the staff, although he was then middle-aged. Inevitably, as his father's control weakened, the inadequacies of young Max became more apparent.

There is a theory about Beaverbrook's ambivalent attitude towards his son, which has some basis in history and psychiatry. Although the megalomania, which afflicts most owners of powerful newspaper empires from time to time, was muted in Beaverbrook's case by a sharp and boisterous sense of humour which he could turn on himself, he was affected by one of the commonest symptoms of the disease – the belief that no one is properly equipped to run the empire after you, the empire builder, go, so it's better to drag it down or let it fade away with you. It's notable that, on a higher historical level, great politicians, like de Gaulle and Churchill to name but two recent examples, each prone to megalomania in varying degrees, were extremely reluctant to nominate successors.

In the case of Beaverbrook, operating on a lower level but dealing with a sizeable newspaper empire, the difficulties were complicated by the fact that his successor, and inheritor, *had* to be his only surviving son: he loved young Max, as a God-fearing son of the manse like himself should; but he also knew, as a shrewd old self-made millionaire, that young Max had not inherited the essential instincts and talents.

When he married Lady Dunn, Beaverbrook was in his eighty-fourth year, and I suspect that he did it, after forty years of fairly merry widowerhood, partly to complicate the inheritance question. She was the extremely rich widow of his old friend and Canadian business crony, Sir James Dunn, and she had been tending to some of his needs for some time; it was hardly necessary to legitimize their relationship to stop the gossip, and it is perhaps significant that the marriage took place in a register office, and was not solemnized in a Presbyterian church. As an indication of how mixed his motives for marriage may have been, he added to the confusion with a characteristic flash of humour by declaring: 'Of course I married her for her money.'

Whatever his motives for marriage may have been, it was clear for some time before it took place that his ambivalent attitude to young Max was not likely to change. It was part of the walking paradox that was Beaverbrook, one of the Calvinist crosses he had to bear on one shoulder unevenly balanced, according to his enemies, by the satanic fork on the other.

The situation was highly complex for those members of the staff whose regard for young Max's professional talents was as low as the Old Man's – and whose relationship with the Old Man himself was the classic love–hate one in varying degrees of that mixture. I was one of the fortunate few with no cause for hate, but the amateur psychiatrist that lurks in most journalists warned me that there was a possibility I could be driven to feel differently, and in addition if I was beginning to lose confidence in the paper because its most talented journalist was also its oldest, perhaps the time had come to part company. So I decided to accept an offer to join the *Mirror* group under the editorial direction of Hugh Cudlipp and write a column for the Sunday paper, the *Pictorial*, which he planned to relaunch as the *Sunday Mirror*, moving it closer to the rich, middle market dominated by the *Sunday Express*, on which he had worked as Managing Editor.

It was one of the most difficult decisions I've ever had to make in my professional life, and it was made only after a long period of agonizing. Although Beaverbrook believed rightly that every journalist on the paper was expendable, with the exception of himself, he could be jealously proprietorial and paternalistic about his editorial staff, particularly those, like myself, to whom he had given encouragement, guidance, support, protection – and a platform on which to air views he didn't always share. Sentiment and loyalty apart, his sharp business instincts undoubtedly made him think that, after visiting most countries in the world at his expense and acquiring a fair amount of valuable jornalistic experience, I was now about to hand it over to a rival newspaper group.

I had been given more than a hint of proprietorial disapproval a little earlier when my book of short stories was published by Hutchinson. Like all fiction, the stories were partly based on personal experience and the character common to all the stories was a newspaperman. The title was *A Ticket for the Peepshow*, and Beaverbrook probably thought he had paid in part for that ticket. The book received more generous review space in rival papers than it did in the Beaverbrook press, and his loaded comment to me was: 'Dangerous pastime for a newspaperman – writing fiction. Ah well, I suppose I should be grateful you kept your fiction out of the paper and gave it to another publisher.'

However he must have forgiven me for most of my professional and personal sins when the final parting came, for he treated me more generously than I probably deserved. His handshake wasn't golden but it wasn't brass either, as it could have been since I was resigning; in addition he let me keep the company car I had been driving, and he handed over a couple of endowment insurance policies he had taken out on my behalf. When we did shake hands at Arlington House on my last day, he said as though echoing my innermost thoughts: 'Maybe you're wise to go. I'll be going myself soon.' I replied: 'Nonsense. I could be under that No. 9 bus before you.' Years before, when crossing Piccadilly with him, setting out on one of his morning walks up Bond Street, a No. 9 had almost got both of us: he had said then: 'That one's meant for us – it stops in Fleet Street.'

Looking back now, I have no regrets about leaving Beaverbrook newspapers when I did. My absence from the columns of his newspapers did not affect them, and had nothing to do with their decline, which had been setting in before I left, continued till his death, and has been noticeable ever since. As he and many others had forecast, young Max, like so many sons who inherit everything except the talents of their outstanding fathers, allowed the inheritance to slip out of his grasp, and into hands even less skilled than his own in journalism and newspaper publishing, or what his father sometimes called 'the black art'.

Certainly the Trafalgar Group which took the Beaverbrook press from young Max is a booming public company with wide-ranging interests in property and shipping, and Victor Matthews, who now controls the publishing subsidiary, Fleet Holdings, is a smart, self-made millionaire whose achievements include helping to keep the Cunard Line afloat. But when he sailed into Fleet Street to take over Beaverbrook's captaincy, he was in perilous waters. It cannot be denied that he has been bold enough to launch a new daily paper, the *Star*, though its main claim to prominence so far is that it was the first national paper to publish pictures of topless girls in full colour. It has also set something of a record by switching its political stance from right to left with such speed that the switch may not have been noticed by readers as they concentrated on right and left nipples. The *Star*, however, has failed to match the remarkable commercial success of Rupert Murdoch's paper, the *Sun*, although it has done its best to equal it in toplessness and patriotism. In fact during the Falklands war, for example, when they were vying with each other in efforts to raise the morale of 'our boys', the *Star* could claim that it outdid its rival by displaying red, white and blue nipples.

However even before the Falklands war, a grateful Prime Minister had given Victor Matthews a peerage, making him the latest – and perhaps the last – of the press lords, but there the similarity with Beaverbrook ends. Indeed, the depressing fact is that Lord Matthews is to journalism what Lord Beaverbrook would have been to male modelling.

Nevertheless it has to be said that, although the journalistic standards have declined since Lord Matthews took over, one of the established papers in the group, the *Sunday Express*, has changed very little in style and general content over the last three decades. When you consider that a newspaper should mirror a constantly changing world and reflect the age it lives in, this is a remarkable feat. It is mainly due to one man, Sir John Junor, who has edited it for more than twenty-five years. He inherited a successful editorial formula, which had been originated by Beaverbrook with Beverley Baxter as Editor, and then developed skilfully under John Gordon's editorship. It was a formula which appealed mainly to the middle class and the middle brow, though it attracted readers on all social and intellectual levels, and it was never defined by Beaverbrook except negatively. He made it clear that he preferred stories about people not things, action not abstraction, success not failure; he favoured a good measure of passion and provocation but shunned pornography.

Although no man could have cherished, and protected, such a successful formula more than Sir John Junor, it is wrong to say that he hasn't changed it in any way at all. Since Beaverbrook's death, he has gradually introduced what could be called soft (suitable for Sunday) porn. Nothing shocking of course; nothing to frighten the horses or *épater les bourgeois*. Just a nice picture on every other page, and sometimes even on the front page, of a nice girl doing something nice like mounting a horse, or emerging from a swimming-pool, or bending to mend a bicycle puncture, so that she is showing a nicely judged expanse of thigh or bust. Unlike their sisters in the *Star*, Sir John's Sunday girls have their nipples discreetly covered and their buttocks, though pneumatic, are never bare.

Like the litanies of television presenters at beauty contests, the captions of these nice pictures of nice girls contain useless information which is amazingly constant. The nice girl is invariably a model who wants to be an actress or pop singer, who is usually going, or has just been, to an exotic foreign island to model bikinis. In other words the pictures and captions have no journalistic relevance whatsoever. They are there to titillate and keep the sales up: Sir John clearly believes that a slice or two of cheesecake on Sunday is good for sluggish circulation. But at the same time, on the leader page, sometimes opposite a slice of cheesecake, in the 'Current Events' column (a pulpit first built and occupied by John Gordon), Sir John might be preaching a stern Calvinistic sermon about the journalistic nadir touched by the 'Dirty Digger', Rupert Murdoch, and fulminating against him for stripping girls to the waist on page three of the *Sun* in a desperate pornographic drive to boost sales. (Sir John overlooks the fact that Lord Matthews does the same in the *Star* – and in full colour.)

If Beaverbrook were still alive, he would, I'm sure, condemn Murdoch's, Matthews' and Sir John's circulation boosters, but he might prefer Murdoch's as at least a bit more honest and less hypocritical – free of the cant that is contained in Sir John's juxtapositioning of fiery Sunday sermon and tempting cheesecake.

Admittedly Beaverbrook himself wasn't entirely free of Calvinistic cant, John Knoxian humbug. The virtuous Beaverbrook persona he liked to present for public scrutiny would have been appalled by some of the things he got up to in private. Piers Brendon, in his book *The Life and Death of Press Barons*, reports that in the period between the wars when Beaverbrook was something of a playboy and installed in Stornoway House overlooking Green Park, it used to be said that the two wooden lions, which guarded the door, winked whenever a virgin crossed the threshold.

But his Calvinistic cant was not exposed unblushingly to millions of readers, and he didn't try to sell his newspapers by publishing pictures of coquettish models posing as nice virgins while he looked on like a winking, leering lion. He would never have allowed Sir John, whose journalistic skills he much admired, to waste any newspaper space on the areas, inviting though they may be, above a dimpled knee or around a swelling bosom.

Of course Sir John can claim – and is never slow to do so – that his paper is the only one in the group that has kept its circulation figures at a highly profitable level. They are declining now in common with those of many other national papers, but they are still high. There is no proof, however, that they could not be just as high, if not higher, under a more innovative Editor, displaying journalistic flair rather than irrelevant flesh.

By sticking rigidly to his inherited formula, except for the addition of cheesecake, Junor has removed the element of surprise that Beaverbrook insisted was essential in a successful newspaper. In his own book *Success*, Beaverbrook wrote: 'Nothing is so bad as consistency ... The man who is consistent must be out of touch with reality. There is no consistency in the course of events – in history, in the weather, or in the mental attitude of one's fellow men . . .' One of his editorial canons was: 'Never be over-cautious and predictable. Surprise the reader and he will buy the paper again to find out what you've got for him next.' But for too many years under Sir John Junor, the *Sunday Express* has been about as surprising as the statement that Sunday is the day after Saturday.

Even at the risk of losing circulation, Beaverbrook with his restless, questing journalistic mind would have initiated changes in style and content. He used to call himself the 'No. 1 Reader': had he lived, he would never have sat back and allowed himself to become the No. 1 *bored* reader.

After I left the paper, breaking the maxim 'never resign', which Beaverbrook's old Irish friend Tim Healy had taught him, but which he often broke himself during his own political career, I didn't see the Old Man again for many months. Then came the invitation to the dinner in the Dorchester Hotel given by Lord Thomson of Fleet for Beaverbrook's eighty-fifth birthday. It was an unforgettable night: one of those occasions that add a footnote to the history books. Beaverbrook had been ill for some time, and until a few hours before the dinner, it had been doubtful if he could attend. Yet when he arrived in a wheelchair, he looked lively and sounded spritely. When I spoke to him just before the dinner, and asked him how he felt, he said: 'Did you read that piece about me in the *Sunday Telegraph* that quoted me saying, "I can piss, but I can't walk"? Well, you'll be pleased to hear I can still piss. I still can't walk, though.'

But walk he did. Powered by his indomitable will, he rose from the wheelchair and, leaning on his son's arm, he walked to the top table. Standing alone and steady, he made a speech that was full of vigour and wry humour – a swan song that was never a dirge. One of its most quoted passages was: 'This is my final word. It is time for me to become an apprentice once more. I have not settled in which direction. But somewhere, sometime soon.'

After dinner he made another, by no means lugubrious, comment about his direction and ultimate destination. For some reason (unexplained to the guests) each of us had been presented with a copy of a lavish cookery book published by one of Lord Thomson's companies. Beaverbrook said: 'Roy Thomson obviously believes there are good cooking facilities where I'm going.'

When he did go almost exactly two weeks later, he would have been surprised – perhaps even disappointed – if he had discovered that Roy Thomson had made a mistake about that ultimate destination.

# The Apprentice
# Godfrey Smith

My appearance in this book is something of a swindle, for I met the Beaver just once. The circumstances were nevertheless comic enough, I think, to justify this brief note.

Robert Edwards, then Editor of the *Daily Express*, turned up for lunch at Cherkley with the Deputy Editor, Harold Keeble, to find the Old Man in a vile mood. Roy Thomson had just filched one of his favourite men, Tom Stacey.

'Who's the best man on the *Sunday Times*?' snarled the Beaver.

'Smith,' riposted Edwards, always quick on the draw.

'Get him,' snarled the Beaver.

In the car going back to London Harold turned to Bob. 'Who the hell's Smith?' he asked.

'God knows,' said Bob. 'But there must be someone called Smith working there.'

A car came for me in the summer of 1960 and swept me swiftly down to Cherkley. The only image in my memory of the Old Man is now hopelessly blurred with Low's celebrated cartoon. Surely he was not really sitting on a high stool, holding a phone, and grinning from ear to ear, yet that is just how I remember him.

The interview was mercifully short. I was to be an assistant editor of the *Daily Express* and my salary was to be doubled. I stayed with the *Express* twenty-one months. It was what a regular army officer might have called his SAS course. The Beaver never asked to see me again. I don't know if this suited him; it certainly suited me.

It was not, however, the last time I saw the Old Man. I was one of the 658 guests at the Dorchester on the night of Monday 24 May 1964 when Roy Thomson gave his epic dinner for Beaverbrook's eighty-fifth birthday.

It was an evening that combined in one mind-bending bonanza all that is the most endearing and the most absurd about our business. There were Mounties and Indians, specially flown across the Atlantic. There were songs of his native land, sung by the Maple Leaf Six, excruciating in their corniness. There was a seven-tier cake, each tier representing a different stage of his life. There was a ceremonial sword, courtesy of the Canadian Guards, to cut it.

The Old Man had not walked for weeks. He had two weeks left to live, yet he crossed that great concourse in the glare of the lights on the arm of his son as if he had been scripted to do it by a Hollywood screenwriter. And what a speech he gave us.

It was, by turns, mischievous and reflective, frivolous and profound. It was, he told us, his final word. The last few lines had clearly been written by that putative scriptwriter from Beverly Hills. All his life, he told us, he had been an apprentice: in business, in politics, in newspapers. 'It is time for me to become an apprentice once more. I have not settled in which direction. But somewhere, sometime soon.'

The standing ovation as he sat down went on for several minutes. We are a sentimental and ruthless lot in the Street of Shame. There must have been few men present who had not crossed swords with Beaverbrook at some time in their lives. Yet the ovation was genuine. It was the only possible reaction to a speech of that brilliance. I am glad I was there to hear it. I am glad I met the Old Man once, just as, I must say in all truth, I am profoundly glad I met him no more.

# Vastly Entertaining
# Robert Edwards

They don't make them like that any more. It is probably a good thing really. The divine right of proprietors is no longer in fashion. That now belongs to Editors, provided they sell their papers.

However, I am one of the small band who look back on their Beaverbrook days with little short of delight. Recalling him is as pleasing a nostalgic exercise as remembering those marvellous films with Sydney Greenstreet, Peter Lorre and Humphrey Bogart. He was vastly entertaining.

I first met him at Cherkley, the large country house near Leatherhead where he entertained Bollinger Bolsheviks, Churchill, H. G. Wells, Cabinet ministers, Stanley Morison (the anarchist who designed the neat, orderly Times Roman type), excellent journalists, singularly dull captains of industry, and goodness knows who else.

Picture the scene. The young Editor of *Tribune* sitting on a large settee, facing a vast picture of a horse by Stubbs. Outside, a menacing, black afternoon sky. Enter the evil Tory Press Baron, his right fist curiously clenched. 'Ah, you must be Mr Edwards,' said the much-imitated voice. 'I'd like to shake you by the hand, but I can't.' Dramatically he unclenched his fist. 'It's full of worms for the fish Churchill gave me.'

Indeed it was.

We entered the garden through french windows in his study. He had lost interest in the fish by now and threw the worms into the pond without a further glance.

'Excuse me, Mr Edwards, I must make water.' Which he did, there and then, facing a distant fir tree.

That night I attended the first of many dinner parties. One famous guest was accompanied by two strikingly plain daughters. I was on Beaverbrook's right hand.

'You realize, Mr Edwards,' he said in a loud voice, 'Mr — has many extraordinary talents. He is a fine politician, none better. He is a superb writer. He was a brilliant editor. But of all his gifts, none is greater than his two beautiful daughters. Don't you think so, Mr Edwards?'

He repeated this with variations throughout dinner.

Later, as we walked towards his private cinema to see (inevitably) *Destry Rides Again*, Beaverbrook held me back for a moment with a light touch on my arm.

'Wonderful fellow, Mr — ,' he said. 'Pity about his daughters.'

I decided it would be fun working for him, if a little dangerous. He finally offered me a job at lunch with Arthur Christiansen (a truly great editor) and Ian Aitken, now the *Guardian*'s Political Editor, a chum I had recommended to him, feeling his name would have a certain pull.

The arrangement was that Chris would nod if he agreed with Beaverbrook's choice, first of Ian and then of me. He nodded – twice.

'I think,' barked the Beaver, 'Bob will make a good fellow journalist, don't you, Chris?'

Thus the Editor of *Tribune* eventually became Editor of the *Daily Express*, but not without resigning a couple of times on the way.

'That's enough,' he said after the second resignation. 'One more and you'll be worse than me during the war.'

The Beaver had wonderful servants. At his villa, La Capponcina, in the south of France, I was in the doghouse (again) and left to write an impossible article with a bottle of plonk and a piece of cold chicken for lunch.

Mr Mead, the butler, and I watched the yacht go out to sea with all the other guests on board.

'It doesn't seem right,' said Mr Mead. 'Them with all of that and us with nothing.'

On another occasion Beaverbrook decided I looked too young for an editor. 'You should wear turn-ups on your trousers,' he said, glaring at the offending objects, 'and they are too narrow at the bottom.'

'Sir,' I said, 'you have no turn-ups and your trousers look the same width as mine.'

He pressed a bell twice. In came Raymond, his valet. 'Get a tape-measure,' commanded the great proprietor, 'and measure the bottom of Mr Edwards' trousers.'

They were fifteen-and-a-half inches. 'Now measure mine,' said his lordship. They were eighteen inches. Beaverbrook had triumphed, but not for long.

'Mr Edwards,' said Raymond insolently, 'has exactly the right trouser-width for a gentleman of his age and position.'

Raymond could get away with murder, like all of the Old Man's staff who weren't afraid of him. I remember a secretary correcting him when he put the phone down rudely on a colleague. 'He was still talking,' she said. She survived.

One year my wife and I were invited to La Capponcina just before Christmas. While there, Beaverbrook attacked me for publishing an article on Scrooge. He thought it was old-hat stuff, and he was right, but I defended the article. The Old Man pressed the bell once and in came Mr Mead. Beaverbrook handed him his Christmas box in an envelope.

'Mead!' he cried. 'Is anybody at all interested in Scrooge nowadays?'

Mead got the picture. 'Oh yes, my Lord,' he said.

Not to be outdone, the Beaver pressed the bell twice. In came Raymond. The performance was repeated exactly.

Beaverbrook sat down and read the article again. Then he threw the paper on the floor. 'Do you know why I've done that?' he shouted, reaching for the paper. 'So that I can pick it up and throw it down again!'


Beaverbrook loved his papers, for all the stick he gave his editors. Every now and then he pretended to show concern over the money they spent.

Once Harold Keeble, the brilliant features executive, had the bright idea of publishing a Photonews picture of all fifty *Daily Express* photographers.

'Good God,' said the Old Man when he saw the picture. But no one was fired.

One day, when Edward Pickering was Editor, we published a marvellous picture of Jackie Kennedy falling off a horse. It cost a shattering £2,000. The day it appeared was my turn to go walking with Beaverbrook. His right eye flickered ominously when I arrived at his flat.

'How much was it?' he asked.

'How much was what?' I replied.

'Oh dear, you're becoming an old soldier,' he sighed. 'The picture of Jackie!'

When I confessed all, he picked up the Dictaphone and shouted to the chairman, 'Mr Blackburn, Mr Blackburn. You're all mad on the *Daily Express*.'

'Well, sir,' I said, 'we all decided we'd rather face your wrath for spending £2,000 than for letting it go to the *Daily Mail*.'

We heard no more.

Shortly before he died, some busybody told him the total *Daily Express* bill for expenses. Sitting by the fish-pond on a lovely sunny day, his feet covered with a car rug, straw hat almost over his eyes, he said vehemently: 'By God, Bob, if it's the last thing I do I'll sort out this racket before I die! Are you in favour of a reign of terror?'

'Certainly, sir,' I said. 'But I think we should take care whose expenses we query.' Then I mentioned the names of some of his favourite contributors.

He picked up the Dictaphone. 'Mr Blackburn, Mr Blackburn. Before the great purge, check every name with Mr Edwards.'

That was the end of that.

These were almost the last words I heard him speak, this unique man who may have broken the hearts of some, but who made the careers of many others.

The best thing to do was to fasten your seatbelt and enjoy the ride.

# Mentor and Tormentor
# Geoffrey Bocca

A couple of years ago on a Caribbean cruise in the Cunard *Princess*, we put in at Nassau in the Bahamas. It was the first time I had been there since I had written for Lord Beaverbrook. I retraced old steps, contemplated Pancake House on the waterfront where he housed his excess guests. I walked up Hill Street, past the Royal Victoria Hotel and around the corner up to the gate where tars of several nations used to wait for Beaverbrook's valet to come off duty. The house was still called Hill House and I walked up the garden path. The place was now a businessmen's club. No one answered the bell, but the door was unlocked and I went in, into the vast drawing-room, where I had once accidentally spilt one of Beaverbrook's famous daiquiris over Sir Oswald Mosley, and into the dining-room which looked out over the gorgeous garden. Upstairs, the bedrooms had been turned into offices.

There was a visitors' book at the entrance. I wrote, 'I lived here in another time, signed Geoffrey Bocca, the ghost of Lord Beaverbrook' and left. End of story.

Max Aitken, Baron Beaverbrook, loved what he considered good writing, although his admiration for the writing of Godfrey Winn entitled some to question his judgement. He also disliked his own company and so it amused him to surround himself with journalistic whizz-kids. Being a whizz-kid for Beaverbrook meant being highly paid, but the work frequently induced the feeling of being a novice lost on the Cresta Run. The Beaverbrook kiss of approval sometimes seemed to approximate that bestowed by Richard Nixon on the likes of Haldeman and Ehrlichman.

But most went into it with their eyes open. When I was whizz-kidding for Beaverbrook between 1953 and 1962 – intermittently quitting and returning – the Beaver's walking wounded abounded in Fleet Street, in English letters and in the House of Commons. Some were old men. Some just looked it – look at Michael Foot. But few could resist Beaverbrook's siren song of gold, glamorous parties, transatlantic voyages in the *Queen Mary* and exotic travels to the Caribbean and the Riviera. I know I couldn't.

Was he totally without scruple? I am inclined to think so. In my office I have a framed note he pencilled to me which illustrates perfectly either his impishness or his cynicism, depending on how one wants to interpret it. It dealt with the abdication of Edward VIII and says: 'Beaverbrook's advice over the years has always been, "Never quit, wait until you are fired." '

Could he have meant it seriously? Would he have advised Nixon to 'hang tough' until he was impeached and America split apart? Would he have advised Alexander Haig to hang on at the State Department until he went *really* bonkers? Would he bring society to anarchy? Or was he just giving me a good quote? Maybe, maybe not. He fired Arthur Christiansen to save Chris's life after his heart attacks. But the firing broke Chris's heart and he died anyway.


Beaver's parties at Cap d'Ail, the Bahamas and Jamaica were wonderful experiences, but I noticed one thing. They were always more relaxed when he wasn't there, when he was taking his afternoon nap or after he had retired to bed. It was rather like Hitler's generals lighting up cigarettes in the Berlin bunker the moment they heard the shot that blew out Hitler's brains. The guests let their hair down. But I also found it was best not to talk about Beaverbrook, because the rich, famous and beautiful people snitch.

I, invariably being the youngest guest at his parties, always sat close to the bottom of the table. One evening, smiling his monkey smile, eyes twinkling under the bushy eyebrows, he called down the table, past Walter Lippman, the Archbishop of York, Captain Simon Wardell and others, 'Bocca, I understand you give an excellent imitation of me and my Canadian accent. Some of us have not heard it. For the amusement of all of us, pray do so.' All the eyes directed at me were hard, worldly, pitiless. The kid had been set up to make a Roman holiday for the quality. But God does keep an eye on things. Some quick thinking saved me from having by decree to make a fool of myself. The previous evening the guest of honour had been one of those baronets who from time to time appear by aberration in the Honours List and then either commit suicide or flee to the Caribbean.

His Cockney accent had made the other guests smile behind their hands. I said, 'Perhaps you meant Sir Joseph Doakes' and went into a routine of 'Ow are yer, Beaver, boy . . .' which got a few laughs and the subject, thankfully, was changed.

Of course, the most exciting times were when Winston Churchill was staying with the Beaver. I found myself briefly alone with Churchill in the Bahamas. He was feeling no pain after lunch and, my heart beating at my temerity, I approached him. 'Sir Winston. I am a writer, and I want to be a better writer. I know how much Gibbon has influenced your writing. Would you recommend me other authors who have impressed you?'

Churchill replied with one word: 'Kinglake.' I had never heard of Kinglake. I didn't dare ask Beaverbrook and be splattered against the walls by his derision. I didn't dare ask Freddie Lonsdale. I waited until I got back to the Charing Cross Road to discover Alexander Kinglake and his *Eothen* and his nine-volume history of the Crimean War.

Almost every memoir concerning Beaverbrook involves name-dropping, but now we come to the greatest bit of name-dropping since the clerihew. I told Beaverbrook about the encounter – for my own protection; Beaverbrook was very possessive about his friendship with Churchill and would not tolerate anyone going to Churchill behind his back. He gave one of his roars of laughter and slapped his knee. 'That son-of-a-gun, Winston,' he said. 'He always claims *he* discovered Kinglake. He didn't because I was there when he first heard about him, at lunch at the Carlton Grill. He heard about Kinglake from Rudyard Kipling.'

Occasionally – very occasionally – one could turn the tables on Beaverbrook. I recall doing it only once. He was always torn between his lust for women and his Presbyterian conscience. He continually said, 'If you don't believe in the damnation of unbaptized children and that, for every one who goes to heaven, nine roast in eternal flames, you are not a Presbyterian.' But he also loved scabrous gossip about those around him, and frequently needled me about stories he had heard about my enjoying the contemplation of a well-turned ankle, as it were. He commissioned me to write my book, *The Life and Death of Harry Oakes*, while I was in the Dominican Republic doing an exposé of Trujillo for *Look* magazine.

Bored one evening, in Ciudad Trujillo, I asked a taxi driver to take me to the area where ladies strolled, and I met an agreeable young person whose name I never learned. A couple of days later I was in the Waldorf Towers in New York, admitted by the unforgettable Raymond, his valet. Typically, the first question Beaverbrook put to me was, 'Who do you think killed Harry Oakes?'

I stammered. 'I haven't the faintest idea, sir. I haven't started my research. A black man, I suppose.'

For some reason I never learned, or could even theorize, the answer made Beaverbrook very agitated. He jumped to his feet. 'No, no, Bocca! That is quite impossible. You must immediately disabuse yourself of that idea! No, no. If Harry Oakes were killed by a black man, it would be for one reason only, that Oakes was going to bed with a black woman. And that's the worst thing a white man can do in the Caribbean.'

I saw my chance to get my own back for years of ill-treatment. Assuming my most innocent expression, and looking puzzled, I said, 'I don't know about that, sir. Only forty-eight hours ago, in Ciudad Trujillo, I myself had a bit of black stuff.'

It almost seems in my memory that Beaverbrook took a step backwards and flung the back of his hand against his forehead, like Harry Wharton face to face with Herbert Vernon-Smith smoking. Then he recovered, and gave a little chortle. Lust had won out over Presbyterian conscience. 'Well, Geoffrey,' he said, 'you're a little bastard. You always were and you always will be.' He was in high good humour over lunch.

For some reason, my work on the Oakes murder bothered him from beginning to end. It could scarcely have been fear. He could hardly have been concerned about his place in Bahamian society. What society? When I wrote to ask if I could stay in Pancake House while researching, he sent me a letter saying, 'You are a cheeky young boy, and the answer is no.' But he had also, unknowingly, left a clue I had come to recognize. He had started the letter, 'Dear Geoffrey'. Whenever I was doing something that particularly intrigued him, I was Geoffrey. The rest of the time I was Bocca.

Then he took me off the job and fired me. But I had already signed contracts with Doubleday in New York, Weidenfeld and Nicolson in London and with several European magazines. I had the financial backing to go ahead, so I was brash. I said to Beaverbrook, 'I'm committed to write the book anyway, and I will wager all Lombard Street to a china orange that the *Sunday Express* will serialize it.' He bared his teeth in a snarl. I interviewed several people, from Canada to the Bahamas, who were friends of Beaverbrook. They would have shown me the door if Beaverbrook had dropped the word. He didn't. From the moment of my firing until the moment of serialization in the *Sunday Express*, I never heard a word from Beaverbrook. And then the invitations resumed. Beaverbrook wanted the book and, as was his wont, he crouched behind his praetorian guard.

Beaverbrook hired me originally to write a biography, unauthorized, of the Duchess of Windsor. The Windsors were furious. I wanted to call it *The Iron Duchess*, a title suggested to me by Elsa Maxwell, but Beaverbrook was set on the title *The Woman Who Would Be Queen*, and kept repeating it, both to me and to himself, chuckling with the delight of invention. He didn't get the title anyway, not in the UK at least, for libel reasons, and it emerged as *She Might Have Been Queen.*

Beaverbrook showed me a lot private papers, but his directions were usually oblique. I was sitting in his living-room at Arlington House while he was talking to E. J. Robertson, his General Manager. The Beaver looked over his shoulder at me and said, 'Go to Portugal and talk to the Holy Ghost.' Then he resumed talking to E.J. It was obvious I was not to ask questions.

I walked down the road to my flat in Little St James's Street and pulled out my reference books. I found the reference quickly, in the Duke's book, *A King's Story*: Ricardo do Espirito Santo Sylva, the Portuguese banker who had put the Windsors up after they had fled the Riviera on the fall of France.

In the home of Espirito Santo, they had met Hitler's Ambassador to Portugal, Baron von Hoyningen-Hühne. The connection between the former King of England and the envoy of Hitler was so alarming that Churchill had sent Walter Monckton to Lisbon to find out what mischief was going on.

I flew to Lisbon, interviewed the baron, then living in retirement in Estoril, and was duly entertained to lunch by Dr Ricardo do Espirito Santo Sylva at his mansion, O Boca do Inferno in Cascais, a home decorated in execrable taste. Espirito Santo, a handsome and eloquent man, was frank and charming and gave me wonderful material. He confirmed that the baron, on instructions from the Wilhemstrasse, had suggested to the duke that once Britain was occupied he should return as *Friedenskönig*, or 'Peace King', with Lloyd George as a Pétain-esque Prime Minister. He left for a moment, and returned with a note that left me gasping. It was scrawled in ink in the Duke of Windsor's hand and it said – I quote from memory – 'Dear Espirito Santo, I enjoyed our meeting last night and hope you will stay in touch with the baron.'

I said, 'Dr Ricardo, I know money means nothing to you, but it means nothing to me either. Name your price.'

I knew I couldn't use the letter, for libel reasons, but I knew that the Beaver would pay anything to own it. Indeed, that may have been his reason for sending me to Portugal. Espirito Santo smiled and shook his head. And then a funny thing happened a few months later. I received a telegram from Espirito Santo from the Lancaster Hotel in Paris, saying it was important I see him. The two of us dined in his suite. He was very nervous, kept cracking his knuckles and said that the letter was a fake, and it wasn't written by the duke, and would I please not use it . . .

I tell the story. Don't ask me to explain it. As my long years with Beaverbrook taught me, the labyrinthine mental processes of the high and mighty are too much for the likes of little us.


We all had agonizing experiences with the Old Man, but the worst of all, for me, did not touch on me at all. I was fresh in Beaverbrook's employ, still seeing stars, and sitting with him in his drawing-room at Cherkley. Max, his son, came in, notebook in hand, to take his orders. The Beaver berated him in terms I would never have used to my son, even if we were alone. 'You are a stupid little fool . . . You will never grow up . . . If you didn't have my name, you would be a messenger boy.'

I wanted to die. Why, I wondered, didn't Beaverbrook tell me to leave the room? Max took it all, head bowed and said nothing. I am sure Max's dislike of me stemmed from that scene to which I was such an unhappy witness.


Neither rain nor snow stopped Beaverbrook's long morning constitutional, always with one or more of his minions. Once he and I were walking through Grosvenor Square. At the corner of Carlos Place, he stopped and looked at the penthouse of a block of flats. He looked for such a long time that several people stopped to see what he was looking at. When we resumed walking, I asked him the question. 'Jean Norton lived there,' he said in a very low voice. Jean Norton had been one of the great loves of his life.

Once I was walking alone with Beaverbrook through Central Park in New York. It was a fresh spring day when the New York air becomes magic. Approaching us from around a corner I saw half a dozen noisy young Puerto Ricans. In such a situation one does not know what is

boisterousness and what is menace until the moment of truth. I felt
the little old man beside me stiffen. I thought of taking his arm but I
knew that would insult his pride. Instinctively I took half a step ahead
of him and covered his left shoulder with my right, bodyguard fashion
(although I had no idea that that *was* bodyguard practice, never having
been a bodyguard). The boys passed us without even looking at us, and
the incident was forgotten. Not then, but later, and even today, I
realize that if they had attacked us, I would have died to defend a man I
so frequently hated.

His relationship with the women in his entourage always intrigued
me. His hostess was a lovely Frenchwoman, Marie Edmée Escarra,
widow of, or divorced from, a former Minister of France. Marie Edmée
spoke English with the classic Maurice Chevalier accent. We were
discussing the Beaver – which, as I said earlier, one did not often do for
it was as if Big Brother lived in the Beaverbrook ménage – and she said,
'Max is an old bas-tard.' The line can be appreciated only by thinking of
it in her French accent with each syllable of bastard given equal stress.

I discussed him rather more bluntly with Beaverbrook's exceedingly
nubile secretary, Josephine Rosenberg. Her answer was succinct: 'Yuk!'
Certainly the shortest verdict on Beaverbrook ever uttered.

But his charm with women was overwhelming. The fact that my
then wife was Canadian like himself, albeit French-Canadian, delighted
him, and he called her his 'little cousin'. He left her gasping. And then
one observed his cruelties to the women who were under his thumb,
which were as incomprehensible as everything else in the Beaverbrook
mythology.

He and Marie Edmée and I were sailing in his yacht off Monte Carlo.
His chef had prepared a magnificent picnic in a basket. The cold roast
chicken had to be carved. There was no steward, and Beaverbrook told
Marie Edmée to carve it. Marie Edmée belonged to a class of
Frenchwoman who could not boil water, let alone carve a chicken.

'I'll do it,' I said, rising, but Beaverbrook pulled me back to my chair.
Marie Edmée cut, sawed, pulled joints apart with her fingers, her
temper getting worse and worse, and she finally slammed down the
plates of shredded chicken in front of us. Beaverbrook maintained a
serious look but I could feel his glee.

Some might think this was just a practical joke between lovers, but
it was not so. Beaverbrook's aim was to break her spirit, destroy her. I
heard belatedly of Marie Edmée's death and wrote my condolences to
her parents in Paris. Her father replied emotionally that she died 'of the

excesses of her life'. He may have meant alcoholism. Marie Edmée had been drinking heavily at the end.


The last time I saw Beaverbrook was also the last time I saw Churchill. I was in Beaverbrook's office at La Capponcina, his home at Cap d'Ail up the road from Monaco. It must be explained that the office looked out over his patio and swimming-pool. The Beaver was giving me an assignment when it was announced that Sir Winston was arriving. Beaverbrook became fretful. He did not like surprises. He said to me, 'Wait here. I don't know how strong Sir Winston is,' meaning whether or not he was senile. Churchill, white as paper, and seemingly half his own size, was carried in by two men, and the two immortals sat on the patio. Both were deaf, Churchill very, Beaverbrook quite, and they both had shouters, like food-tasters at Renaissance courts. The time is easy to remember, the autumn of 1961. The Berlin Wall had just gone up, and Vice-President Lyndon Johnson had gone to West Berlin to arm Berliners to the teeth with ballpoints labelled 'Lyndon B. Johnson'.

I heard Beaverbrook say, 'What do you think of Lyndon Johnson's visit to Berlin, Winston?'

Churchill's shouter yelled, 'Sir Winston, Lord Beaverbrook wants to know what you think of Lyndon Johnson's visit to Berlin?'

I heard a Churchillian mumble.

'Lyndon Johnson, Sir Winston! Sir Winston, Lyndon Johnson is the Vice-President of the United States.'

Another mumble, and the shouter shouted again. 'Lord Beaverbrook, Sir Winston wants to know what *you* think of Lyndon Johnson's visit to Berlin.'

'Barnum and Bailey circus, Winston,' said Beaverbrook. 'Barnum and Bailey circus.'

The shouter gathered his breath once more. 'Sir Winston, Lord Beaverbrook thinks it was a Barnum and Bailey circus. *Barnum and Bailey circus, Sir Winston! Barnum! Bailey!*'

Beaverbrook came back into the office to dismiss me until dinner. He was smiling, tanned and walked briskly. 'Go and do some work,' he said. 'Five thousand words will do.'

Beaverbrook was born in 1879, four years, six months and five days after Winston Churchill. Beaverbrook died on 9 June 1964. Churchill outlived him by seven months and fifteen days.


Nearly twenty years later, what are my feelings towards Beaverbrook, my mentor and tormentor? Hate? N-no. No. Love? *No!* Admiration? Not a whisper. Resentment? Twenty years ago I might have said yes. Now it is more – curiosity. How could Beaverbrook with all his power and comprehension of life, deliberately seduce so many talented but innocent and inexperienced young writers into projects that served his own obscure interests while knowing that the results could damage the writers' reputations and careers? Not only without any compunction, but even it seemed, with some relish. Of course, the writers were then bound all the more tightly to the Beaverbrook chariot.

Do I miss the old bastard? Hell, yes.

# The Proprietor
## Alan Brien

In his autobiography, Sir Michael Redgrave recalls crossing Blackfriars Bridge on his way to play the leading role in Ibsen's *The Master Builder* at the Old Vic. His hands were shaking. Was it just first-night nerves, or perhaps, as it turned out, the onset of a nervous disease which was to plague what should have been the crowning years of a distinguished, and adventurous, acting career? The evening was to face him with a challenge neither he nor any of his audience could have anticipated.

I was there, as drama critic of the *Sunday Telegraph*, in my usual seat on the aisle, about six rows back from the stage. My mind, as I waited for the curtain to rise, was not very securely on the play or the performance I was about to witness. For several weeks now, whenever I switched off from work, and sometimes while I was trying to concentrate on work, I found myself worrying about a libel action recently mounted against me, and the paper for which I wrote a weekly essay column, the *Spectator*, by Lord Beaverbrook.

When I had hammered it out at my typewriter in an ill-lit, dark-panelled backroom in the paper's offices at Gower Street between 11 a.m. and 2 p.m., working up to the last second of a deadline, the offending piece had not seemed to me to be dangerously damaging to his lordship, or indeed very novel or surprising stuff. I had regarded it as largely a repetition, perhaps with a little more detail and some personal anecdotes, of an accusation that had often, over the years, been made against him – that, after retiring from active participation in politics, he had pursued a policy, under various more-or-less transparent subterfuges, of arranging that the history of Britain for the period between 1914 and 1945 should be written, or rather rewritten, to make him a key figure in our island story.

I had suggested that this was the reason he had cornered some of the most valuable archives available to scholars who were even then researching those decades – the Lloyd George and Bonar Law papers, his own extensive documentation – and farmed them out to writers who would be permitted to use them only by his licence and with his approval. I did not claim, nor do I even now believe, that any of them would write what he instructed them to write. The whole point was that they should be, and should be seen to be, independent witnesses, though clearly they could scarcely help being influenced by the first-hand evidence of someone who was by then often the only surviving participant in many of the events.

My aim had been simply to leave, hidden away in the back numbers of the *Spectator*, a warning to the next generation of historians, fifty years in the future. They should not assume that, because several of their predecessors, figures varying from Oxford Tory dons to left-wing journalists, all agreed on the same version, this must be the un-challengeable truth. I wanted them to know that one possible thread linking Robert Rhodes James, Frank Owen, James Cameron, Tom Driberg, Randolph Churchill, A. J. P. Taylor and others might eventually be traced back to the great spider, Max Aitken, Lord Beaverbrook, at the centre of his web. Some would be bound only by his charm and courtesy, others by his advice and assistance, an occasional one or two by a guarantee against the publisher's advance or, in Driberg's case, by his payment of the author's debts.

After I had left my copy with the Editor, I had taxied off for a late-lunchtime drink at El Vino and forgot about what I had written. It had been with a shock then, a couple of weeks later, that I had found on my desk at Gower Street the long, fat envelope that signifies the solicitor's writ. It had been unusual in that the statement of claim had run to several pages of closely typed abuse, written in a style that I had recognized as dictated in my former employer's unmistakable idiom. Not only had my opinions been stigmatized as outright lies, but my motives had been located as deeply rooted in long-standing malice, hatred and personal spite. Unless the enclosed grovelling apology, plus a total withdrawal of every word I had written, was published in the next issue, action would be taken in the courts.

My immediate impulse had been to give way. I had sufficient experience of the British libel laws to know that though, in theory, the old Fleet Street adage, 'The greater the truth, the greater the libel,' may not be accurate, in practice this often turns out to be near enough what is demonstrated in the courtroom. I also knew that when such a multi-millionaire plaintiff sets the wheels in motion, he can afford to leave the rest to his professional hirelings, suffering barely a ripple on the surface of his life. Even if he loses in the end, all he has lost is money, the one thing he has plenty of. But a poor defendant cannot afford to forget the prospect of defeat, knowing that if he is faced eventually with damages and costs, he may have to sell up all he possesses. For him, even victory will have consumed much of the time he would otherwise has spent earning his living, and have bitten deep into his savings, if any.

Fortunately, I had been spared such a humiliating show-down. The *Spectator*, though a small and shoe-string publication compared to the least of Beaverbrook's papers, proved to have gutsy and gallant steersmen at the helm. Its owner was then the young Ian Gilmour, a rich and radical Tory aristo, who immediately offered to risk the hefty sum, for those days, of £40,000 to fight the case. And its Editor, the pugnacious Iain McLeod MP was actually eager for the fray. 'The little monster will never dare go in the box,' he chortled. 'And if he does, we'll crucify him. I've been waiting for this chance for years.'

Nevertheless, though emboldened by such fighting spirit expressed by my trainer and manager, sitting in my seat at the Old Vic I could not help feeling a tremor of cowardice from time to time, reminding myself that after all, I would be the one to put on the striped shorts and go into the ring against the best bruisers Lord Beaverbrook's money could buy.

So I turned a glazed eye on Bernard Levin, fellow drama critic, when he stopped beside me on the first night of *The Master Builder* and said, 'Who's a lucky bugger then?' He did not pause for an answer. 'When Emile Littler sued me, what happened?' he demanded. 'Did he die, or did I have to apologize?'

'You had, er, to, well, you know . . .' I burbled.

'Never mind,' he said. 'When Henry Sherek sued me, did he die or did I have to apologize? When . . .'

'Never mind,' I said, a light dawning. 'Who's died then?'

'BEAVERBROOK!' he shouted. 'You jammy happorth. You've won and you don't even know it. It was on the six o'clock news.'

I felt as if my blood had been drained away and my veins transfused with Bollinger. I hardly heard the man in front of me whispering. It was 'Binkie' Beaumont, head of H. M. Tennent, the most important theatrical management in Britain. I had looked at the back of his neck on many openings though we had barely exchanged more than a word.

'Excuse me, Mr Brien,' he was saying in a quiet, intimate voice. 'I could not help overhearing. Did Mr Levin say Lord Beaverbrook is . . . dead?'

I nodded, still drunkenly bemused. What did it matter to him?

'Is that certain?' he asked in lowered tones. 'I mean, there can be no mistake?'

'Absolutely,' I replied, getting a little tetchy. 'Bernard doesn't make mistakes. Anyway, he heard it on the news.'

'Binkie' stood tall, with his back to the stage. 'HURRAH!' he cried. Several heads turned. 'Binkie' searched out friends all over the front stalls. 'Beaverbrook's dead,' he beamed in every direction. 'It's on the news.'

The audience was fired by the announcement, and it ran along the rows like flame through a cornfield. As the curtain rose, the first-nighters were still crackling with it. I had never realized that so many undercover enemies of Beaverbrook were just waiting for his departure to release their feelings.

Redgrave appeared on stage. Perhaps it was a marvellous performance. Nobody could tell. Every line about the ageing martinet at the end of his domination was greeted by muffled laughter. Redgrave clearly sensed he was evoking the wrong mood and executed the experienced performer's 'September Morn' check-up of his costume, one hand running over his flies, the other exploring his wig. He carried on but the lines of fellow players produced now more open mirth. By the end, it was like the climax of a birthday party. Redgrave and the cast received their cheerful applause with wary puzzlement.

Afterwards, in the back bar of the stalls, Emlyn Williams, the play's translator, was in despair. 'How can you put on a tragedy,' he complained, 'when Beaverbrook's death turns it into a comedy?'

I have described this occasion at some length, not in order to obtain any kind of posthumous revenge upon Beaverbrook. Even in those weeks before his death (which I, of course, did not realize was so near) I had not been able to help feeling a certain sense of gratification, mixed with my apprehension, that he should have thought my criticisms of him important enough to justify taking what was for him an unprecedented action. And afterwards I was even rather proud that his writ must have been among the last public decisions he made on this earth. I have committed the description of it to paper because I regard it as a revealing and interesting piece of social history of Britain in the sixties which otherwise might have been lost to posterity.

It is not mentioned in A. J. P. Taylor's life, though the bare bones of the libel suit must be in the files that Beaverbrook left for Professor Taylor to protect and administer. But then his biographer made, as he has explained, a deliberate decision to avoid relying upon what he characterizes as Fleet Street gossip and bar-room tales about the press lord he confesses to having 'loved'. I have never been able to understand this approach. As I put it to him, when we debated his book on BBC television on the day of its publication: what would he think of a biographer of Napoleon who refused even to listen to the oral testimony of the emperor's marshals, or even corporals, however biased, inflated or romantic it might seem? What is the criterion which can elevate letters, diaries, memos and published memoirs above the spoken evidence of those who knew the subject of the work, often on surprisingly intimate terms? It seemed to me he did not have a convincing reply. And I can only suppose that he ignored all of Beaverbrook's journalist employees below the rank of Editor, and quizzed not many of those, largely because he was afraid they might tell him things he did not want to hear.

And yet it seems to me that Beaverbrook, if not the greatest reporter, certainly the best-equipped gossip columnist, whose words ever appeared anywhere in the Beaverbrook press, was exactly the kind of man who comes alive only in the tales of his hired hench-persons. He lives on in El Vino, the Cheshire Cheese, the Garrick Club and other drinking holes where they still foregather, with a vivid presence that will not be found in Whitehall, the City, English country houses, Jamaica, the south of France or even New Brunswick, where his mercurial, many-sided influence was felt for half a century.

Like almost all former Beaverbrook employees, I think of him as the only proprietor for whom I ever worked whose eye I could feel burning along every line I ever wrote, however trivial, specialized or obscure the part of the paper in which they appeared. This was often an illusion, but none of us could count on that. Just when you thought you had disappeared in some dense thicket amid acres of newsprint, there would come a message to you by name, sometimes handed down by proxy from above, sometimes delivered in person by telephone. It might be words of praise or criticism, a correction or an elaboration, encouragement or reprimand, but at least it meant you were being read inside, as well as outside, the office – not as common a practice as non-journalists might think. And if you were one of those singled out, for reasons not always immediately apparent, to meet the Little Old Reader face to face, the same principle operated only on a larger scale.

In the late fifties, Beaverbrook appointed me film critic of the *Evening Standard*. It was an odd choice, for several reasons, most particularly in that at around the same time I had been plucked from my post as underpaid critic/book reviewer/roving columnist of the lively but tiny-circulation weekly, *Truth*, and given the job as the *Observer*'s first full-time TV reviewer. David Astor, the Editor, and effectively, the owner, of the *Observer*, and Beaverbrook, the owner, and effectively the Editor-in-Chief of the *Daily Express*, the *Sunday Express* and the *Standard*, were not on good terms. The *Standard's* Londoner's Diary and the *Observer's* Pendennis frequently sniped at each other's proprietor and mocked each other's policies. And there was I, in the middle, commuting between the two offices, the person most likely to be blamed for leaking gossip in either direction, when all I wanted to be was a famous Fleet Street by-line.

The *Standard's* Editor was not very enthusiastic about my appointment, but I soon realized this mattered little so long as Beaverbrook's magic hand hovered over my head. I knew he must want me for some good reason of his own since the interview that settled my contract had originally appeared to go very wrong. Most proprietors would have decided from my answers to the questions asked then that I was quite the wrong type.

I had attended Beaverbrook at his Arlington House eyrie overlooking Green Park, just behind the Ritz. He had begun by asking about my politics.

'I'm a socialist,' I said.

'What kind of a socialist?' he asked, smiling benignly.

'A socialist socialist,' I said.

There was a pause so long I thought one of us had passed out.

'Good,' he said briskly. 'Then you're against Gaitskell. So am I. What do you think about the royal family?'

This had to be it, I thought. All press lords love the Queen if only because she sells papers.

'I'm a republican,' I said.

'Even better,' he said. 'So am I. I'd abolish them only it's not practical politics. And the House of Lords too. What is your religion?'

'I'm an atheist,' I said.

He stood up, gave me a courteous hand, and escorted me to the door.

'That seems very satisfactory, Mr Brien. I appreciate your candour. I think you may find that the Editor will look upon you favourably.'

And so he did, though I thought I detected a certain relish in his voice when he sent for me a few months later. 'You seem to have upset the Old Man by something in your film column,' he said. 'You're to go to see him at 10.30 tomorrow.'

That following morning, at his flat, Beaverbrook did not appear so welcoming. He dropped the 'Mr' and called me just 'Brien'.

'Who's this "Billy Bunter" you mention this week?' he demanded irritably, picking up the name as if with a pair of tongs. 'I've never heard of him. Nobody I've spoken to has ever heard of him. Don't you know it's not only bad journalism, it's bad manners, to mention obscure figures that only confuse your readers.'

I was taken aback. On the way I had prepared my defences against what I considered might have been the source of his displeasure – praise for Danny Kaye, said by all Beaverologists to be top of his blacklist of overrated entertainers; or leading the column with a review of a Soviet film at the Everyman, Hampstead, in the week of the Hungarian uprising. There was nothing for it but to play the 'candour' card again.

'I'm sorry, Lord Beaverbrook,' I said. 'But with all respect to you, Billy Bunter is possibly the most famous character in British literature of this century. I do not honestly believe there is a single person brought up in these islands who does not know who he is.'

He stared at me for a few moments. And his hand reached for the telephone. 'Get me Max Aitken,' he snapped. Then, with the beginnings of a twinkle, he explained to me what he was doing. 'We'll consult my son, the young Napoleon. He runs all my papers now, you understand. I've retired from business.' When the telephone rang back, he launched into a lecture to Max Aitken as though I were not present. He complained about the lead story in the *Sunday Express* ('If it's worth those big headlines, why is there nothing about it in the other papers on Monday, not even the *Daily Express*?') He wanted to know why the Beaverbrook city editors were still not pushing something called 'Mexican Eagles'. He suggested that it was about time the *Standard* carried another leader on 'Dirty London'. Then, just before he rang off, he asked, as if as an afterthought, 'Who is Billy Bunter?'

He listened for a brief second or two, then interrupted fiercely. 'Whaddya mean what do I mean by Billy Bunter? I mean Billy... Bunter. Have you heard of this Bunter fellow or not? Yes or no? Oh, I see. You're certain now? Well, goodbye t'ya.'

He turned slowly to me again. 'Young Max says this Bunter is a fat fellow, a famous fat fellow. Where does everybody read about him?'

I assured him Bunter was on view every week in a couple of boys' comics, the *Magnet* and the *Gem*, even in Canada. Possibly I looked too smug. He made a note on his pad.

He opened the door, and shook my hand again. 'You're doing a good job, Mr Brien. I shall tell your Editor so.'

A week later, the Editor stopped by my desk. 'Thought you ought to see this,' he said, dropping a torn-off strip from an airmail-weight letter. It read: 'TELL BRIEN MAGNET-GEM NO LONGER EXISTS. HE MUST CHECK HIS FACTS MORE CAREFULLY.'

'What's Magnet Gem?' he asked.

'I have no idea,' I said. 'Who are Mexican Eagles?'

The next confrontation came a few months later and concerned my least favourite subject for debate, money. It began with a telephone call from Beaverbrook, succinct and steely. 'I have decided I can no longer share you with Mr Astor's *Observer*. You must write for him or for me. You will not lose by staying with us. Make your decision and come here to discuss it with me.'

It was not an easy choice to make, and my discussion with David Astor is practically a comic short story in itself. But in the end I opted for the big bad press lord. And I turned up once again at Arlington House determined not to be short-changed.

His Lordship came straight to the point. 'You will never regret this,' he said. 'Name your figure.'

I added the two fees I had been getting together, watching him closely, and wondered how much more I could add.

'I think forty . . .' I mused slowly. He began to rise. 'Forty-five, that is . . .' I went on.

He rose. 'Fine,' he said. I realized it was too little, though a handsome weekly salary in those days.

'Net, of course,' I added.

He stared at me strangely. 'What is "net"?'

' "Net",' I repeated, playing for time. 'Why, correct me if I'm wrong, "net" is a well-known financial term, at least on my level, signifying a sum paid after all other amounts have been deducted.'

' "Net",' he said. 'You mean take-home pay. You want £45 a week in your pocket, is that it? How much would you need to be paid to get that after tax and such?'

'I don't know,' I admitted.

'How can you ask for a salary you don't know what it is?'

'Well, Lord Beaverbrook. Put it this way. The *Standard* must have a chief accountant or whatever who can take a slide rule and tell us how much will bring in £45 a week, net.'

He lifted the telephone. 'Get me the chief accountant at the *Standard* . . . This is Lord Beaverbrook. We have a young man on our paper called Mr Brien. No, don't go away and look him up. Take my word for it. I forget what he is paid now, but from next week he is to receive £45 a week. Net. Yes, net. Are you not familiar with the word? I am informed that it is a well-known term signifying a sum arrived at after all other deductions. Yes, £45. No, I do not know how much will be necessary to produce this sum. I believe it can be calculated with a slide rule.'

For once, I felt I had triumphed in the money market. What could Lord Beaverbrook have meant, as he politely ushered me to the door, observing: 'I trust this arrangement will always operate to your advantage.'

Not long after, against all my experience of budgets, a Conservative chancellor decreed a reduction in tax for incomes over £2,000 a year. Most of my colleagues found their pay packets fatter without having had to ask for a raise. Mine remained the same.

I rang the chief accountant.

'Have you forgotten?' he asked. 'Your salary is net. If deductions go up, you can't lose. But if they go down, you don't gain. You're on £45 until the next time Lord Beaverbrook rings about my slide rule.'

I didn't see much of Lord Beaverbrook for about a year. But when I left film criticism to become the *Standard* correspondent in New York, and he passed through the city, I used to find myself being summoned to the Waldorf Towers to fill in some of his empty hours. I don't kid myself that he had any particular affection for me, though I think he preferred me over the other Beaverbrook press staffers in Manhattan because, during my early post-Oxford year of devilling for Randolph Churchill, I had been forced to study English political history between 1910 and 1940 in some detail. So I was able to listen to his reminiscences of Bonar Law and Asquith, Lloyd George and Bonar Law, Baldwin and Chamberlain, Curzon and Lord Derby, with more than simulated attention, making an occasional informed response, even extending that sometimes to disagreement and dispute. But mainly it was the result of something I had discovered with my increasing sophistication – the rich, famous and powerful, especially as they grow old, are often more lonely than outsiders can imagine. It was a time of many odd, nerve-wracking, occasionally rather endearing, encounters with someone already passing into legend. The man about whom Raldolph Churchill observed, 'He has never espoused any cause which was both honourable *and* successful.' The man of whom Evelyn Waugh remarked, 'Of course, I believe in the Devil. How otherwise would I account for the existence of Lord Beaverbrook?'

The meetings I most dreaded in advance, but enjoyed most in retrospect, were those when he insisted on wandering around Manhattan, moving through the crowds like a fragile, hypercritical extra-terrestrial, followed at a discreet distance by his attentive space-capsule, a chauffeur-driven Cadillac. I have never kept a diary, but in those days I fancy my supposed diary kept me. Beaverbrook had got into his head that, each night, I wrote down a Pepysian account of the day's events and often would fill me up in the evening with all sorts of arcane, complex accounts of long-gone plots and conspiracies which, owing to the strength of his rum-punches, I forgot by the next morning.

I recall walking round the lake in Central Park. He gripped my arm. 'Some day – make a note of it – they will discover oil wells under here. Look at the gleam of petroleum on the water. I know about these things. Remember that.' It didn't seem very probable, but the next day I went back to have another look and, after much peering, thought I could just see what he was talking about. I asked the man who looked after the boats if he'd ever noticed this rainbow sheen. 'Sure,' he said. 'It's what drips off when I grease the rowlocks.' Who was fooling whom?

Another day, he stepped off the pavement looking in the wrong, that is, the English, direction for the traffic. He was almost, like his great friend, rival, pensioner and patron, Winston Churchill, savaged by a speeding cab. I saved him with a swift drag on the collar of his beautifully made, dinky little overcoat. He ought, then and there, to have made provision for me in his will. Instead, typically, he discharged his adrenalin by trying to find some aspect of the city about which he knew more than I did.

'I'll take you to see the antique shops on Third Avenue,' he said. 'I don't suppose you've ever been there.'

Without thinking, I said, 'There are no antique shops on Third Avenue.' I was still in the grip of the delusion that what every tyrant wants is someone who will tell him 'No'.

He insisted in vain, block after block, in proving me wrong. But there were no antique shops. At last, he stopped in front of an empty window. It was, to me, clearly a place that had recently been vacated and was waiting for a new occupant.

'Now here's an antique shop,' he said. I stared at the bare room in which there was only a single, ordinary kitchen chair, placed for obvious reasons under a bare light bulb, where some workman had left it.

'Why hasn't it got any antiques in it then?' I asked. I realized I was now very near to terminating my employment. He looked at me, and there was almost entreaty in his eyes. He was an old man, and near exhaustion.

'Because,' he said, 'they are displaying just this one chair, possibly the only one of its kind in existence. It is worth a fortune. This is an antique shop.'

'If you say so, Lord Beaverbrook,' I said.

'No,' he insisted. 'This is an antique shop, isn't it?'

'Yes,' I lied.

He summoned the Cadillac. 'Why do you always have to contradict everybody?'

I got used to having to give way in the end, whatever we were discussing. And I adopted the habit of saying then, 'Up to a point, Lord Beaverbrook.' I counted upon him not recognizing this borrowing from Waugh's *Scoop*. It made it seem less like sycophancy.

One day, he asked, 'What is this up-to-a-point business?'

I explained that this was what the editors in *Scoop* said to their proprietor, Lord Copper, when they disagreed. When they agreed, they said, 'Definitely, Lord Copper.'

'Never read it,' he snapped. 'I'm told it's a very poor book.'

'I don't think so,' I said. 'You should read it. Some people think Lord Copper is meant to be you. But there is little resemblance.'

Immediately he was interested. 'You don't say?' he said. 'What sort of fellow is Lord Copper?'

'Well,' I said, taking a deep breath. 'Lord Copper is shy and retiring, rather stupid, and not at all attractive, or successful with women.'

Beaverbrook stood still in the middle of his hotel room and stared at the wall. 'How'd you like to be a diplomatic correspondent?' he said.


However friendly we occasionally seemed, the gap was always there. I was working for him. Even supposing I was the best that money could buy, still I was bought and he was the buyer. Once when I made some remark about politics that had not occurred to him before, he regarded me like a disappointed father. 'When I was your age, I had made a million dollars,' he said. I knew what he was thinking – the old New York Jewish insult: 'If you're so clever, why ain't you rich?'

Our parting came after a dinner at the Waldorf Towers. For some reason, I had grown very nervous about his invitation, and popped several tablets of the then wonder relaxer, Miltown, before downing a couple of large Scotches. By the time we came to the bananas *flambée*, during which he almost barbecued himself lighting the brandy, I was well away. In the presence of another of his editors, I replied to his demand to tell him what was wrong with the *Evening Standard* by telling him what was wrong with the *Evening Standard*. He went into the next room and we all could hear him dictating my criticisms on a Dictaphone for the benefit of the Editor of the *Standard*. I protested, pointing out that I had made these criticisms only under orders, and after his promise that what was said would not be repeated outside that room. We looked at each other over the smoking dessert. 'All right,' he said. And he added to his dictation the instruction: 'Delete all remarks by Brien about the *Standard*.'

A few days afterwards I returned to London, laden with the treasures and junk of a two-years' sojourn, plus a new wife-to-be. Looking back, I marvel at my innocence. I rejoined the *Standard* as chief feature writer, everything I wrote winning golden opinions from the Editor I had once thought resented me. It must have been a fortnight before I unearthed at the bottom of one of my many suitcases an envelope entrusted to me by Beaverbrook for his private office in the *Express* building. Praying it wasn't urgent, I dropped it in. The next day, the axe fell. The Editor told me that everything I was writing was stale, boring, tired and virtually unprintable. I realized then that he had received Beaverbrook's account of what I had said at that drunken, drugged dinner, so I resigned on the spot.


Beaverbrook forgave me. The day I cleared out my drawers, he sent me a letter, topped and tailed in his own hand, wishing me well, speaking highly of my talents, and prophesying (since he had convinced himself I was returning to New York) that I would become 'a second Alistair Cooke, only better'.

That was the last I heard from him until the writ flopped on my desk.

# That Printer's Devil
## Eve Perrick

The voice on the telephone I had picked up from the desk I share with three other reporters had a transatlantic twang and responded to my 'Eve Perrick speaking' with 'What is a lug?' Now a lug, in the sense in which my caller posed the question is – according to the *Concise Oxford Dictionary* – 'projection on an object by which it may be carried, fixed in place, etc.' But one does not have a dictionary at the ready on a reporter's desk, and without such precise information available, 'a lug' is something which is impossible to describe verbally, especially in the state of shock brought on by the Editor's secretary rushing in to whisper into my free ear, 'It's Lord Beaverbrook on the phone.' They were the first words he ever said to me.

I had better explain the circumstances leading up to this bizarre predicament. I had been writing a small daily column in the four-to-six-paged *Daily Express* of 1947/48. It was headed 'Signing Off' but was without a by-line. Thus I had no recognized identity to attract invitations and interviews and had to rely on gleaning possible copy-producing material from the news editor's discards, usually via his waste-paper basket. One invitation I got this way was to attend an event in a pub in Hammersmith at which the Earl of Dudley was going to reveal to an apparently breathlessly waiting world a 'lug-less bicycle'. He did, too, and rode it and fell off. All this was duly reported by this conscientious columnist. It was a good piece. Editor Arthur Christiansen in his famed 'bulletins' pronounced it 'good enough for the *New Yorker*; no, good enough for the *Daily Express*'. Anyway, good enough for Lord Beaverbrook to call Chris, ask the identity of the writer and then have his call put through, unannounced, to me with my mixed emotions of surprise, gratification and embarrassment. Which was about par for the course with all my subsequent encounters with that printer's devil, the legendary press lord, Beaverbrook.

Our first meeting in the flesh was at one of his Savoy Hotel tea parties at which tea was about the only beverage not served – but Lord Beaverbrook couldn't bear to have the word 'cocktails' on his invitations, and the current chummier 'drinks' was not then in use. To these spasmodic events the editorial executives and selected specialist staff were invited.

I was early among those pounced on by Chris, in his party role of procuring for his lordship's entertainment those chosen few who might, by their wit, erudition or – and more frequently – some frightful gaffe, create such fun. Caught with an empty glass in one hand, a chewed olive stone in the other and at the same time struggling with the veil of my hat which had become stuck, visor-like, so that my face was locked in, I was nevertheless borne along the length of the River Room to the inner 'throne room'. Which may have been the reason I answered Lord Beaverbrook's seemingly politely interested enquiry of how I became a journalist and joined the *Daily Express* with, 'Oh, I got picked up in the Quality Inn in Argyle Street.' As *Punch* is rumoured to have it, 'collapse of stout party', the stout party being my astonished Editor. 'Surely,' said Lord Beaverbrook in his best Presbyterian minister's manner, 'Mr Christiansen does not go around recruiting staff that way?' There followed some fraught minutes of amplification and explanation absolving his Editor and any *Express* personnel from any part in that incident, before I was led away, my shamed face mercifully obscured by the imprisoning veil.

Soon after came the summons to have a cup of tea with Lord Beaverbrook at Arlington House. Now, someone should anthologize the tales of the traps set by the host for novice guests visiting Lord Beaverbrook in his various lairs. I have collected a few such: Wolf Mankowitz was ushered into the presence only to find Beaverbrook with his trousers rolled up, earnestly scratching his leg; Marius Pope (then Features Editor of the *Evening Standard*) was shown into an apparently empty room into which, after about ten minutes' wait, a small figure emerged on all fours from behind the sofa where, he explained, he had several newspapers laid out on the floor and would Mr Pope be kind enough to help him search for a certain item. Marius, who is a big and burly six-footer, went down on all fours beside the pixie-dispositioned peer, and said he felt like Papa Bear trotting out Baby Brumas (the pre-Panda star attraction at the zoo at that time). Kathleen Sutherland, taking round the finished portrait to the sitter because her husband Graham was unwell, has told me of how Lord Beaverbrook looked but briefly at the painting, propped it against a wall out of vision, then engaged her in general chit-chat without mentioning the picture at all until she was leaving. *Then* he said: 'It's a work of genius.'

Of course, during the time I was being exposed to these tests of one's aplomb as it were, I was not aware I was in such good company. I thought these spider-and-fly parlour games were coincidental with my visits. At the Arlington House flat, the butler showed me right on to the balcony of the sitting-room where Lord Beaverbrook was discovered engrossed in an intimate and lengthy telephone conversation. In a room, one could have backed away out of earshot; on a tiny balcony with closed french windows, one is trapped. I have often wondered whether there was actually anyone on the line at the other end. It was at that tea-for-two session that Lord Beaverbrook, having told me I was a good journalist, said, 'You must either listen a lot, or read a lot. All good writers do one or the other, or both. Except,' he added, 'Beverley Baxter. I don't think he's ever opened a book in his life, and no one can get a word in edgeways when he's talking.' (I'm certain, though, that Lord Beaverbrook never lost control of any conversation, Sir Beverley or no Sir Beverley.)

My second summons to take tea with the Principal Reader of the Beaverbrook publications – his chosen designation instead of plain 'Proprietor' – was to Cherkley. There he was sitting on the terrace, a towel over his head which was almost submerged in a bowl of steaming Friar's Balsam (or whatever was the upmarket, updated equivalent of the inhalant my grandmother used for her asthma). Again, with hindsight or rather hindhearing, I've learned how Lord Beaverbrook could summon an attack at the most awkward time. Harold Keeble, the Deputy Editor, told me of the time he was with him in a taxi when there was a sudden hissing sound, causing the driver to stop and look for a suspected punctured tyre. It was Lord Beaverbrook performing the breathing exercises prescribed by his doctor. It was then suggested that Harold should join him in the exercise – for his, Keeble's hay fever. And there were the two of them, hissing away in the middle of a traffic jam in Piccadilly.

The next call came in New York, the night before I was returning home at the end of the Queen Mother's American holiday trip. Tagging along had been, for the most part, an enjoyable assignment, except for the nagging cables I was getting from London in which I was instructed to convey to Her Majesty the fact that Lord Beaverbrook was much in favour of her becoming Governor-General of Canada. I had failed in this mission, so I was somewhat apprehensive about the summons to his apartment. Could one, I pondered, be incarcerated in the Waldorf Tower for insubordination amounting to treason? But it was a benign Beaverbrook who received me – in bed with a cold and electric-blue pyjamas. We had quite a cosy chat and I think I made him understand that the charming and gracious lady did not actually want to be Governor-General 3,000 miles away from her beloved family and friends. I must have given him the impression that I had really tried to persuade her but had been talked out of it, though naturally, I had not dared to. However, he suddenly reached behind his pillow and took out twenty-eight dollars in crisp new notes. Said Lord Beaverbrook, 'I like your work. You're a good girl and I was going to take you to dinner tonight. But, as you see, I can't go out. So take this and buy yourself dinner.' Thus, alas, passed my one and only chance of dinner *à deux* with the bold baron.

From this distance in time I may fantasize about the way the dialogue just might have gone, to the point where Lord Beaverbrook off guard and slightly dopey from the anti-cold drugs he'd taken, would talk about himself. I am not, however, aware that he ever did talk about himself to anyone. Anything I've ever heard about him has come from the company he kept. And the stories about dear Max, while probably apocryphal, have come from such illustrious storytellers, Somerset Maugham for one, that they have helped embellish the legend without revealing the man.

Anyway, for the record, let me set this down: I did once ask Lord Mountbatten what was the reason for the historic bitterness between them. He replied, 'I never did know. Probably Beaverbrook was bored and just decided to start a feud all on his own. He was a man who loved keeping people guessing.'

# The Elusive Essence
# Christopher Dobson

I have always fought shy of writing about Beaverbrook even though as a young man I was associated with him for more than ten years, acting at various times as baggage master, itinerant journalist and general fixer, and I owe him both my career and some years of anguish. I suppose that what scared me off writing about him previously is that I have read a number of books about him and not one has told his story properly, with the honourable exception of the late war correspondent Alan Wood. It is a vast story concerning great men and turbulent events and it needs a big person to write it. Most of those who have written about this extraordinary man have been overawed by their subject, able only to produce cameos of their own roles in his life and revealing more about themselves than the elusive essence of Max. The two men who should have got it right were Tom Driberg and A. J. P. Taylor, but both failed. Driberg's book was disgraceful; he savaged the hand which had saved him on more than one occasion from public humiliation and even imprisonment, but then, he was a double-crosser all his life. Taylor's failure is harder to explain. His admiration for his subject is total and that is difficult to understand in a professional historian. Perhaps he felt in Beaverbrook's mischievous perversity a reflection of his own rebellious nature. Whatever the reason, he fell too much in love with his subject, did not apply his usual stringent criteria and failed to show us the man 'warts and all'. And, as those of us – both male and female – who were called to conduct business with him while he sat in his bath, knew only too well, he had plenty of warts, both on his body and on his soul. He knew about his blemishes. He feared no man but both dreaded and was fascinated by the hell to which he was sure he would be consigned by a vengeful Jehovah. The sense of impending retribution surrounded him towards the end of his life and he would say: 'The hand of the Lord is upon us.'

It was a feeling that those of us who worked for him felt every day, and the retribution that he inflicted was not always just.

My involvement with him started in 1950 when I was a researcher on the 'Crossbencher' political column for John Junor, now knighted and Editor of the *Sunday Express*. John fell ill one week and there was a panic to get the column written. I wrote it. Beaverbrook liked it. And to my astonishment I found myself, three days later, travelling to New York with him on board the *Queen Mary*.

It was not, however, a pleasure cruise. As soon as we boarded at Southampton – we being his valet, secretary, nurse and myself – he gave me two diaries, both kept by him but giving different accounts of the Abdication Crisis and his role in it. It was rather like a tradesman keeping two sets of books, one for public perusal and the other telling the true story. 'I want you to produce a single story out of those two diaries,' he said, and dismissed me. I sweated over this task throughout the crossing, hardly leaving my cabin while the unsavoured delights of an Atlantic voyage on the great *Queen* went on all round me, until, as we steamed past the Statue of Liberty, I presented him with the single account. He started to read it, asked me for the original diaries, looked at them and then threw my work on the floor. 'I gave you the wrong diaries,' he growled, and never mentioned it again.

It was an incident which set the pattern of our relationship. He was 'the Old Man', 'the Lord' and, as far as I was concerned, his word was law. He could charm people into doing what he wanted, and if charm failed, he used money or fear. He was rich, he was powerful, a dazzling example to a young man. And sometimes I hated his guts. Once at a dinner he gave for local dignitaries in the Lord Beaverbrook Hotel in his Canadian fief on the banks of the Miramichi, he called me to him and said 'Dobson, there are too many flies in this room. Get rid of them.' There was nothing I could do; they were coming off the river in swarms. He knew that. So did everybody else in the room. It seemed to me that he had simply tried to demonstrate that he could order me to do anything he wanted. Perhaps I had been enjoying the evening too much. Anyway, I simply said, 'Yes, sir,' and returned to my seat. But at that moment I hated him with a very fine hatred indeed.

However, most of the time I admired him, and I was fascinated by him all of the time. He made life interesting even when he was being a bastard. And, of course he repaid loyalty. Shortly after we returned from that first trip to New York and Canada, he summoned me to La Capponcina, his villa at Cap d'Ail, sat me down in the summerhouse overlooking the sea where Noël Coward had composed one of his hits and put me to work on another aspect of the Abdication Crisis. I was a dreadful failure; I could not make the words work. So after a week he sent me home to the *Daily Express* for a two-year stint on the subs' table 'to teach you to be a real journalist'. I have always been grateful for those two years. They made me a professional.

They also, however, started the process of my questioning my loyalty to Beaverbrookism. The warts began to show. It was a process which took ten years and came to a show-down only after I had become a foreign correspondent and been to war. It came after an arduous year and a half in Moscow, where I had been sweating it out under Soviet censorship and restrictions. It was always exciting; Khrushchev was at the height of his rambunctious power and there were stories to cover, but as each day passed, it became increasingly evident to me that communism was a cruel sham maintained only by the use of naked force. (There is nothing like living in the Soviet Union as a cure for any lingering belief in socialism.) So when I returned to London for reassignment to Washington I wrote an angry story revealing some of the facts that the censors, unseen behind their green baize door in the Central Telegraph Office, had refused to allow me to write from Moscow. I regret that story now for one reason only: it caused my successor in Moscow some grief with the authorities. *Pravda* devoted half a page to my iniquities, heading its story: 'Mr Dobson is a liar.' Beaverbrook hated it because at that time he had come to believe that the only way he could leave his mark on the world was bringing about a *rapprochement* between the Soviet Union and the West, and he saw the *Daily Express* as his catalyst. He based this belief on his wartime mission to Moscow in which he had come to a successful agreement with Stalin. He admired Stalin almost more than any other man. 'It will not be long before he is spoken of as Stalin the Great . . .' he used to say.

There is a case to be argued that Beaverbrook was at heart a Marxist, but I suspect he admired Stalin simply because he was a man of power and envied him because he had achieved total control, something which Beaverbrook had striven for and failed to acquire throughout his life. He had been deluding himself, of course, in this last great enterprise. Far from his wartime mission being the success his newspapers had claimed, the agreement had been struck only because he had given in to all Stalin's demands, and it had served as a prototype for the sell-outs at Yalta and Potsdam. Either he was, in his own expression, 'in cahoots' with Stalin or the cynical Georgian had conned him. And it was the suggestion that the *Daily Express* was being conned by Stalin's successors into using dispatches which had been savagely censored which so enraged him about my story. He never forgave me, never spoke to me again, put me in cold storage in

Washington – the word soon got round the *Express* office and my stories were treated accordingly – and after a year I was brought home and fired.

It was a terrible blow. In those days in Fleet Street you were either an *Express*man or a lesser breed. I was an *Express*man through and through despite the erosion of my Beaverbrookism. My whole life revolved round that shiny black building 'on the sunny side of the street'. I am grateful now because I have made a new career, but then it was as if my whole world had collapsed. I might just as well have woken up one day and discovered I was a leper. And this is another reason why I have always shied away from writing about Beaverbrook. The hurt is still there. Perhaps I am frightened of revealing too much about myself rather than about the Old Man. Perhaps I have already done so in this piece.

So I am going to let him speak for himself. Some time ago I came across a forgotten folder of his memos to me dating from the years 1956–58 which I spent in New York as the *Daily Express*'s chief correspondent. They were good years, with splendid stories to write at a time when the *Express* was really interested in foreign news: the Suez Crisis at the United Nations; the launching of the first satellites; Broadway and Hollywood; the sinking of the *Andrea Doria*; the Cuban revolution; Eisenhower's presidency. And all the time Beaverbrook deluged the office with memos on a hundred subjects, occasionally descending on New York like a tornado, with him in the calm eye of the storm while everybody else spun in panic around him. He would take up residence in the Waldorf Towers with his trilby set square on his frog face, his shoulders hunched in his blue suit, his small feet encased in the brown shoes he always wore with his blue suits, and call for his secretary and his Dictaphone. And the memos would flow.

I have one before me which admonishes me: 'The extent to which you make use of new envelopes in sending me old material is a distressing experience. I suggest that you use old envelopes and send me new material. Economy should always be practised. It is always essential. I have to request that you will send to the ship for me, in an old envelope, *Time, Newsweek, New Yorker, US News and World Report* and the *Reader's Digest.*' Anyone who ever worked for him will recognize the tone and content of this memo. One can almost hear the flat Canadian voice drawling out the damning phrases in the style of an Old Testament prophet.

Economy was his watchword and the use of new envelopes drove him to rage. He never used his own stationery if he could use someone else's. Some of the memos I have before me carry the letterheadings of the Waldorf Towers and the *Queen Mary*, for he always took care to clean out his suite's stock of headed notepaper before he left the hotel or disembarked from the liner. I quite often ran out of used envelopes, but rather than risk his wrath I would go round to neighbouring offices and beg them for their old ones. He was completely aware of the chaos caused by his demand for old envelopes and enjoyed every bit of it.

His sense of economy was wide-ranging. He kept his supplies of drink in the municipal liquor store in Fredericton, New Brunswick, and whenever he held a party, I would have to go down to the store, draw out his booze and wheel it to the hotel on a porter's trolley. And immediately each function ended, my first task was to mark the level of drink remaining in each bottle – 'You can't trust these waiters.'

He was fascinated by the techniques of saving pennies, and one afternoon I walked with him down New York's Third Avenue – it was a warm sleazy place before it was tarted up – as he compared the prices of bowls of chicken soup in the greasy spoon joints which then lined the avenue. He had no intention of drinking any soup, he simply wanted to find out which restaurant was undercutting the others by a cent a bowl and how they did it. It was my first experience of what has become known as investigative reporting.

The need to economize was constantly reiterated in his memos. He sent me a memo from his expensive estate in Nassau which said: 'When you are shipping to me by air cargo or otherwise, please put the lowest possible value on the goods you send me. The higher the value, the more duty I have to pay. On this parcel of books you sent me, you appear to have paid $6.00 freight. That's too much. I would rather you put it in the Post Office.'

Whenever I was asked to buy something for him, the request was certain to be accompanied by a demand for economy. I have one note asking: 'Would you be good enough to buy me a copy of *Why England Slept* by John F. Kennedy, and hold it for me.' The note is typewritten, but added to it in Beaverbrook's handwriting is the admonition: 'Second hand'.

He was convinced that, if it became known he was interested in buying anything, the price would be doubled, and so he demanded secrecy. When the New York Public Library announced the sale of ten paintings including works by Turner, Gainsborough, Constable and Reynolds, including the latter's 'Boy in a Red Velvet Dress', he wrote saying: 'If this sale of pictures takes place, I am a possible bidder. But it is of the utmost importance that it should not be known.' However, despite his care he was later duped by an unscrupulous art dealer, but that's another story.

My folder of memos also demonstrates his avid interest in the theatre, films and books. At Cherkley he was more often then not content to rerun the Marlene Dietrich/James Stewart classic: *Destry Rides Again*. I dined there with him and a group of journalists and politicians one Sunday, and as the meal drew to an end, he asked, 'Waal, what shall we do now?' Nobody said a word, so he answered himself: 'We'll see a film. Now what film shall we see?' Again, nobody answered. 'I know,' he said as if suddenly making up his mind, 'we'll see *Destry*.' As we trooped off to his cinema, the late Frank Owen peeled off from the end of the line, protesting loudly: 'No. I've seen this fucking film forty fucking times and I'll be fucked if I'll watch it again.' Beaverbrook did not turn a hair.

His tastes seemed to blossom in New York, however. He wanted to see the latest smash hits from the very best seats. As his requests were usually made at the very last moment, they often caused trouble. He refused to allow me to go to the 'scalpers' and pay more than the official price for his seats – although I often did and charged the extra cost to office expenses – and so getting him into the hit Broadway shows was often a problem. On one occasion I was forced to plead with producer David Merrick to get some virtually unobtainable seats. Merrick replied that he would be delighted to help – on condition that Beaverbrook fired his 'illiterate' theatre critic.

In the days before one of his descents on New York, the memos would flood in: 'I want two tickets for *The Music Man* for Tuesday, 25 February. If they are not good tickets, don't take them . . . Some time ago I asked you to book three seats for the night of 26 February for the play *Sunrise at Campobello*. I have not heard from you whether you were able to do this. Please let me know what theatre tickets you are holding for my visit to New York . . . Have you got the tickets for *The Music Man*? . . . Please get me tickets for *West Side Story* at the Winter Garden Theater for Saturday night, 26 October . . .'

*West Side Story* was one of my disasters. I could not get the tickets he wanted and, out of pique, he refused to go on the following night for which I did get tickets, writing to me that 'the tickets for *West Side Story* was a very sad story'. It turned out well in the end, however, because my wife and I used the rejected tickets.

Gramophone records were another fountain-spring of memos: 'Would you be good enough to send me an album of hymns by Tennessee Ernie Ford? . . . Lord Beaverbrook is wanting up to six records by Belafonte, the West Indian calypso singer. He does not wish to have the "Banana Boat Song" . . . Would you be good enough to buy me a recording by Debbie Reynolds called "Tammy" . . . There is a recording of the Red Russian Choir, brought out by RCA, I understand. Please have a copy of that record ready for me when I go to New York.'

Then there were the books: 'Would you please send me a copy of John O'Hara's novel *Ten North Frederick* . . . Would you please send me a copy of *The Family of Man* by Edward Steichen, a photographic collection. The price is $1 . . . Please send a copy of the American edition of *Men and Power* [his own book] to Robert F. Kennedy . . . Send me a book called *Are Men Gay Deceivers!* by Mrs Frank Leslie. It was published in 1983 by Neely's Library of Choice Literature.'

There were also more esoteric requests, all of which had to be carried out with the utmost speed and precision while, at the same time, the business of the office had to be conducted and the stories of the day covered. It was an ageing process. For example: 'Please send me one hundred packets of Sanka instant coffee, just like the enclosed sample.' This request was closely followed by 'Please do not send me any more Sanka, I have been given some.'

He suffered severely from asthma and some of his memos were a cry for help, pathetic in their admittance that this powerful man was as vulnerable as the rest of us. 'Please send me two bulbs for my asthma-spray. Your office has been supplying me with asthma-sprays and bulbs for years. You can buy the asthma-sprays and bulbs from Gimbels. It is not the spray I want this time. Just the two bulbs, because they wear out. It is the bulbs with which you blow the adrenalin through the spray.'

The memos were always couched in the politest of terms. But when he was displeased, the snarl bit through the courtesy: 'Here is an envelope I have received from the New York office. It has been insufficiently stamped for express. This is the second time this has happened.'

I was able to explain that neither of the offending letters had been sent by my office but had come from a young woman journalist in whose career he was interested, and who made her own postal arrangements. But there were other rebukes I could not escape. Some were justified; others were not. But there was no point in trying to wriggle out of responsibility. He had an unerring feel for the weak point in any excuse and was on it like a terrier. The best thing to do was to accept all responsibility and make a fulsome apology. That would delight him and he would forgive with a show of gruff grace – but, at the same time, he would store the incident away in his computer-like memory bank for production on a future occasion when it could be used to screw you into the ground.

I once made a howler which even now makes me blush with shame.

He had asked me for the name of the American Ambassador to Switzerland. I had replied, not knowing that the man I had named had been replaced. Beaverbrook had written a letter to the wrong man, and had been put in the embarrassing position of receiving a mildly chiding letter from the new ambassador, Mr Henry Taylor.

The Old Man sent his letter on to me and added: 'I received the enclosed letter this morning. And I am ashamed of it. You need not return it. Simply keep it in your records.' I knew very well that it would never be expunged from *his* record. What made it worse was that Ambassador Taylor's son, Harry, was a great friend of mine. A foreign correspondent, he was later killed in the Congo.

But among the rebukes and the often impossible requests, a certain kindness and thoughtfulness showed through – allied, of course, to thrift: 'I would like to send some flowers to people in New York, to be delivered on 24 December. And I should be grateful if you would go along to Goldfarb at 160 East 57th Street, or another reasonably priced flower shop (not Constance Spry for example) and order them. But please, if possible, go to the store yourself and conduct the business. The telephone is not a good medium for important transactions.'

There were also occasions on which his generosity outweighed his love of economy: 'Please pay — $50 for her article on juvenile delinquency in the United States, although we will not print it.'

Above all, his memos demonstrated his love for popular journalism and his ability to smell out a story: 'There is a wedding at St Patrick's between Judie Rathvon and Julian Plowden. Is the girl rich? And if so, then that is a good story for the *Daily Express* ... Sir Winston Churchill is sending out his collection of pictures to New York. You can so report if you wish.'

Sometimes his reasons for suggesting a certain story were not immediately apparent and only later did his real motives emerge. They were usually based on either enmity or friendship. There were other stories, however, for which every *Express*man had his own built-in warning device. Anything touching on Lord Mountbatten or GATT (General Agreement on Tariffs and Trade) or the Canadian raid on Dieppe set all the alarm bells ringing. But my own very special problem was covering the United Nations Organization. His distrust of the UNO – what he called 'Youno' – was well known, but it still had to be covered. When he was in New York it was a sometimes hilarious but almost always exasperating business because he literally refused to allow me to go there. Normally this did not matter overmuch, but during the Suez Crisis, the Editor, Arthur Christiansen – no man to cross – was demanding personal coverage of the Security Council debates.

I had to go, of course, but Beaverbrook took perverse delight in ringing me when he knew the debate was in progress. My secretary would tell him that I was out of the office on a story and he would reply: 'How strange it is that he is always out on a story when Youno is talking. Ask him to come and see me. Goodbyeee.' And down would go the telephone. My secretary would then get me paged at the UN and I would dash round to the Waldorf Towers where he would greet me with: 'Where have you been? You've not been to the Youno, have you?' It was more a statement than a question. I would lie and give the impression that I would never go near that den of iniquity. But he would know, and I knew that he would see my story from the UN in the *Daily Express* the next day. Still, honour had been satisfied.

In these circumstances the United Nations were the subject of a number of memos. In one, urging me to write a story about lavish cocktail parties being held in the UN, he wrote: 'These cocktail parties cost the governments a lot of money. It represents an invisible item of additional expenditure. It is said that Puerto Rico is in default of fees payable to the United Nations and, at the same time, has given a cocktail party costing $10,000.' I must say that over the years I have come to agree with him about the United Nations. It is an organization to be profoundly mistrusted.

The Old Man is gone now, having borne his final, terrible, illness with typical courage, irascibility and humour. When he died, I regretted not having made my peace with him, and now, reading his memos again so many years after they were written, I regret it even more, for they conjure up all the excitement of those heady days. And I miss that.

The last item in my folder is a cable written on *Queen Mary* notepaper. It was to his son, Max, and it was a choice example of the Beaverbrook style: 'Max Aitken. Pay my chauffeur £5 gift from me. Tell Escarra picture dealers should provide frames free. Thanks for telegram. Keep your staff occupied and they will be happy. Idleness breeds discontent.'

# I am in Favour of Economy

Letters from Lord Beaverbrook

26th March 1941

Dear Farrer,                    _Cannot_

    I am so sorry to hear that you have
water on the knee.

    I am just as sorry to say that I have
water on the eye.

    And I hope that you will soon be well
enough to come back and help poor Thomson who
keeps his water in the right place.

       Yours sincerely,

*Beaverbrook*

David Farrer, Esq.

From Lord Beaverbrook          Somerville House,
                               Fredericton, NB.


                               14th September, 1956

Dear Dobson,
          Can you find out and let me know what
is available in paper caps, suitable for use by
roundsmen when delivering milk. I want caps that
will withstand the rain, possibly a waxed surface
would be best for the purpose. And I want the name
of the dairy inscribed on them.
                    Yours sincerely,

                         *[signature]*


Christopher Dobson, Esq.,
London Daily Express,
50 Rockefeller Plaza,
New York.



From Lord Beaverbrook             Aitken House
                                    Nassau
                                    Bahamas


                              13th November, 1956



          The distant reader gets a weird opinion of a
newspaper; rather like a rewrite of a morning story
in an afternoon edition. But that impression does
not prevail if the newspaper is the DAILY EXPRESS.
          The news is so vigorously treated and the
correspondence of foreign representatives is so
brilliantly descriptive of events that the reader
is fascinated and absorbed by a journal as readable
a week after the event as on the morning of issue.
          To the staff of the DAILY EXPRESS I send my
compliments and congratulations on a performance
unrivalled by the Black Art at home and abroad.

                         *[signature]*

LORD BEAVERBROOK

SOMERVILLE HOUSE,
WATERLOO ROW,
FREDERICTON, N.B.

12th September, 1957

Dear Dobson,

I see by correspondence that the New York office
called up Newcastle and Fredericton about the Blessing
of the Bells. It seems to me that one telephone call
would have done. I am in favour of economy.

Please have your office look up the pools of opinion
on the Democratic Nominations in the Presidential Election.
I am under the impression that Kennedy leads in that Poll
with Kefauver second. Kindly look up the facts and let me
know.

Would you be good enough to send me Baruch's book
which was published the other day.

If the type is large enough for me to read in
"Queen of France" by Harper, please buy the book and
hold it for my arrival in New York.

Sir Winston Churchill is sending out his collection
of pictures to New York. You can sole report if you wish.

Yours sincerely,

*Beaverbrook*

Christopher Dobson, Esq.,
London Daily Express,
50 Rockefeller Plaza,
New York.

LORD BEAVERBROOK'S OFFICE
121/8, FLEET STREET,
LONDON, E.C.4.
FLEET ST. 8000

12th.April 1957

Dear Chris.,

Would you kindly send to Lord
Beaverbrook here 12 packages each of
10 of Sanka coffee.

You will of course mark them as
gift.

Regards,

Yours sincerely,

Christopher Dobson, Esq.
London Daily Express,
50 Rockefeller Plaza,
New York,20, NY.

---

FROM LORD BEAVERBROOK

SOMERVILLE HOUSE.
WATERLOO ROW.
FREDERICTON. N B

17th September, 1957

Dear Dobson,

Please do not send me
any more Sanka. I have
been given some.

Yours sincerely,

Christopher Dobson, Esq.,
London Daily Express,
50 Rockefeller Plaza,
New York.

---

FROM LORD BEAVERBROOK

SOMERVILLE HOUSE.
WATERLOO ROW.
FREDERICTON. N B

September, 1957

Dear Dobson,

Would you be good enough
to buy me a recording by Debbie
Reynolds called "Tammy", and
hold it for my arrival.

Yours sincerely,

Christopher Dobson, Esq.,
London Daily Express,
50 Rockefeller Plaza,
New York.

COMING
END OF
WEEK

From Lord Beaverbrook      P.O. Box 1028

Nassau

Bahamas.

8th November, 1957

Dear Dobson,

I congratulate you on your article in the "Daily Express" on poor old Ike. It was extremely good. It was followed by another good article.

Please give me the advertising rates of the "Times" and the "Herald Tribune", for classified advertisements; that is the smalls.

Send me, please, a note of the minimum salary of journalists from the beginning up to six years.

I see that Lowrie gets $193.00 a week in the form of salary and rent allowance. I am taking up the question of Singleton.

On the whole, I think, compared with other salaries in New York Lowrie gets very good pay.

Please send me Dr. Creighton's account with the Gladstone Hotel.

I enclose a cutting from a Nassau paper. You can associate with this story the activities of the English delegates to U.N.

No doubt William Aitken told you he gave a big cocktail party. These cocktail parties cost the Governments a lot of money. It represents an invisible item of additional expenditure.

It is said that Puerto Rico is in default of fees payable to the United Nations and, at the same time, has given a cocktail party costing $10,000.

Yours sincerely,

*Beaverbrook*

Christopher Dobson, Esq.,
London Daily Express,
50 Rockefeller Plaza,
New York.

*× if you do tell a story*

11 pounds. minimum!

6 pounds 14 oz weight limit

parcel post
customs declaration
83 first 4 oz.
= 14 + en add.
4 oz

2+ weeks
22 limit
45 first pd.
22 ea add pd.

1st class   8d first oz.
            4d ea add.   = nb limit 70 for

From Lord Beaverbrook     P.O. Box 1028
                          Nassau
                          Bahamas.

9th November, 1957

Dear Dobson,

       When you are shipping to me by air cargo
or otherwise, please put the lowest possible
value on the goods you send me.

       The higher the value, the more duty I have
to pay.

       On this parcel of books you sent me you appear
to have paid $6.00 freight.  That's too much.  I
would rather you put it in the Post Office.

                    Yours sincerely,

                    Beaverbrook

Christopher Dobson, Esq.,
    London Daily Express,
    50 Rockefeller Plaza,
    New York.

From Lord Beaverbrook

Aitken House,
Nassau,
Bahamas.

November 11th, 1957.

Dear Dobson,

     Would you please look for a book called
"Pushing to the Front" by Orison S. Marden.  It
was probably published about 1850 or some time
then.  It is ~~about~~ the fore-runner of Mrs. Baker
Eddy.

     There is a concern down on 4th Avenue,
which has nearly every book in the world.  I don't
wish to buy it if it is expensive.  I don't want
it if it is a precious book.

         Yours sincerely,

               $3.00


Christopher Dobson, Esq.,
London Daily Express,
50 Rockefeller Plaza,
New York.

From Lord Beaverbrook

P.O. Box 1028,
Nassau,
Bahamas.

February 16th, 1958.


Dear Dobson,

Here is an envelope I have
received from the New York office. It
has been insufficiently stamped for
express.

This is the second time this
has happened.

Yours sincerely,

*Beaverbrook*

Christopher Dobson, Esq.m
London Daily Express,
50 Rockefeller Plaza,
New York 20, N.Y.


From **Lord Beaverbrook**      To London Daily Express

23rd February, 1958.

Please pay Sarah Rothschild $50 for her article
on juvenile delinquency in the United States, although
we will not print it.

*B.*

From Lord Beaverbrook     To London. Daily Express,
                                     New York.

26th February, 1958.

(1) The extent to which you make use of new
envelopes in sending me old material is
a distressing experience.

I suggest that you use old envelopes and
send me new material. Economy should be
practised. It is always essential.

(2) I have to request that you will send to
the ship for me in an old envelope "Time",
"Newsweek", "New Yorker", "U.S. News and
World Report" and the "Readers' Digest".

Dear miss manney

       Lord beaver brook has asked me to write to you

to let you know that he is sending a television set to the Old Manse

Library as a Christmas mocnéc present. He instructs that this set

is to be kept as a surprise until Christmas morning and that it is

to be used only by the little children. It is to be kept for those

under thirteen in the upstairs room

                         yours sinderely

*Louise Manny*

# All Mouth
## Charles Douglas-Home

I met Lord Beaverbrook twice, first in April 1961, and for the second and last time in November 1963. Our first meeting occurred shortly after I had returned from Budapest where I had incurred his displeasure by not being available to follow up a story about light aircraft, which had appeared in another paper. My appointment was at Arlington House, 4.30 p.m. I had a haircut and then walked up all nine flights of stairs because I had heard that he did not like one to be either early or late.

A butler answered the door and showed me into a dining-room looking out over Green Park. A tape machine chattered somewhere in an alcove along the corridor and from the drawing-room I could hear the voice of 'the Lord' dictating letters into a Dictaphone. He shuffled down the passage, pausing for a visit to the loo, leaving the door open and causing the maximum noise effects.

He was tiny – tinier than I had ever realized. His mouth was all of him. He wore funny little soft blue suede shoes, one of which he took off. I regarded the little blue stockinged foot with mixed feelings. 'Gout,' he said, 'and if that is all you have got when you are my age, you'll be lucky.' His eyebrows were huge too, and the eyes beneath them never gave up for a minute. They were very bright – too bright for eighty plus – and very penetrating.

Was I married? he asked. No. Best not to be. What did I earn? I told him I earned the minimum. 'We never pay the minimum, Mr Home. You have already doubled your salary in a year? That is good going. You must be doing well. Do you write well?' I told him I was trying.

And so it went on, relentless questioning, testing, probing. The bright eyes laughing like laser beams through me, my 'sirs' in danger of running out of control through my sheer awe and the incipient panic caused by the little man. He was wrong about the minimum, since I was on it, but I could not possibly tell him. As I left, he said, 'And what are you writing about today?' And when I said something about aeroplanes, he said, 'Ah yes – of course, you were in Budapest.' Point taken.

I had not met him again for two and a half years when he invited me to lunch, probably interested in me as the new Prime Minister's nephew. Again I was amazed by his tininess and the large mouth and the bushy eyebrows, which were, if possible, even more craggy and shaggy than they had been before. The other guest at lunch was Mike Wardell, whom Beaverbrook called 'the Captain'. They mixed a cocktail for themselves, and Beaverbrook chuckled away like mad when the captain was supposed to have 'frightened Mr Home' with stories about liver cirrhosis, apropos my teetotalism.

We went into lunch. The Old Man drank whisky throughout. The captain had wine. I had water. I cannot remember much about the food, a sort of cheesy fish as a main course and baked jam roll, or something like that, for pudding, followed by delicious cheese. He asked me a lot about Alec and said you had got to give it to Macmillan for the masterly way he outwitted everybody in engineering Alec's succession. I said I hated Macmillan. He said, 'Maybe, but you have got to give it to him.' We talked about fox hunting and how the foxes barked at Cherkley, and how 'we on the *Daily Express*' have never attacked field sports. There was a great blizzard going on in Canada at the time, and he was desperate to get through to Lady Beaverbrook, but had been unable to do so.

After lunch, we adjourned to the drawing-room without the captain. 'How much do you earn?' he said, long before I sat down. '£40, – £10 in expenses.' 'Would you like more expenses or just salary?' 'I am satisfied with my expenses,' I said.

He lifted the little microphone clipped to his Dictaphone. 'Mr Blackburn,' he said as though starting to read the lesson in church. 'Mr Blackburn, put Mr Home up from £40 to £50 and leave his expense allowance as it is at £10.' Click. It was done. 'You are very kind,' said I. 'You are worth it,' said he. It was a nervous moment.

He said he thought the Labour Party would be in government without much trouble, and smiled at the thought. Then he asked about the office. Was it happy now? We had to get rid of Roger (Wood) – the previous Editor – he said, too many libel suits coming in.

It was time to go. He came right out and played with the lift button, walking in a rather strange way, flaying his arms around like antennae, and just correcting his balance from the walls. His skin was a funny, mottled brown, but the eyes continued to blaze, and there was that amazingly infectious snarling laugh. The voice was now always a growl, coming up over cataracts of phlegm and old age before spreading out from those latitudinous lips. I never saw him, or spoke to him, again.

# Man of Surprises
# Harry Fieldhouse

If I had to characterize Lord Beaverbrook, it would be as a man of surprises. He liked his papers to be full of surprises, he liked stories to have surprise endings, and the only predictable thing about what he did was that it would be surprising. Beverley Baxter once asked him how he got started making his fortune. The answer was perhaps more surprising than Beaverbrook realized: 'Well, there was a bank in my home town when I was seventeen. Now it was obvious to me that this bank was under-capitalized.' Baxter could not get over the idea that to a boy of seventeen such a thing could be obvious.

Reducing situations to clarify issues, however, was another Beaverbrook characteristic. He made a distinction between 'articles', which he viewed as fresh and to the point, and 'essays', which he abominated as indecisive rigmaroles. In the Dictaphone notes with which he goaded his key employees, a favourite complaint was the tendency to lapse into writing essays. 'Essays have got to be stamped out,' he said. 'I have been trying to do it now for a lifetime. Can I get any help, please? I've got only a little while left and I am most anxious to carry through this revolution before I die.'

Along with the telephone, the Dictaphone was the chief instrument of his newspaper proprietorship. He had no office and never came into the *Express* building in Fleet Street, but with these devices to hand, he might as well have been next door. However remote the control, there was no doubt who exercised it. Seasonal migrations took him to Canada, New York, the Caribbean and back to the French Riviera by way of London – but the messages kept coming. Only Jamaica rendered him incommunicado, though never for long. The mobility that computer link-ups are supposed to be going to give us was something he already had thirty years ago.

My first surprise when I was hired by the *Sunday Express* to write the 'Crossbencher' column was that he was still in full command. I joined under the impression that he'd retired. After all, he was seventy by then and, anyway, I remembered reading of his retirement years before. A phone call soon put me right. It instructed me to report to Arlington House behind the Ritz after dinner the same evening, and to be sure to bring a notebook. I was shown into his sitting-room where the great man was holding court for various grandees such as Arthur Christiansen, the Editor of the *Daily Express*, and Herbert Gunn, the Editor of the *Evening Standard*. As they filed out of the room, Beaverbrook advanced on me carrying a typescript that proved to be what I'd written earlier that day. Far from having retired, I found, he took a detailed personal interest in the column I was going to write.

So began several years of journalism under his tutelage. He overflowed with ideas, comments and information, not all of which were committed to the Dictaphone. A fair proportion would be delivered by telephone at what are now called unsocial hours – like the crack of dawn or last thing at night. This was an era of frantic notetaking to catch the Old Testament flavour of his phrases. It was frantic not only because I'd never learnt shorthand, but because he liked to conduct our consultations while taking his daily constitutional. I became practised at wielding notebook and pencil while accompanying him around Green Park or promenading down Bond Street.

Back at the office, the latest Dictaphone thoughts would be waiting. 'Tell the boy Fieldhouse . . .' was a recurrent beginning. 'Tell the boy Fieldhouse to look up Callaghan, the fellow down in south-east Cardiff . . . to watch the Co-op papers . . . to get out a list of admirals and generals with jobs in the City . . .' When in full spate, his output was such that action could not keep pace with all his promptings, even with the best will in the world – and the will of the harassed is not always of the best. Occasional defiance was inevitable. But it gave only temporary relief, as a new version of the neglected message would soon turn up.

Like all those on the receiving end of his notions, I often grumbled about them, but rereading some of his notes now, I must admit that even the rejects strike me as more practical than they did at the time.

Beaverbrook never minded a dissenting point of view, but getting into an argument with him was unwise, especially if it was about politics. For one thing he was so exceptionally well informed – after fifty years in, or on the fringes of, politics he knew nearly everybody of importance. For another thing he was a disarming tactician. He once objected to an item I'd written that exactly reflected what he'd told me twenty-four hours before. Full of righteous indignation I burst out with 'But it's what you said.' He was unmoved. 'If it is,' he said, 'then I was *wrong*! We're all ashamed of what we do sometimes.' There's no comeback to that one.


Fleet Street legend tends to portray Beaverbrook as a ruthless employer, but this was not my experience of him. He was exacting and exasperating, but always encouraging. He also paid generously. I spent nearly ten years on two of his newspapers at the height of their success. No doubt success itself makes for an improved atmosphere, but I've never worked anywhere livelier, or more congenial.

His principal Editor, Christiansen of the *Daily Express*, was an inspired choice, but Beaverbrook's own quirky mind set the paper on its zestful course. I remember how he once made journalistic capital out of a boring rail strike. Instead of droning on, like the other papers, about the awkwardness of the railwaymen, Beaverbrook decided we needed a fresh topic. We should take up the canals, came the edict. We all thought the Old Man (the in-house term for him, except from his butler Albert, who referred to him as 'the Lord') had gone barmy. Anyway I wrote a series of leaders about the neglect of the canals, their continuing potential and the need to restore them. The news pages carried canal reports. Within days the canals were a public issue. The canals authority put out statements, rival papers weighed in and the outcome was an official programme of rescue for these backwater highways.

When Beaverbrook appeared in cartoons in his own newspapers, he was generally shown as a grinning imp. There was more to this than flattery. He did seem to get a kick out of puzzling his staff. I was once instructed to report to his Daimler parked outside a house in Harley Street. I arrived and climbed into the car to wait. Beaverbrook duly appeared and told me to get out again – he'd been visiting his doctor and wanted company for a walk home across Mayfair. Another time, just back from the south of France, he received me at Cherkley, his country home, surrounded by open suitcases and piles of clothing. He was standing in the middle of this unpacking scene stark naked, but for a white sports cap. A colleague, Douglas Clark, once phoned the office from Cherkley in a high state of excitement because Beaverbrook was driving to have dinner with Churchill and Clark had been told he would accompany him in the car. He came crestfallen into the office next day: Beaverbrook had dropped him off at a country stop and told him he could catch a bus there to the nearest station.

Beaverbrook had a knack for finding out when members of his staff were going away, and was inclined to issue a summons just as the hour of departure neared. It was like a battle of wits for him. Holidays in general seemed to provoke him – perhaps because he worked wherever he was. His chief executive, Robertson, was once so pestered by phone calls on a rare holiday that he chose to return early. A Paris weekend I planned was once stymied by a last-minute task, but Beaverbrook did dictate a note to the management saying that as I'd obliged him by delaying my departure I was to be expected back correspondingly later.

One day, on the way back from one of our walks, he paused at an antique shop next door to Arlington House and pointed to an unmarked bureau in the window. 'How much do you think they're asking for that?' he said. I should have known it was no idle question. I had no idea what the bureau would be worth, would never have dreamt of owning it, and thought the price not worth knowing, but he was not to be deflected. He coaxed me for a guess, and seemed genuinely disappointed by my reluctance to be drawn. It was not till I was reading a new edition of his book *Don't Trust to Luck* long afterwards that I tumbled to his purpose. The following passage leapt out at me:

The key which opens the door of success is the trading instinct, the knowledge and sense of the real value of any article. Without it a man need not trouble to enter business at all . . .

I had failed a test.

# The Enchanter
# Anne Sharpley

Mine is an unabashed love story: I adored the man. It was certainly not my intention to do so, but was one of those unexpected, irreversible enchantments that may have been – and, I expect, was – a daily occurrence with him but was unique in my experience.

As a very young journalist on the *Evening Standard* in 1954, I had written something that had caught his eye and was summoned to meet him. I remember how enraged I was at the obvious importance of this first meeting. I had battled my way through the journalistic jungle from the age of sixteen (recruitment was much less formal then), and having just got on to the paper I'd always intended to join, now came this appalling test of acceptability.

It was a sunny summer's day and I had a very red nose as a result of some imprudent sunbathing at the weekend, which may have contributed to my angry mood – it's always well to look one's best at such moments and, most resentfully, I knew it. I was wearing what every aspiring girl reporter wore those days – a plain little suit with a hat and yes, white cotton gloves. Oh, those gloves, how essential they seemed then, how astonishing now in retrospect. But we wore them everywhere – and washed them nightly. Into Arlington House at the back of the Ritz I stormed, thinking, as I took the lift to his flat: 'What does it matter what the old so-and-so thinks of me?'

I glared my way past somebody deferential who opened the door but who wasn't going to win any notice from me at the time. Later I came to appreciate the state of permanent amused fascination that all his staff were in – more enchantments.

As I had been warned, he was standing with his back to the window so that he could read my face as I came into the room. As I advanced towards a figure (a tiny one) whose own face was shaded, I wasn't smiling as there was nothing to smile at yet.

When he turned towards the light, my anger evaporated. I found myself looking into a face that reflected such amusement and pleasure at the angry young woman in front of him that I remember being absolutely suffused with relief and delight. 'Oh, I *like* you!' I thought to myself as I gazed at that Hallowe'en-pumpkin face with the huge mouth and goblin charm. The deep rustling voice matched the face and the tiny neat body – all magic. I was hooked!

From that moment began an exciting ten years. Looking back I am amazed at how much care and attention he devoted to one of his youngest reporters: telephone calls, letters, cheques, invitations to lunch, tea and dinner; if I boarded a plane to cover an overseas story, then fruit or flowers would appear at the gangway and occasionally a letter of introduction to someone of importance he knew at my destination. It was like an intense, if unconsummated, love affair.

What he especially did was praise and encourage. *Buckets* of flattery, it seemed at the time. 'You are like Harris's meat pies, always good' was my favourite. Everything I wrote was commented on, and usually in such terms. What a way to make a reporter work, and didn't I work!

And for some reason, which can only be put down to that initial encounter when he charmed me off my perch, I was never harassed. I knew other journalists who were being hagridden, and dreaded what might happen if he started on me as it was not in my temperament to put up with too much. Indeed there was a fleeting occasion when it nearly happened. He gave me three stories. I checked them and found them not to be true. 'Aaargh, you won't take stories from me then,' he growled. 'I'll take them from anybody if they stand up,' I replied. That was the first and last time. I wish I'd known then that the danger was past! But the *Standard* was an uncommitted, lively paper and he had need of independent reporting, and that may have been the reason.

Because he always looked at me with such amusement and affection, I always felt encouraged to be cheerful, cheeky and probably a bit absurd. He was on my side, so I'd say and do anything that came into my head. We really had the greatest fun. I could always tell that, when he tapped his toe, there was some surplus energy around that had better be diverted. And yet he could be crooningly tender. He would hold my hands, admiring them, a long time – the only man in my considerable experience of men to notice that they are small. Another time he said to me, 'Sit there, I want to admire you. You're a woman in her prime.' And I sat an hour, while we gazed at one another – the old magician.

Since I often got notice that my presence was required, there was always a likelihood of being summoned any minute. We developed a formula for these last-minute arrangements: 'What are you doing?' he'd ask, and I would always reply 'Nothing,' whatever may have been the truth and I would find myself in a car being swept out to Cherkley or, on occasions, the south of France. Even getting to Arlington House, which was no problem, was made velvet-smooth by the arrival of a limousine.

One evening my boyfriend was taking his turn at doing the cooking (lovers of women reporters had an early experience of women's lib) when the telephone rang.

'What are you doing?'

'Nothing.'

'I'll send round the car.'

And I went, of course. As we ate, a telegram arrived – it was the days when telegrams could actually get instant delivery.

KINDLY DATE SHARPLEY EARLIER IN FUTURE. WE WERE ABOUT TO DINE

'Aaargh, you've got a jealous boyfriend,' he said, delighted.

From that time, the battle about whether I would go and cover the States ensued. Jealous boyfriends may not be easily got rid of, but the object of their affections could be removed! I didn't want to go to the States because I was more interested in reporting the Middle East, such stories as Cyprus and Suez, and I particularly adored going to Africa, so I refused to go and take over the *Evening Standard* office in New York. However the Queen and Prince Philip were going to Canada and the States in the autumn of 1957 (just around the time when Lord Beaverbrook made his annual stay), and while I could refuse a shift of base, I couldn't, in my view, turn down a story. So off I went, to find him divertingly ensconced in the Waldorf Astoria, surrounded by amazing people as usual.

He had seen the Queen that afternoon at the United Nations where she had made a speech at a special session of the General Assembly. He had been enthralled. Despite the somewhat touchy relations between the royal family and the Beaverbrook press, he had been genuinely captivated by her and said how proud he had been to see her delight and command that motley assembly. 'God save the Queen,' he kept chanting. By one of those quirks of fashion that sometimes occur, we were slightly ahead of the American women in shortening our skirts and in wearing that much derided style, the Sack. So the Queen's skirts were considerably shorter than New York had seen for quite a time, a point not lost on Lord Beaverbrook who commented on her 'pretty legs.'

A couple of years later, she was to visit Fredericton, and I was not surprised to find myself in delicate negotiation with Buckingham Palace. Would they make it clear that his presence was welcome? Fredericton *was* Lord Beaverbrook; everything was named after him, including the hotel where the Queen was to sleep. 'It would be rather like the play without Hamlet,' agreed the palace official, but it was up to the Canadians to make sure he was there. So no personal invitation was forthcoming, and Lord Beaverbrook stayed away. A pity.

Needless to say, that first trip to the States proved fatal to my private life as somehow my arrival coincided with the return to London of the then correspondent and, I was told, somebody had to run the shop. Before he set off on his annual winter migration to the West Indies, I saw a great deal of Lord Beaverbrook. Usually we ate the not very distinguished food of the Waldorf, or so I thought it, but in truth I was not ordering it. One evening, great excitement: I was to be taken to the Pavillon, then the leading restaurant. We had walked over there without booking a table and the place was full. He simply stood there, and I think they must have taken out a couple of the diners and quietly shot them because we were quickly seated. I looked at the complicated French menu with enthusiasm, thinking I was at last to have some good food. Instead Lord Beaverbrook's voice cut across my intentions as the waiter appeared. 'Bring us some soup and some beef,' he growled. And that was that.

As always he walked me round to the *Evening Standard* office in Rockefeller Plaza, so I could do my evening stint before turning in. He was a real press lord, and reporters, however well wined and dined, still had to do their job. And yet he could make it seem the most courteous and delicate of attentions.

He was back again in the spring and I was still stuck in the States, much to my fury; only after he had completed the visit was I allowed home. That got rid of that boyfriend, more or less. When the next appeared, he was summoned to the presence and thoroughly harangued on what a serious matter it was to consider marriage with such a splendid creature. Rapid reconsideration on both sides led to no marriage.

I never supposed for an instant that I was, in any real sense, important to Lord Beaverbrook; he was manipulating dozens of other lives in just the same way. But he had the knack of making it fun and worthwhile.

A perfect instance of his handling involved the memoirs of Lady

Diana Cooper. I was staying at La Capponcina in the south of France and he had the galleys of one of the volumes she had written, and wanted my opinion of them. As a stroppy young radical, I thought very little of them (though I do rather admire her now) and read bits of them aloud in a mocking voice. I remember him laughing as we sat in the sunshine by the roses. I don't think his laughter was cruel; it was simply that there was fifty years' difference in our ages and he enjoyed my youthful lack of respect.

I was surprised therefore to be given the book to review when it came out, under Lord Beaverbrook's instruction. I did a very thorough job. Before it went into the paper, it was sent to him and he was promptly on the telephone asking me to be more kind. I refused. A rumble came over the line and he started one of his biblical laments: 'Oh, what shall I do? Oh woe. You're a peasant and I'm a peasant, and she's a beautiful princess I have known nearly all my life. I shall have to jump out of the window if you won't change it.' Still I refused. A further rumble and he reached for his bucket of flattery. 'Aaargh,' he said, 'you *beautiful* women, what a problem you are to me.' I was so won over and amused by this perfectly absurd line that I said that, while I wouldn't change it, he could give it to someone else to review. Another much more appreciative review duly appeared in the *Evening Standard*, but typical of Lord Beaverbrook, I received the following note: 'Your review was one of the most brilliant I have read and I have ordered it to be put in the archives.' Preposterous, but quite enchanting.

However, change was on the way in the formidable but, to me, very likeable person of Lady Dunn. After some ill-judged remarks about the notes of luxury (bearskin rugs and gold ewers) she had introduced into the somewhat tatty Cherkley, I was not around much, although Lord Beaverbrook summoned me to tea, secretly, several times. Lady Dunn's wonderful nursing of her late husband, Sir James Dunn, was something I knew could be relied on as news of Lord Beaverbrook's illness came through.

When I received my invitation to the great dinner that Lord Thomson was to give on his eighty-fifth birthday, I was delighted, because Lord Beaverbrook of all newspaper proprietors had been keen to use and encourage women in his newspapers and indeed he had often said he wanted to make me an editor. So when it was decided that no women were to be invited except Lady Dunn, now Lady Beaverbrook, his wife of a year, I looked at the printed card withdrawing the earlier invitation with some bitterness. It seemed the cruellest and most nonsensical of exclusions. I knew he was dying and couldn't bear not to see him again.

Then one evening that sad spring, the telephone went.

'What are you doing?' He remembered the old formula.

'Nothing' – I could surely remember my line – and the car arrived to carry me out to Cherkley. I sat with him on the sofa putting, and keeping, my arms around him, trying to save him from pain and death.

On the Saturday before his birthday I went out to Cherkley again to do the *Evening Standard* interview with him for his birthday. It was one of those marvellous May mornings that showed Cherkley – ugly house, magnificent grounds – at its best. We went out on to the lawn, he leaning on me and walking slowly, but full of his old spirit. He gave me a lovely interview, teasing and serious at the same time, the true, ambiguous nature of the man. He waved his hat for the photographer with a great grin, then saw me slowly but as courteously as ever to the car. That was the last time I saw him alive, though I spoke to him when he telephoned to say he had doubled my salary. Doubled!

Nehru died that week and I found myself, as usual without time to pack, dashing straight out to Heathrow to catch the first plane to Delhi – and literally running across the tarmac and hitching a lift on the special plane laid on for Lord Home and Earl Moutbatten. The Beaver would have enjoyed that; he liked his reporters to be cheeky – and lucky.

On my return I was asked to go to Cherkley the following Sunday, but the lunch was cancelled. He died on Tuesday afternoon and I went out to do a story for the *Evening Standard*. It was again a beautiful day and no curtains or blinds were drawn in the grey Victorian mansion, so that every room seemed to blaze with sunshine and the green light reflecting from lawns and trees. I wandered about and stood for a while in the shade of the two great yews he had called John Knox and Winston Churchill and where, in the past, he too would stand every day.

I said goodbye. Later I was to see him dead, but our real goodbye was then. I miss him still.

# Fellow Immigrant
## William Davis

When news of the assassination of President Kennedy was flashed to London, I was Lord Beaverbrook's guest for dinner at his flat in Arlington House. Like everyone else, he was shattered; a small portable radio was brought to the table so that he could keep up with developments. We talked about the likely consequences, and I asked him how he thought Wall Street would react. It seemed an insensitive question, at such a moment, but I was the City Editor of the *Sunday Express* and it was obvious that a new column would have to be written in a hurry.

'Oh,' the Old Man said, 'Wall Street will have a boom. They *hated* Kennedy. You'd better get over there right away.'

Beaverbrook was right, of course. He knew how financial markets worked and I frequently consulted him. Inevitably, though, there were times when we argued. On one occasion at Cherkley, we were discussing the likely course of the London stock market. He took a gloomy view (which I shared), but added: 'You mustn't say that to your readers.' Sunny optimism, I knew, was almost mandatory at the *Sunday Express*. But I was a very earnest chap in those days and pompously explained that a City Editor had a duty to his readers. He was in a different position from other columnists; his job was not merely to entertain but to make honest judgements. Many small investors backed his judgement with their hard-earned cash. If a City Editor genuinely felt that the market was headed for the rocks, he had an obligation to say so. 'All right,' the Old Man conceded, 'but tone it down a bit, will you?'

On another occasion, I was dispatched to Canada to write about the mining boom. I knew all about Beaverbrook's fondness for that country, and I knew what kind of column was expected from me. But when I got there, prominent members of the financial community in

Toronto told me that the boom had got out of hand. Many investors were being taken for a ride by unscrupulous operators. I duly reported this, and promptly received a call from the *Sunday Express* office in London. 'We can't print this,' they said. 'Lord Beaverbrook wouldn't stand for it.' I decided to telephone him and explain my dilemma. 'Well,' he growled, 'if that is the situation you had better say so. I'll have a word with the Editor.'

I learned afterwards that the Editor, John Junor, was far from pleased with my action. He got his revenge a few months later. I had written a piece which criticized a new unit trust. He insisted on dropping it because, he said, the unit trust had advertised in the same issue. I took the matter to Beaverbrook, who had frequently urged me to warn readers against sharp practices in the unit-trust business. The Old Man told me to come and see him. I did so, and was shocked to find him very ill. He was in bed, his head propped up by half a dozen pillows, and he was clearly in an irritable mood. I told him my side of the story, but he would not listen. 'It is very naïve of you to expect that we can take a man's money and then criticize him,' he said. 'The Editor says you give him a lot of trouble. Do as you're told or leave.'

I said I would think it over. Later that day I was summoned by his son, Sir Max Aitken, and the ultimatum was repeated. I resigned. Happily, Charles Wintour, the Editor of the *Evening Standard*, wanted me back, so I returned to the *Standard* as City Editor and was given a free hand. Well, almost. There was another skirmish, not long afterwards, which I lost despite the fact that I had Charles Wintour's full support.

Beaverbrook had asked me to write a diary piece about Roy Thomson. The Old Man frequently used the *Evening Standard* to snipe at influential people who, for one reason or another, had incurred his displeasure. He had been kind to Roy at first, in a rather patronizing way, but when his fellow Canadian bought *The Times* and *Sunday Times*, he grew jealous. My instructions were to look into his financial manipulations. I went to see Roy and asked him a lot of searching questions. I discovered, among other things, that his whole empire was, in effect, controlled by his grandchildren, who were still in school. Roy proudly gave me their photographs. He volunteered a good deal of other fascinating information and the Editor agreed that it was worth more than a diary paragraph: he told me to write a feature article. It was sent to Beaverbrook, who exploded. This was not at all what he had in mind; it made Thomson look *good*. The article was not to be published. Charles tried to argue with him, but was curtly informed that the proprietor's decision was final. Davis had overstepped the mark again: why couldn't he obey orders? The affair blew over, but I had become disillusioned with the Beaverbrook group and when, a year later, I was invited to become Financial Editor of the *Guardian*, I accepted with alacrity, even though it meant a cut in salary.

I would not wish to give the impression that I was constantly fighting with Lord Beaverbrook, or that I resented his interference. I admired him greatly and, of course, I fully recognized that they were *his* papers. I was also grateful (and still am) for the useful lessons he taught me and for his many acts of kindness.

I was twenty-four when I first met him. Beaverbrook had wanted to start a financial newsletter, similar to one published by the *Investor's Chronicle*, but his city editors didn't think much of the idea and didn't want to be bothered. The Old Man persisted and eventually the then City Editor of the *Evening Standard*, Alexander Thomson, told him that there was a young man in his office – me – who could probably do the job. I had been trained on the *Financial Times* and was writing the *Standard*'s daily stock-market report.

Beaverbrook did not waste time with questions about my education (I had left school at fourteen) or any other personal details. I wondered, nervously, what he would say if I told him that I had been born in Germany. But he never asked. He tersely explained what he had in mind and I eagerly agreed to have a go. Who was I to argue with the great man? I stayed up all night to work on a 'dummy' and showed it to him the next morning. He was clearly pleased with my enthusiasm and told me to go ahead. A separate office was hurriedly set up and someone painted the word 'EDITOR' on my door. It was heady stuff.

During the months that followed, I saw him regularly. He gave me a great deal of advice, interspersed with quotations from the Bible ('Where your treasure is, there your heart will also be') and I incorporated it all in the modest new publication. He also passed on his views on writing. 'Keep your sentences and paragraphs short. Don't use the word "very"; it's usually superfluous. If you criticize someone, praise his good but irrelevant qualities before you put the knife in. Say: "He dresses well, and he is kind to his mother: pity he's incompetent." That way, readers will think you are a fair man.'

Beaverbrook appointed all his own City Editors – not surprisingly, he felt that he was best qualified to do so – and after eighteen months he made me City Editor of the *Standard*. I was still only twenty-five, which many people considered ludicrously young. His famous memos, typed on flimsy paper, arrived almost daily. And I learned some other lessons. One day I asked him why his papers were always expected to be optimistic. He said that, when he bought the *Daily Express*, it had been in bad financial shape. Nothing had seemed to go right. One of the advertising people had come to see him and had said that he had trouble getting business because the paper put people in a gloomy mood. Beaverbrook had thought he had a point. He added: 'Always remember, young man, that a happy reader is a spending reader.' I have never forgotten it: it was a piece of advice that came in handy when, many years later, I became the Editor of *Punch* with a brief to restore the magazine to profitability, and when I subsequently launched a new magazine called *High Life*.

He also taught me never to bluff. It seems that, during his days as a Member of Parliament, he had quoted some inaccurate financial statistics, had tried to cover up and had been made to look foolish. He wasn't going to let it happen again, to him or to the readers of his papers. 'If you're not sure of your facts,' he said, 'admit it. Don't try to bluff your way out of it. Say you don't know, and check at the first opportunity.' He devised little tests to catch me out. Once, in a taxi, he suddenly said: 'Interlocking shareholdings are a very bad thing, don't you agree?' I had no idea what he was talking about, but thought it wise to say yes. 'Well,' he said with a smile, 'how would you explain that to your readers?'

I had been the *Standard*'s City Editor for about a year when the rival *Evening News* asked me if I were prepared to do the same job for them, at a substantially higher salary. I said that I would think about it. At 8 a.m. the next morning, the telephone rang in my office. It was Beaverbrook. How was I getting on? Fine. How was my family? Fine. Did I like my work? Yes, I loved it. 'Good,' he said, 'anything else?'

Alarm bells rang. I decided to come clean. 'As a matter of fact,' I said, 'the *Evening News* has asked me to be its City Editor.'

'So I heard,' he said. 'The bastards. How much are they offering?'

I mentioned the figure. 'Right,' he said, 'from today you get that. I take it you won't be leaving.'

'No.'

'I didn't think you would. Come and see me when you've finished work. Goodbye t'ya.'

I went to Arlington House later on, still marvelling at the Old Man's efficient grapevine. 'I'm glad you are staying,' he said. 'You have a great future here. You don't want to be a city editor all your life, do you?'

The obvious implication was that, if I played my cards right, I might end up editing one of his papers. I never did – though I was offered the editorship of the *Daily Express* fourteen years later, after Victor Matthews had bought the group. I declined with thanks; Victor was no Beaverbrook, and he didn't share the master's view (and mine) on the merits of optimism. At the time of Beaverbrook's hint, though, it was an exciting prospect. I was hooked.

Soon afterwards, I got involved in another new project. I thought there was scope for a Sunday business paper and took the idea to the Old Man. This was before the *Sunday Times* and others launched their separate business sections, and Beaverbrook liked the proposal. A 'dummy' was prepared and managers were ordered to look at the financial implications. It quickly became clear that they opposed the concept. The company was doing well enough out of its existing publications: why rock the boat by taking on a heavy additional burden? Beaverbrook gave in. I have often wondered whether he would have done so if he had been twenty years younger.

For me, one of Beaverbrook's greatest qualities was his infectious enthusiasm. One expects it in an ambitious young man, but he was in his late seventies when I first met him. I marvelled at his *joie de vivre*, his impish sense of humour, his unerring eye for a good story – including a good financial story – and his willingness to consider new ideas, however daft they may have been.

He could, of course, be ruthless, and he had some odd ways of judging people. One of his earlier City Editors had been invited to accompany him to Canada. He and Beaverbrook had shared a railway carriage and had done some serious drinking. Unlike his lordship, the poor fellow couldn't hold his liquor and had soon been legless. Beaverbrook had promptly sent him home and had thereafter contemptuously referred to him as 'the man who gets drunk on trains'. His career at Beaverbrook Newspapers had ended soon afterwards. Another financial journalist was dismissed because his fingers were stained with nicotine.

Even those closest to him were sometimes subjected to criticism. I was once present at one of those embarrassing sessions when he ticked off his son, Max. 'He's a nice boy,' he said to me when Max had left, 'but he doesn't understand money.' On another occasion, I was invited to lunch at Cherkley with Beaverbrook and the formidable Lady Dunn. They got into a heated argument about the stock market and, ignoring my presence, he told her that she was 'talking rubbish'. He later said to me: 'She is very clever, really. She has more money than I have.'

There were times when he exasperated those who worked for him, and I was no exception. But he also inspired respect and affection. He wasn't concerned with what your father did, whether you had been to the 'right' school or how old you were. He was sympathetic and helpful if you ran into problems which were not of your own making. He was patriotic in a way which perhaps only fellow immigrants, of which I am one, can ever truly understand. He knew the power of money, but unlike so many millionaires, he was more interested in what human beings would do to get it than the thing itself. What mattered (or seemed to matter) more than anything else was that you were what he considered to be a good journalist. He had an enormous influence on my life, as he had on the lives of so many others, and I was genuinely moved to tears when I listened to that last, magnificent speech he made at the dinner Roy Thomson gave for him shortly before his death.

# Lapsed Calvinist
## Alan Watkins

Lord Beaverbrook's chief characteristics were his love of mischief, his inability to organize his life (or, rather, his possessions) entirely to his satisfaction, his reluctance ever to make himself wholly clear to his subordinates, his energy and his fear of death – or, more precisely, of going to hell.

As to his love of mischief, in his *Beaverbrook*, A. J. P. Taylor denies that, during the Conservative crisis over the succession to Harold Macmillan in 1963, Beaverbrook sang 'We'll sow the seeds of discord' to the tune of 'Polly put the kettle on'. The story was originally mine, and I was right, but I foolishly got the tune wrong. It was 'The more we are together', which, as a moment's humming will demonstrate, allows the words to scan:

> We'll sow the seeds of discord
> Of discord
> Of discord
> We'll sow the seeds of discord
> How happy we shall be

Beaverbrook had so many houses that whatever he wanted was rarely to hand. Thus, if he wished to consult, say, the Authorized Version he found he had only the Revised Version, and some luckless minion would then be dispatched to acquire the volume that was needed, in the backstreets of New York, Nice or wherever he happened to be. His reluctance to make himself clear – his ability to cause endless confusion over the simplest aspects of the administration not so much of newspapers as of life itself – may have been deliberate. He may have thought that, by constantly muddying the waters, he was emphasizing his own primacy and causing confusion in others, so keeping them keen and alert.

His fear of hell led Malcolm Muggeridge to think that Beaverbrook was only too conscious of his own wickedness, but this conclusion by no means followed for, as a lapsed Calvinist, Beaverbrook may merely have feared that he had not been numbered among the elect.

Muggeridge and Anthony Crosland (for example) considered him evil, whereas A. J. P. Taylor and Michael Foot thought him, not exactly saintly, but a good kind man. They said they loved him, and one cannot argue with love, any more than one can argue over whether something is, or is not, funny: but both views, Muggeridge–Crosland and Taylor–Foot, still strike me as exaggerated and somewhat sentimental. He was not like this at all. I know because for five years I worked for one of his papers, the *Sunday Express*: first as a general features writer, then as the New York correspondent, finally, for a year, as the author of the 'Crossbencher' column. Unlike some journalists I know I did not go out of my way to seek his company. He certainly did not go out of his way to seek mine. There was very little reason why he should. Of my existence he was only vaguely and intermittently aware. Ian Aitken (who was not a relative but knew him better than I did) tells me that he was under the impression that my name was Watkinson. Though, as will appear, we met several times, he never called me by this or indeed any other name. Our connection, at the beginning anyway, was indirect.

One day in February the Editor, John Junor, called me into his office. 'Have you ever heard of Anthony Praga?' he asked. I confessed I had not heard of him. The Editor explained who he was. In the 1930s, so it appeared, Praga had written a series of articles for the *Express* in which the plots of well-known, unread, lengthy novels were summarized. 'Like short stories,' said the Editor.

The series had been successful. Beaverbrook, at any rate, had been pleased with it. Some thirty years later he wanted to revive the idea. The Editor read to me part of his dictated memorandum. He wished, for a start, to have summarized, in short-story form, *East Lynne*, *Lorna Doone*, *The Scarlet Letter* and *Three Weeks* by Elinor Glyn, maybe on account of her relationship with Lord Curzon or perhaps for some other reason. However, he foresaw trouble owing to her advanced views.

'Elinor Glyn,' he wrote, 'may present difficulties but we should be able to overcome them with tactful treatment.'

The assignment, I confess, did not greatly appeal to me. The prospect of reading *Lorna Doone* was particularly distasteful. This was a book I had been at pains to avoid. It had been on a school reading-list and I had failed to progress beyond the first chaper. To have to read it now, in Fleet Street, at the request of Lord Beaverbrook, would be to suffer some kind of defeat in life.

'What about Bob Pitman?' I asked. The late Robert Pitman was then the Literary Editor of the paper. 'Bob is much too busy with other things,' said the Editor, which seemed a comprehensive enough reply. 'You are the only other person on the staff with enough literary ability to do this job.'

The flattering effect of this opinion was slightly spoiled by what came next. 'I may say,' the Editor went on, 'that this series will appear in the *Sunday Express* over my dead body, but as the idea comes from Beaverbrook we have to go through the motions at first.'

It was one of the Editor's several virtues that he was a by no means obedient follower of his proprietor's frequently incomprehensible instructions. One of Pitman's functions was to decode the strange, garbled messages which would issue from Cherkley, Montego Bay or the south of France. 'Bob has a genius for seeing what's in the Old Man's mind,' the Editor would say.

When the instructions were deciphered, Junor would sometimes procrastinate or deliberately misunderstand them. However, he was rarely as frank about his ultimate intentions as he was on this occasion. I cannot say I was wholly discouraged by the promise of non-publication. I had no wish to acquire a reputation, however slender, as a compressor of the works of Elinor Glyn. 'He wants the first piece to be on *East Lynne*,' said the Editor. 'Just to see how it goes.'

I bought a Collins' Classics edition of Mrs Henry Wood's work and, hour after hour, sat reading it at my desk. Occasionally the Editor would pass by on his errands of encouragement or reproof to his staff. 'You're a slow reader, I see,' he would say, and laugh as if he had made a joke.

Eventually I produced a piece of about 1,500 words which was dispatched to Beaverbrook. 'He thought it was all right,' said the Editor some days later. 'Now he wants you to have a go at Elinor Glyn.'

Happily I never did have a go at Elinor Glyn. I pretended to forget the task, the Editor made no more references to the matter and Beaverbrook, as far as I am aware showed no further interest. Elinor Glyn, like *Lorna Doone*, remains a gap in my reading.

Beaverbrook next impinged on my work when a Labour MP appeared to be in trouble with his constituency party over a divorce case in which he was involved. (Eventually, I believe, there was no trouble.) On this general issue, as on a few others – bishops, the royal

family, the powers of the House of Lords, access to Ascot – Beaverbrook's views were broadly radical though, as will appear, he was not
entirely consistent. This time, however, he did not require an 'opinion
piece' or a polemic but an historical article about the effects of divorce
or similar irregularities on the careers of politicians. Over the
Dictaphone came a list of suitable cases for inclusion. Inevitably that
of Parnell appeared on it. He had been brought down, Beaverbrook
stated, because at a meeting of the Irish MPs he had said: 'I am still the
master of the party,' to which Tim Healy had interjected: 'Who is to be
the mistress of the party?' Collapse of Parnell: or so I was given to
understand.

Perhaps rashly, I decided to verify the story in Tim Healy's own
published reminiscences. He was clear that the interruption had not
come from him but from some other, unnamed Irishman. Nor was the
remark in the form of a neat question; rather the phrase 'the mistress of
the party' had been heard above the general noise of the meeting. I
consulted various other political memoirs of the nineteenth century.
They all told the same story. This was decidedly worrying. I faced the
choice of either taking Beaverbrook's perhaps first-hand version or
preferring the accumulated evidence of others. I chose the latter. The
Editor was alarmed. 'Do you realize,' he said, 'that Beaverbrook is a
great historian?'

I produced Healy's reminiscences together with other works. The
Editor was slightly mollified but still unconvinced. We compromised
on retaining the question 'Who is to be the mistress of the party?',
attributing it not to Healy but to an unnamed Irish MP. Beaverbrook
accepted this version. 'He says he must have been mistaken about
Healy,' said the Editor.

Some months afterwards I was sent to New York as the paper's
correspondent there. 'Scrub the nicotine off your fingers, don't light up
unless he gives you permission and don't argue with him unless you're
very sure of your facts,' the Editor advised me. 'If you make a bad
impression on Beaverbrook it could have a fatal effect on your career.
After all, it's his newspaper.'

One of the curious features of life on the *Express* was that it was only
in New York that an employee was likely to come across Beaverbrook.
In London, senior journalists had grown grey in his service without
once setting eyes on him. In New York, on the other hand, the most
junior reporter might find himself suddenly called upon to accompany
his proprietor on his constitutional in Central Park, which was less
dangerous in those days. Indeed on one of these expeditions, a
predecessor of mine, Arthur Brittenden, had succeeded in losing his –

and Beaverbrook's – way. For hours, so the story went, the two of them had wandered about, lost. Subsequently an instruction had gone out to the effect that every member of the New York office must acquaint himself with the geography of Central Park. The conversation on these tours consisted chiefly of questions from Beaverbrook about the value of skyscrapers or other buildings which caught his eye.

'How much would ya say that was worth?' he would ask, and as his companion was usually ignorant of, and uninterested in, New York property values, the only possible response was a desperate guess. Oddly, these answers – quite literally, as I have explained, made up – would not anger or even amuse Beaverbrook but made him appear worried, particularly if the sums were on the high side.

'Ten million dollars? Ya really think so? Now why d'ya say that?'

'Well, it's in a good position.'

'It's in a good position. But ten million dollars. Ya can't be right.'

Every day he would telephone the office, generally between seven and eight in the evening. Perhaps he did this to satisfy himself that the staff had not all departed. On the whole, however, I do not think that this was the reason.

'What's the news?' he would enquire in jaunty and hopeful tones. Alas, as most members of the New York office spent their time rewriting agency copy or reproducing stories from American newspapers, transmitting the results to London at great expense, there rarely was any news. 'Oh, I see,' Beaverbrook would say, disappointed, and replace the receiver.

He made his presence felt in less obtrusive ways. In a corner of the office was a cupboard which contained stationery. It also contained a supply – about a dozen tins – of Campbell's tomato soup. I asked a secretary why they were there.

'That soup belongs to Lord Beaverbrook,' she said. 'It's the only kind of soup he likes, and one day he couldn't get any, so we have to keep a supply. You leave it alone.'

From time to time the secretary or one of her colleagues would take a foolscap envelope from the cupboard and then maltreat it, screwing it up, scoring it with pencil and even skating it across the floor. The envelope, it turned out, was to contain copy to be sent to Beaverbrook at the Waldorf Towers. He considered it wasteful not to reuse envelopes. The secretaries quite reasonably considered it irksome and uneconomic of both effort and storage space to hoard used envelopes. They therefore processed new ones to look like old. Everyone was satisfied.

Eventually a summons to lunch arrived. It was communicated by the butler, Raymond, a reddish-haired man of uncertain age with protruding eyes, a surprisingly strong handshake and a camp conversational style.

'Oh, the old bugger. He's in such a *temper* these days. I pity you all, I really do. Some of the things, you wouldn't believe.'

Peter Hopkirk and I presented ourselves at Beaverbrook's suite in the Waldorf Towers. Ian Aitken was already there. Beaverbrook questioned Hopkirk and me about the stories we had lately sent. He appeared satisfied though unenthusiastic. Then followed a waddya-think-of session. Though the subject matter of these conversation pieces might vary, the form was unchanging. First Beaverbrook would ask 'Waddya think of . . .' – it might be Kennedy or Khrushchev or Harold Macmillan. Whatever the answer might be, he would go on to ask: 'Now why d'ya say that?' Whether the reply to this question was satisfactory or not, he would conclude with 'Oh, I see.'

A Washington correspondent, one 'Lobby' Ludlow, once got drunk and announced: 'We're going to play the game differently this evening, Lord Beaverbrook. We're going to ask *you* the questions.' He was afterwards dismissed. 'He is a bad man,' Beaverbrook was reliably reported to have remarked. 'If he spoke to me in that manner, what would he say if he met the President?'

On this occasion there was no encouragement to behave in such a dangerous fashion. At any rate there was no opportunity to get drunk, because no drink was provided. Nor did matters improve at lunch itself. We ate boiled carrots and peas. We drank water. However, the only woman present, Lady Dunn (as she then was), consumed steak and a large baked potato. For most of the time Beaverbrook talked about Bonar Law. He summoned Raymond to cool his coffee, which he did by pouring it repeatedly from one cup to another until the required temperature was achieved.

Afterwards, in the sitting-room, we were talking in a desultory way when a large man appeared in the doorway and advanced towards Beaverbrook with hand outstretched. 'Lord Beaverbrook . . .' he said.

'Go away,' said Beaverbrook. 'I can't see ya today. I am much too busy to make any arrangements now. Ya must make an appointment. There are no vacancies on my newspapers.'

He spoke these words gently, almost timorously. Then he raised his voice and shouted: 'Raymond, that man is here again.' To Ian Aitken he whispered in tones of appeal: 'Ian, get rid of him. Tell him to go away.' Aitken was fully equal to the situation. He rose and took the man by the arm, leading him into the tiny entrance hall of the suite.

When Aitken returned, having handed the intruder over to the charge of Raymond, Beaverbrook said: 'He is an Australian. He has been pestering me for a job. I have told him that no jobs are available but he will not listen.'

'He must be a good reporter,' said Aitken, 'to get in here at all, past all those people.'

'Takes more than cheek to make a good reporter,' said Beaverbrook.

Some weeks afterwards I was working late in the office one Sunday when a telephone call came from Beaverbrook's granddaughter, Lady Jean Campbell, in Montego Bay. She asked me to listen carefully to her instructions: Lord Beaverbrook wished to have dispatched to him quantities of honey, coffee and cider vinegar, all of specified brands with which I was unfamiliar. In fact I did not have the slightest idea of where to obtain these commodities at eight o'clock on a Saturday in the middle of New York. I went to several delicatessen stores and did the best I could.

However, I rebelled against packing a parcel: partly as a gesture of protest, partly because I have an intense dislike of, am highly incompetent at, packing parcels. Instead I left the assortment of groceries on the desk of the chief of bureau, Henry Lowrie, together with a note saying they were to be sent to Lord Beaverbrook clearly marked 'unsolicited gift' – a point on which Lady Jean had placed great emphasis. The goods were duly sent off but they were the wrong goods. I had made a mess of things, obtaining 'White Rose' instead of 'Red Rose' coffee – or it may have been the other way around – and committing various other more or less fundamental errors with regard to the honey and the cider vinegar. Beaverbrook blamed Henry Lowrie. 'The New York office,' he wrote in a letter of reproof, 'is going to rack and ruin.'

One might have expected him to take a close interest in the 'Crossbencher' column. In fact, in his later years anyway, he rarely intervened.

Returned to London, I was puzzled to receive, via the Editor, a dictated memorandum in the following terms: 'There is a man in the West Country called Bessemer or something like that I believe he is a Liberal I have a good opinion of him I commend him to your attention you might mention him in your political notes.' He usually referred to the 'Crossbencher' column as 'your political notes'. His memoranda were rarely punctuated as those responsible for taking them down were frightened of putting the full stops and commas in the wrong places, thereby altering the meaning, if any.

An examination of the list of Liberal candidates produced the name of Peter Bessell, who was standing for Bodmin. A colleague said he thought Mr Bessell was in the habit of writing to Lord Beaverbrook about the Common Market and other matters. Enquiries showed this to be so. Indeed, if anything exceeded Lord Beaverbrook's high opinion of Mr Bessell, it was Mr Bessell's high opinion of Lord Beaverbrook. However, I could think of nothing sufficiently flattering or interesting to say about him. Besides, I did not see why the column should, for no very good reason, devote space to obscure parliamentary candidates. The Editor agreed with me. We decided that for the moment we would ignore Peter Bessell.

About six weeks later the Editor sent for me. He bore a slightly concerned expression. He read out part of one of those dictated messages. 'Some time ago,' it went, 'I offered you a piece of advice about your political notes I see that you have not taken this advice perhaps you could give me the reason.'

'Look,' said the Editor. 'No one's asking you to attack anybody. You're being asked to praise. There's no question of principle remotely involved. Just write a short paragraph saying something nice about this chap. It would make all our lives a lot easier.'

And so I wrote the paragraph. I said that Mr Bessell had inaugurated the Liberal revival at Torquay in 1955 – which was, as it happened, true – and that he would win Bodmin for the Liberals at the general election. This also turned out to be true. It must have been one of the few correct predictions I made.

The next intervention occurred when the Editors of the *Sunday* and the *Daily Express* were both away at the same time. Beaverbrook moved into his flat in Arlington House and began to interfere. 'I haven't enjoyed myself so much for years,' he said.

On the Friday afternoon his new secretary, Colin Vines – a put-upon individual who wrote an extremely funny book, *A Little Nut-brown Man*, about his master – asked me to send the 'Crossbencher' copy to Arlington House. I was to follow later.

'Tired old notes,' said Beaverbrook when I arrived. 'Ya political notes were tired,' he added as if to leave no room for misunderstanding on the point.

I did not dissent.

'Tired old stuff on Home and Wilson. Home is not worth bothering with. He has not made good. He is a failure.'

Again I did not quarrel with this judgement.

'What I suggest to you,' Beaverbrook went on, 'is a note on the financial position of the Liberal Party. That will be something fresh. Have ya got a pencil?'

I said I had a pencil.

'Take down these notes. Have ya heard of Lord Sherwood?'

Lord Sherwood, I subsequently discovered when working on a book about the Liberals, was an obscure benefactor of the party. At this earlier time, however, his name was unfamiliar to me. I admitted as much to Beaverbrook.

'Ya never heard of Hugh Sherwood?'

The gap in my knowledge seemed to present him with endless possibilities for wonder and amusement. 'Ya call yaself a political writer and ya never heard of Hugh Sherwood? Well, ya better learn about Hugh Sherwood, that is my advice if ya wish to be a political writer.'

Beaverbrook dictated some material of chiefly historical interest on the Liberal Party's funds, or lack of them. He then asked how I passed my working day. In the course of my reply I said – not entirely truthfully, I must confess – that I spent a good deal of time making assiduous enquiries by telephone. This, it soon became evident, was the wrong thing to say.

'Vines,' he suddenly yelled. 'Drat that Vines, where is he?'

Colin Vines appeared.

'Vines, I wish to send an urgent message to the staffs of my newspapers about the use of the telephone.'

Vines stood at the ready.

'Mr Brittenden,' went the message (for during this period of activity Arthur Brittenden was editing the paper temporarily), 'a member of your staff tells me that he spends a good deal of his time on the telephone I do not recommend this practice have nothing to do with the telephone that is my advice rip out the cord and throw it away two feet after the subject of your enquiry that is the way to beat the agencies and get exclusive news.'

The use of the telephone at the *Express* did not, however, noticeably decline as a result of this message.

Beaverbrook's last instruction to me concerned Anthony Nutting. I never discovered what Nutting's crime had been. Certainly his behaviour at the time of Suez (the official house reason) did not seem fully to explain the ferocity with which he was pursued. Anyway, Beaverbrook discovered that Nutting was the Conservative candidate for Oldham East. This was well known – had been well known for many months – but it came as news to Beaverbrook. He therefore demanded a paragraph attacking Nutting. I refused to write it both because the information was scarcely fresh and because the attack was supposed to mention some divorce proceedings in which Nutting had been involved. So the matter uneasily rested.

And then Beaverbrook died. *Cadit quaestio*: or so one might have thought. But no. In the same week the Editor called me in and suggested that 'as a tribute to Beaverbrook' I should carry out his last known instruction and attack Anthony Nutting. In the circumstances this seemed to me unnecessary and irrational, not to say bizarre. I said as much and perhaps more. However, the attack duly appeared, written by someone else. Shortly afterwards I moved to another job.

# Always Taller
# Tom Hutchinson

He was taller than I had expected. Legend, with the connivance of the cartoonist Vicky, had made him out to be a rotund, compact rodent with a wicked smile and sharp teeth perfectly suited to gnawing away at the Establishment as beavers do at tree trunks. It was a pretty conceit, but meeting him in that flat near Green Park, I was aware only of Beaverbrook's height, when compared with my anticipation of him. His torso, clad in clerical-grey suiting, bulked, giving a formidable impression of strength.

I had joined the *Daily Express* as a show-business reporter and, although I met Beaverbrook only a few times, he made an impression on my memory of a most peculiar and particular kind. It is a memory that stretches and heaves around like the introduction to a cinematic flashback being photographed by a director wishing to indicate a delirium of emotion. One moment Beaverbrook is vivid and real and charcoal-distinct; the next the image of him bends and wavers as though too much drink were squeezing all reality out of him.

Remember, I was young and impressionable and in terror.

'Goodday t'ya,' he said. There was no desk, just two armchairs facing each other. I may have taken in the fabled paintings which were supposed to be in that room, but I can't remember now, perhaps because I couldn't focus properly then. His hand was as silky and slithery as parchment. Somebody – I think there was a butler – fetched us a drink. He eyed me over what seemed to be a whisky winking with soda; his voice was less of a rasp than I had expected, the Canadian burr in it sounding almost Cornish.

He liked show business, he said. People in it were so much larger than life, he said. Like politics, he said. That's why he made it a point to talk to newcoming journalists specializing in it, about their subject . . . Did I understand? Now, was so-and-so a homosexual? Was this star sleeping with that star?

I remembered advice from a friend long in the *Express* tooth: always have an answer ready. There was the story about the local journalist who was asked by a visiting Beaverbrook how many laying hens there were in the vicinity of his area. The reporter made up a figure and spluttered it out. He was appointed as the *Express* agricultural correspondent that day!

So, what I didn't know, I made up, conjuring facts from the air. It seemed to please him. Not that I think he believed me; it just was soothing to him to see me put on a performance on his behalf. He chuckled over the thought that a British male star, so adored by millions of young females, was solely devoted to the flesh of members of his own sex. It was, I gathered, the irony of the situation that entered the soul of his amusement.

Then: 'I know you from somewhere else!' It was a statement, brusquely interrogative as though it were without a question mark. I knew exactly what he meant. I explained that once, sitting in Green Park, I had stared at him and his companion walking there. He had stared back at me aggressively, not wanting to be looked at so closely. Then he had walked by. But that had been six years before when I had been in London, away from my home city in the north, trying to get a job. But he had remembered all right.

'Never forget,' he said. 'Memory is a weapon you can always use.'

I met him several brief times after that and, then, on one memorably long occasion. It was during the prolonged, exorbitant hullabaloo surrounding the making of the film *Cleopatra* in England. So much trouble had attended the production, that the departure of Elizabeth Taylor into the London Clinic for treatment for an undefined illness seemed but one more plague-boil for the Jobian producers to bear.

A group of us reporters hung around the entrance to the clinic, awaiting statements, asking what the trouble really was. An abortion? A terminal illness? Rumour ran ripe and rife. But a bland, blank wall was lowered; Miss Taylor was safe from our conjecture on the other side.

In that sort of doorstepping situation, you try anything. I remembered taking a clinic nurse for a drink and passing on money for her to talk. I think she probably made it up, but glandular fever was her reason for Elizabeth Taylor's incarceration. For me, it was some sort of break. Nobody else had got as much as that. I wrote it up and filed it for publication.

The story didn't appear next day. Nor the day after. Nor after that. I sent in a complaining memo to the Editor and there was a summons from 'the Lord'.

'A good story, that,' he said. But it hadn't been used . . . He looked at me with an astonished severity that pruned his face into even more wrinkles: 'I suppose you're one of those who are more interested in people than facts. Facts are what make people. Fact is that I have money in *Cleopatra* and that the *Express* doesn't want any adverse publicity. Had too much already that film . . . Facts. I spent my life with facts. Use them. You can rely on them; don't let you down. You should have known about my investment. You're the journalist. You should have known.'

All these years after, I see him looking at me with a kind of amused outrage on his face. He is always taller than I had expected, or perhaps it's memory whose myth elongates his presence above and beyond me. The sense of power moving upwards into a place where stature is not measured by ordinary means. Actual height, of course, has nothing to do with it.

# The Seeds of Discord
# Peter Grosvenor

Lord Beaverbrook's rare visits to the *Express* offices in the earlier years were invariably attended by panic and not a little unconscious hilarity. Arthur Christiansen recalls his visit to the Manchester office where the slight figure in trilby and drab black overcoat was unrecognized by the doorman. During the course of an angry exchange the Old Man drew himself up to his full but diminutive height and exploded angrily: 'Do you know who I am? I am Lord Beaverbrook.' To which the doorman, unimpressed, replied with world-weary sarcasm: 'And I'm Cecil Parkin' – a famous Lancashire bowler of the day – 'and I say you can't come in.' The irony was quite lost on Lord Beaverbrook who had no interest in sport, least of all cricket, of which he had declared: 'Many readers hate cricket. Most of them know nothing about it. The cricket public is dwindling every day.' So it was that, soon after the Manchester incident, he told the general manager: 'Parkin has guarded my property well. See that he gets a rise.'

In later years, Beaverbrook never came near the office. He did not need to. His presence seemed to be everywhere. Just by picking up the telephone, he sent shivers through the entire building. Even the threat that he might phone at any time from anywhere in the world was enough to keep us all on our toes.

How he loved to stir things up. I remember being in the Editor's office when the late Peter Baker was deputizing. Some government crisis was going on, and Beaverbrook was anxious to poke his oar in and spread a little mischief. Like Beelzebub, whose appearance was presaged by a rumble of thunder, his voice came crackling over the speaker and broke into song. To the tune of 'The more we are together', he sang: 'Sow the seeds of discord, sow the seeds of discord...' It was not unmusical. Discord was duly sown.

Another time the familiar rasping sing-song voice came through on my phone. Many people had a recording machine for just such occasions. I did not and, my shorthand being primitive, I remember desperately motioning my secretary to pick up the extension and take a note. For my sins, I used to write the page-one blurbs extolling the *Daily Express*'s merits as an advertising medium. It was a great story to tell no doubt, and it was always proclaimed with shrill egotism: 'The *Daily Express* is the only truly classless newspaper. It has thirty-three per cent of all readers in all classes – A B C D and E. No other newspaper in the world can match this unparalleled pulling power...' Certainly it was an extraordinary achievement to appeal as much to dukes as to dustmen (who, in any case, would have been C-class readers), but we also reached in equal proportion those poor souls in the E group who are said to be below subsistence level.

What appeal! But there was a limit to the number of different ways you could tell the same story. After you had altered the word classless to all-class ('Surely "classless" implies no class, Peter' said a nervous editor – Beaverbrook's editors were usually nervous, not surprisingly when he once sent 147 directives in a single day), it was difficult to think of many variations on the eternal theme. So on one ill-advised occasion, desperate for inspiration, I decided to put the Great Advertising Story into sporting metaphor: 'The *Daily Express* is always on the ball. It is goal hungry – eager to help you reach *your* goals of bigger and better sales. Rest assured, you will score and score well every time in the pages of the *Daily Express*... Home and away, reader or advertiser, the *Daily Express* is your one sure banker.'

This frivolous approach to the serious matter of money and of advertising 'revenoos' deeply pained Lord Beaverbrook's Presbyterian soul: 'Oh Mr Grosvenor, Mr Grosvenor,' he thundered like an Old Testament prophet. 'The *Daily Express* is a great noospaper. It is not to be likened to some football team.' The last two words were spat out in contempt. 'Let us start again: "You can always tell the quality of a noospaper by the quality of its advertisers. The greatest firms in Britain and the world advertise in the columns of the *Express* – for the *Daily Express* is a great noospaper. It is also a quality noospaper. No other noospaper in the world ...' and so on.

'There you are, Mr Grosvenor, that is the way to sell advertising space in the *Daily Express*. And never forget, advertising is a very serious business.' But like the Bible, whose cadences he was always echoing, he was not particularly consistent; he could always find a different text to suit the needs of the moment. So it was one Thursday morning when he rang to find out why my 'Books' page was not in the *Daily Express*.

Anyone who ever contributed a 'regular' column in the *Express* in those days, be it the mighty Sefton Delmer or a mere tyro Literary Editor like myself, was subjected to the frequent irritation, if not humiliation, of having his column yanked out at the last moment in favour of an extra advertisement or the latest excitement. It might not have been a better story, but it was later, and in the curious way that newspaper offices operate, a story that has never been published can get to seem like an old story merely from having been on a feature editor's schedule a couple of times. Book pages are destined to be items of this sort. But nothing escaped Lord Beaverbrook's eye.

'Mr Grosvenor, what has happened to your book page?'

'Well, sir, it's been held over, indeed held out for reasons of space. We had an extra woman's feature and I gathered there was also a last-minute ad on page fifteen.'

'Oh, this is bad, I shall have to speak to the Editor.'

There and then in my hearing he proceeded to dictate a memo to the Editor. Let us call him Smith, for in common with eight other ex-*Express* editors, he is still alive and prospering: 'Mr Smith, what has happened to the book page? The *Daily Express* is a quality noospaper. It has the highest AB readership of any noospaper in the land. In future, these readers must be served with a regular book page. Do not give me that old story that there is too little space or too many advertisements. If there are too many advertisements, throw them out, throw them out.'

About half an hour later, the Editor came on the line: 'Ah Peter, I've been thinking about your book page. I'm very annoyed it was left out this morning. The *Daily Express* is a quality newspaper, you know. We have the highest AB readership in the country. In future we must have a regular book page for these people. Do not let them give you that old story about too little space. If there's any problem, come and see me. If there are too many advertisements on the page we will, um, well, um, we will rescheme the page to get you a proper show.'

And so it continued for several years until Beaverbrook reached his 'late final' and died on 9 June 1964. I was sorry to see him go. I liked to think he had a shrewd eye for talent, almost as great as his own talent for mischief. Sometimes it was evil mischief, but I encountered only the mischief-mischief.

'There is surprise after surprise for the man who is connected with a newspaper. Every day a newspaper grows more exciting,' he would say. 'You must always surprise the reader' was another of his mottos. And the best way to do that was always to surprise his staff. As a recipe for a bright, quixotic newspaper that 'leaves all the others gasping . . .' (to quote a cliché from one of my blurbs), it was a formula that never failed.

# Exactly Like the Bust
# Angus McGill

Tudor Jenkins had edited the 'Londoner's Diary' for twenty years. He was a shy and gentlemanly man who treated his staff with scrupulous politeness. There was rarely a rebuke. All the same, he sometimes felt obliged to remind his reporters that everything we wrote was read by Lord Beaverbrook.

I knew only that everything I wrote was rewritten by Mr Jenkins, and I couldn't help wishing our stories covered a slightly wider canvas. 'I have news for Mr Nubar Gulbenkian, 64,' they would begin. Or 'To town comes Sir John Ellerman, 56.'

So I can't understand how I came to be writing about the ducks in St James's Park. That wasn't Mr Jenkins' style at all. Still, this story about ducks appeared more or less intact one Tuesday morning. It promptly disappeared after the first edition but not before one reader at least had seen it.

I was called to Percy Elland's office. Mr Elland, a rosy, smiling Yorkshireman, was Editor of the *Evening Standard*. Had I written that piece about ducks? he asked. Well, Lord Beaverbrook wished to see me. Arlington House. Four o'clock. Better get a new tie, lad.

Well, it could happen to anyone at any time, we all knew that. You caught Lord Beaverbrook's eye and next thing you knew you were film critic or something good like that.

I took it in my stride, of course, I told no one except the rest of the staff, some people I knew and my mother. Mr Jenkins nodded down the table at me, and I got on with the morning's work with a will. 'Unamused is Lady Docker, 53 . . .'

I spent lunchtime buying a new tie – stripes, very smart – and took a taxi to Arlington Street, arriving with a bare two hours to spare. This gave me time to adjust my new tie properly and to stare a lot at Arlington House, the rather ordinary-looking block of flats where Lord

Beaverbrook lived when he was in London.

At 3.45 I took the lift to the top floor and stood around a bit. Then on the strokes of 4.00, I was ringing the bell of the flat and walking down a corridor and being shown into a large dishevelled room with pictures in stacks against the wall, books in piles on the floor and Lord Beaverbrook looking at me over half-moon spectacles.

He looked exactly like all the photographs and cartoons and the Epstein bust in the *Express* lobby, and when he spoke, the voice was unmistakable too. *Everyone* could imitate Lord Beaverbrook.

'HA! Mr McGill!' he said. 'You have been visiting the ducks in St James's Park!'

'Yes,' I said. He looked at me, expectantly. 'I went there yesterday,' I said.

'Did you indeed?' he said. He was standing at a reading desk and he gazed for a long moment at some paper there. Then he took off his glasses and we were away again.

'You are interested in the parks?' he said.

I wasn't particularly. 'I certainly am,' I said, sounding keen.

'What is that park there?' he said.

'That is Green Park,' I said. A bull's-eye, but something more seemed to be required. 'It is a very fine park,' I said.

'Is that so?' said Lord Beaverbrook.

Conversation flagged. He seemed to have lost interest in parks. Worse, he seemed to have lost interest in me.

'Well,' he said, 'it was good of you to come to see me. Good day t'ya.'

I said good day to him too and left. It was three minutes past four.

A disaster! It had been a disaster. I had had my big chance and I had blown it. I didn't even have a Beaverbrook story to tell, not much of one anyway, but that did not stop me telling it to anyone who would listen, my imitation of the famous accent getting ever more assured.

'What is that park there? Is that so?'

The months passed, and the seasons changed, and the Editor changed, and the Editor of the diary changed and changed again, and I took over a column called 'Mainly for Men' which dealt largely with men's fashion. I put this down to the fine striped tie I had bought for my now remote interview with Lord Beaverbrook, and which I had worn just in case ever since.

I embraced my new role with enthusiasm. We were now in the 1960s and men's fashion was all the go. Kipper ties are *in*, I cried. Striped shirts are *out*! But though no one could have shown more devotion to the width of the lapel, I did occasionally stray from my brief. I went to the races. I went to the Palais. I went to the zoo, and there was a new baby giraffe.

I was called in by Charles Wintour, the new Editor. Lord Beaverbrook had been reading my piece about the baby giraffe, he said. He was at his villa in Cap d'Ail, and I was to go there that morning. I should go and pack now – I would need to take a dinner jacket – and should then collect some packages from Mrs Ince at the *Daily Express* and an envelope for Mr Wintour, and catch the noon plane to Nice. From there I should take a taxi to La Capponcina, Lord Beaverbrook's villa. I was to tell Lord Beaverbrook that I had caught the bus.

An hour and a half later I presented myself to Mrs Ince, a large suitcase in one hand, a grip and a raincoat in the other. I was clearly going somewhere for a month.

Mrs Ince was one of Lord Beaverbrook's many secretaries, a figure of influence and power. She had several things for me to take, large and awkwardly shaped packages, one of them a bag of limes. I managed to get them all in somewhere and moved on to Mr Wintour who gave me a large, fat envelope. It was a very old, creased envelope with an earlier address and a number of franked stamps all crossed through. It was, in short, a disgraceful envelope. I transferred the contents to a new envelope, and got this in the suitcase too.

I then set off for the airport, flew to Nice, got a taxi to Cap d'Ail, paid off the driver at the arched entrance to the villa and walked down the steep slope of the drive, pleased to have got there in such good time.

A worried young man stood waiting in the open doorway. This was Colin Vines, another of Lord Beaverbrook's secretaries. 'Oh, thank goodness,' he said. 'You've got Lord Beaverbrook's letters? Just leave your things downstairs and come straight up. He is wondering where you are.'

Lord Beaverbrook was in his bedroom, sitting up in bed and staring expectantly at the door. It was a large bed and Miss Kits, yet another of his secretaries, sat on the far end of it, notebook open.

'HA! Mr McGill!' said Lord Beaverbrook. 'Have you anything for me?'

I said I certainly had and handed the packets over. 'Sit down, sit down,' said Lord Beaverbrook and picked up Mr Wintour's envelope. Something about it seemed to trouble him. He turned it in his hand. He gave a sharp intake of breath. He opened it and looked inside. He then pressed a switch on a small recording machine at his side.

'Mr Wintour,' he said. 'I ask you to use old envelopes. You use new envelopes. You persist in this wasteful practice.'

I was appalled. Should I own up? But there was no interrupting Lord

Beaverbrook now. He had begun to work through the pile of papers on the bed.

Some were read, crumpled up and dropped on the floor. Others were thrown without comment to Miss Kits. Some were held tightly while he dictated replies and were then thrown across the bed. Others were thrown across with a muttered instruction: 'Thank him,' or 'Tell him I agree,' or 'Tell him nicely I'm too old now.'

In half an hour the floor was covered in paper, Miss Kits was on her way to her office, and it was my turn.

He enquired most courteously about my journey. How had I come from Nice? By bus? Good. He apologized for being in bed. He was very old, he said, and he had gout. Did I know anything about gout? I said it was caused by an excess of uric acid. I had a friend, I said, who had gout in his ear.

Lord Beaverbrook stared at me over his spectacles.

'Is that so?' he said.

He picked a cutting from the bed and looked it over. It was, I saw, my article about the baby giraffe.

'What are your plans for this afternoon?' he said.

'Well . . .' I said.

'Prince Rainier has a very fine zoo,' he said. 'Why don't you have a look at that?'

'Well . . .' I said.

'Then you can come back here and write a very good article about it for the *Evening Standard*. And you can read it to us after dinner.'

I don't remember much about Prince Rainier's zoo. It was a small zoo, I remember that. I remember the keeper. He had little English; I had little French. There were a lot of monkeys I think and a lion or two. They hadn't much English either.

Back at the villa Mr Vines found a typewriter for me and I pounded away on it in my room. By 6.30, I had some sort of article more or less finished and there was no more time. I hastily showered and changed and went down.

There were three of us for dinner. Lord Beaverbrook sat at the head of the table. Lady Dunn, widow of his old friend Sir James Dunn, was on his right. I was on his left. There seemed to be yards of tablecloth between us.

Lady Dunn did her best to put me at ease. She plied me with questions. She wanted to know about my parents, my schooling, my wife . . .

I didn't *have* a wife? She perked up perceptibly and so, it seemed to me, did Lord Beaverbrook. He now joined in. How did I manage? What did I do about meals? Did I cook them myself?

I often did, as it happened, but was this the right image? I ate out as a rule, I said. In restaurants.

'What restaurants?' said Lord Beaverbrook.

'Well,' I said, 'there is a steak house under my flat. I often eat there.'

'And what,' said Lord Beaverbrook, 'is the most popular meal in London today?'

'The most popular meal in London,' I said, beyond caring, 'is prawn cocktail, followed by rump steak and chips, followed by ice cream.'

'How much does this cost?' said Lord Beaverbrook.

'Six shillings and sixpence,' I said.

Lord Beaverbrook turned in his chair. The recording machine was there on a small table beside him. He pressed the button. 'Mr Wintour,' he said. 'The most popular meal in London today is prawn cocktail, followed by rump steak and chips followed by ice cream. It costs six shillings and sixpence.'

He turned back to me. 'And what did you make of Prince Rainier's zoo?'

There was nothing for it. I took the manuscript from my pocket and, with such sang-froid as I could muster, read it out.

It didn't seem very good.

It really seemed rather awful.

I finished on what had seemed, so short time ago, a light note. I refolded the pages and returned them to my pocket. There was total silence in the room.

Lady Dunn sat as though turned to stone. Lord Beaverbrook appeared to have weighty matters on his mind. Then he stirred, looked up, spoke. 'Very good,' he said.

Mr Vines informed me in the morning that I was returning to London before lunch that day and he had a number of packages for me to take. I delivered these that afternoon to the secretariat in the *Daily Express*.

Mr Wintour did not seem in the least surprised to see me back so soon. He did not mention the switching of the envelope. And the following day an interesting paragraph appeared in the Londoner's Diary: 'The most popular meal in London today is prawn cocktail, followed by rump steak and chips, followed by ice cream. It costs 6s 6d.'

During the next two years I returned to Cap d'Ail several times and survived a little longer. Others were asked from time to time too, of course, some far more often. It was the same for us all. We would arrive unsuspectingly at the office in the morning and would find ourselves on the midday plane carrying papers and letters in much-used envelopes.

Lord Beaverbrook was getting noticeably more frail. He often said he was an old man and indeed he was. He had his eighty-third birthday. Then his eighty-fourth. The brown spots on his skin got more marked. The lines got deeper. He seemed smaller.

All the same, he got no less formidable, and dinner continued to be a testing time for me. Whoever the guests were, Lord Beaverbrook batted the conversation my way. He wanted no passengers. At other times it was again just Lord Beaverbrook, Lady Beaverbrook – the former Lady Dunn – and me, and at such times my domestic arrangements continued to arouse close interest. My cleaning lady's *mother* washed my shirts? How much did I pay her?

Information, that's what Lord Beaverbrook always wanted, and I noticed he loved a bit of gossip too. He couldn't hear enough about the doings of Somerset Maugham in his even grander villa on the next Cap, and received with glee accounts of another old friend, a distinguished bachelor living further down the coast, struck by a soldier while giving him a lift!

I hadn't any good gossip like this for him, but I chatted away about London and what the kids were up to, about the Beatles and the twist as we walked slowly round the pool that no one ever seemed to swim in, Lord Beaverbrook tightly gripping my arm and stopping when the gout was too bad.

Once, halfway round the pool I recklessly put in a plug, for a friend. Had he read Maureen Cleave? I asked. She did wonderful interviews.

It was a mistake. Next morning he sat in his study looking grumpy. Maureen's interview with Nana Mouskouri was on his desk. 'Nana Mouskouri,' he said, making heavy weather of the name. 'Have you heard of Nana Mouskouri?'

I said I had. Miss Kits said she had. Lord Beaverbrook switched on his recording machine.

'Mr Wintour,' he said. 'Why does the *Evening Standard* devote a whole page to a Greek singer no one has heard of?'


I remember, very clearly, our last meeting. I had been there for three days, a record for me, I was off soon to catch the plane, and I had come to say goodbye. Michael Foot, his great friend, had left earlier in the day and now Lord Beaverbrook sat in the shade on the terrace, wearing his broad-brimmed hat. He seemed to want company and he waved me to a wicker chair beside him.

'I worry about Michael,' he said. 'He is such a fine boy. Do you think he will ever get anywhere?'

Then he began to talk about his father. He had been thinking a lot about his father lately, he said. He had been a good man, but he had found it hard to bring up five children. Those had been hard times. His father, he said, had never been able to make money. Lord Beaverbrook shook his head, puzzled.

'I often wish,' he said quietly, 'that I could have been there to help him.'

# 'A Foul-Weather Friend'
# A. J. P. Taylor

I got to know Beaverbrook so late in his life that I almost missed getting to know him at all. I met him first when he was in his late seventies and became a close friend of his only when he had passed the age of eighty. Now when I look back at those few joyful years, there seems hardly an age-gap between us. We made each other younger or perhaps it was merely Max's company that made me feel younger.

What brought us together in this abrupt way was a common interest in recent history. I had been a professional historian all my life and, in the years when I knew Beaverbrook, was writing the concluding volume in the *Oxford History of England*, entitled *English History 1914–1945*. This was very much Beaverbrook's own period. Years before, he had published *Politicians and the War*, an account of how Lloyd George became Prime Minister in December 1916 – or should I say an account of how Beaverbrook had made Lloyd George Prime Minister? The book, though in my opinion first-class history, had appeared at the height of the financial crisis in 1931 and had attracted little attention. Beaverbrook, always doubtful of his gifts as an historian, was much discouraged and did not publish any further instalment until 1956 when he produced *Men and Power*.

I had never concerned myself with Beaverbrook's writings, which I had assumed were not much above journalism. Terry Kilmartin, Literary Editor of the *Observer*, offered me *Men and Power* with the words, 'I don't suppose it is much good but you can have fun at the expense of a press lord.' I began to read and was entranced: this was personal history on the highest level. I rang Terry and said, 'I can't attack this book. It is as fine a work of history as any I have ever read.' Terry replied, using a phrase that was a favourite of Beaverbrook's, 'If that is what you think, you are entitled to say it.'

And that is how I unwittingly changed the whole course of

Beaverbrook's life. For the first time, he had been taken seriously as an historian. His self-confidence was restored and he resolved to write more works of history in his declining years. I had no idea of this until after Beaverbrook's death. Now I understand why I got to know him so easily. The next approach came from me. Beaverbrook, when describing how Lloyd George had imposed convoy on an unwilling Admiralty, had written, 'He took his seat at the head of the Admiralty Board' – incidentally an unprecedented act. I was pretty sure that the Admiralty Board had not met that day so I wrote and asked for Beaverbrook's evidence. He answered by inviting me for lunch.

Beaverbrook did not answer my question beyond saying, 'I am sure it happened: I'll ask Churchill.' I replied, 'But Churchill had nothing to do with the Admiralty in 1917.' And Beaverbrook brushed off my objections with a phrase I got used to later, 'Ah, you are a very clever fellow.' The topic was soon forgotten. I was entranced by this little old man with the mind and spirit of a boy, an historian who could range over the twentieth century and hardly ever make a mistake. As to Lloyd George at the Admiralty Board, I discovered later that Beaverbrook invented the story as what he called 'balancing': livening up a narrative with an anecdote. Looking over the proofs of Men and Power after Beaverbrook's death, I found that he had added the anecdote by biro to the final galleys. This was not the only occasion when I learnt, if rather late in the day, that the most entertaining episodes in twentieth-century history derived from Beaverbrook's invention and not from the real course of events.

Our first lunch went on for a long time. Beaverbrook asked me question after question. Where was I born? What had my father been? What were my politics? How many books had I written? How many children had I? Beaverbrook carried the answers in his head and would produce one or other unexpectedly years later. Two things surprised me about him. The first was his gentle, old-world manners. He was an elegant Victorian gentleman, with great patience and consideration. At dinner parties he took trouble over all his guests, accommodating himself to each one. He had one touch of male chauvinism: he was glad when his male guests smoked cigars – indeed at our first lunch he not only offered me a cigar but pressed the entire box on me – but he did not approve of lady guests smoking cigarettes. There were plenty of cigarette-boxes in his house but the boxes were empty. When one lady guest asked for a cigarette, Beaverbrook replied, 'If you ring the bell, the butler may be able to find you one.' More knowledgeable ladies brought their own cigarettes. I thought his attitude admirable.

The second characteristic of his which struck me was his uncertainty and his craving for affection. Of course he took resolute decisions when conducting his newspapers and running his finances, or so it seemed. But he was hesitant in ordinary life, unsure in his personal relations. He could not convince himself that he was liked for himself, and was the more grateful for affection that had no calculation behind it. Certainly he was unfailingly kind to me and I was devoted in return. As the brief years passed, Max Beaverbrook became the human being I had most loved, and my loyalty went on after his death.

Beaverbrook has been rightly called 'a foul-weather friend'. I had a little experience of this myself. I went out to Cherkley one miserable autumn evening; Beaverbrook was in bad shape, crippled with gout and low in spirits, and I, too, was gloomy. I had reached the year 1931 in my history of England and was stuck, bored with the financial crisis and reluctant to face the foreign affairs of the 1930s about which I had written already. Beaverbrook hardly spoke over dinner. Afterwards he said feebly, 'What are you doing now, Alan?' I began to tell him: how I was stuck with my book and thought I should have to give it up. Beaverbrook realized I was in trouble.

An extraordinary change came over the little old man. He rose unaided from his chair, kicked off his gout-shoe and began to walk up and down the room, declaiming as he went. He described the excitements of the thirties: the break-up of Labour; the National government; Ottawa; his Empire Crusade and its failure; the Abyssinian crisis. The name of Baldwin occurred again and again: 'What a rascal! He was cunning. He dethroned a monarch! He tricked us all.' And then, with a roar of laughter, 'His private life was beyond reproach.' After which he marched across the room and rang the bell, saying, 'Now let's have some more whisky.' Most of what Beaverbrook had said was, I thought, very great nonsense but his zest inspired me. That evening Max Beaverbrook saved my intellectual life. I went home, sat down again at my typewriter and never rested until I had completed *English History 1914–1945*. By then Beaverbrook was dead, but the book was as much his as mine.

I have never known a more restless man. That is why he called himself a journalist and liked running newspapers: they were different every day. His first question each morning was 'What's new?' and then to his Editor, 'What are you going to say about it?' having already prepared his own answer. His principal anxiety in life, or so he said, was to write more works of history, but he could never decide which one to write. He jumped from one to another: more about Lloyd

George; two biographies, R. B. Bennett and Sir James Dunn; the beginnings of an autobiography (a beautiful little work entitled *My Early Life*); and two ambitious fragments never pulled into shape – *The Age of Baldwin* and *Churchill's Victories*. To complete all these was an ambition still bubbling in his mind at the age of eighty-five.

He was equally restless in his residences. As soon as he arrived in Cherkley from the West Indies, he was talking about moving on to the south of France, and no sooner was he in his French home, La Capponcina, than he was making plans for a move to Canada. He had a fantasy that one day he would find a real home by returning to New Brunswick, and he kept up this fiction by spending some weeks at Fredericton, New Brunswick, in the early autumn. He had never lived in Fredericton as a boy, and his only association with it was as Chancellor of the University of New Brunswick. I joined him there in September 1961. He had a busy programme, inspecting the university buildings, going over the art gallery he had created, and interviewing the university staff. He had twice tried to pin himself down to Fredericton by buying and furnishing a house in which he could live. On each occasion he took fright before the house was ready and presented it to the university. When I was there he had a bedroom in the Beaverbrook Hotel (not his property) and spent his days in a basement flat that had been prepared for the curator of the art gallery. In the morning he transacted local affairs, in particular harassing the Vice-Chancellor and some of the professors. He always became increasingly impatient for the moment when he could telephone Beaverbrook Newspapers in London. Then he had a happy half-hour giving his instructions to managers and editors in Fleet Street. Maybe he had an hour's rest after lunch, though he rarely gave me any. After that he rang Montreal for news of its stock exchange, and by the late afternoon he was on to Wall Street. I don't think he wanted to speculate on either of these exchanges: he merely wanted to know what was happening.

This was my first, indeed my only, visit to the New World. Beaverbrook was anxious to show me his native province or, to be correct, to show me the province in which he mistakenly believed that he had been born. He took me over to Newcastle where his father had been a Presbyterian minister, and where he himself had lived as a boy. Now no Aitken remained in Newcastle and few of Beaverbrook's boyhood friends. His father's manse had become the municipal library, heavily endowed by Beaverbrook – also heavily censored by him: only books that he approved of were included in it. Beaverbrook had acquired the entire town square and restored its eighteenth-century appearance, not that even Beaverbrook with his vivid imagination could have imagined that he lived in the eighteenth century. By the end of the afternoon his dream of returning 'home' had vanished. He said to me, 'I am glad I shall never live here.' Actually his ashes rest in the restored eighteenth-century square so his former dream was fulfilled after all.

Beaverbrook gave a last defiant announcement of his restlessness. In the winter of 1963–64 he was obviously failing physically though he was still ransacking Lloyd George's papers for new ideas. Lord Thomson proposed a grand dinner for Beaverbrook's birthday on 25 May 1964. It was uncertain until the last moment whether Beaverbrook would be fit to attend but he had determined on it. 'I'll be there all right,' he told me a few days earlier, the last time we met. So it proved: he walked resolutely up the Dorchester dining-room, leaning on his son's arm. He spoke in a clear forceful voice. His last words reiterated his guiding principle in life: 'It is time for me to become an apprentice once more . . .' Then he went home to bed and died on 9 June. He had been restless to the end.


In one sense that ends the story of the Beaverbrook I knew. But it also marks the beginning for me of many different Beaverbrooks whom I came to know. These were the Beaverbrooks who survived in letters and documents accumulated over a lifetime. Beaverbrook had always been a hoarder of manuscripts, his own and those of others. The collection had been erratic, depending on the efficiency or otherwise of his secretaries. Years before, I had asked Beaverbrook whether he would like me to write his life. He replied grumpily, 'I should like it very much,' and never mentioned the subject again. I thought this was commission enough and so, generously, did the members of his family.

Beaverbrook's archives from 1904, when he first opened a financier's office in Montreal, lay open before me. I now know the Beaverbrook of those early years. I know how he made his first fortune, how he married, and how quite accidentally he moved to England. I know the Beaverbrook, or to be more correct the Max Aitken, who much to his own surprise became a Conservative candidate for Parliament and, to his even greater surprise, and maybe regret, became a member of the House of Commons. I know how Max Aitken MP became Lord Beaverbrook, much to his delight at the time, and even more to his regret later on. I know the activities of Lord Beaverbrook as Minister of Information during the First World War. I have even read the speech in his own vindication which he claimed to have delivered in the House of Lords but which in fact he fabricated in order to please his dear friend Arnold Bennett. I know of Beaverbrook's many acts of charity, and of his more occasional feuds. I learnt that Beaverbrook and Baldwin had been brought together by common devotion to Bonar Law and had great difficulty in sustaining their apparent feud later. I followed Beaverbrook's fluctuating sentiments in regard to Winston Churchill: friendship, affection, hero-worship and then disillusion in his feeling that Churchill had 'betrayed' him in the political crisis of February 1942.

If I were to recount all the Beaverbrooks I learnt to know, I should have to write a whole book, as indeed I did. All I can say here is that the more I read and learnt about Beaverbrook, the more entertaining I found him, the greater my admiration for him and, above all, the deeper my affection. I am proud to have been numbered among his friends.

# 'A Bad Man'

Extracts from a programme in the BBC2 television series, *Reputations*, broadcast on 28 June 1981

Written and presented by Anthony Howard

MALCOLM MUGGERIDGE: ... Beaverbrook's influence was extraordinarily strong in his papers. I would always say of him that I dislike almost everything about him except that I have to admit that he was a very brilliant journalist. He knew what was good for a paper ...

... Some people rather liked him. I never got to like him, and the reason I didn't get to like him is that he did something which I considered to be very evil. And that was he rejoiced in developing and encouraging people's weaknesses. If someone was a drunk, he would ensure that they got more drunk. And poor old Tom Driberg whose weaknesses we all know ... he encouraged him when he ran into trouble for some of his little ways. Beaverbrook protected him and sort of lured him on. I think that is to say that Beaverbrook was a man who enjoyed stimulating in people what was basest in them ...

... Beaverbrook loved getting into bed with society ladies, you know, aristocratic ladies – and performing rather resolutely there ... Well, you would always know this was afoot. You would simply get a scribbled note that we should do a paragraph on Lady Mary somebody or other: she's witty, she's beautiful, she has taste in clothing, she's very intelligent and so on. If he hadn't pulled it off, then a little later you'd get a different account of Lady Mary: that she was a rather troublesome and scandalmongering lady who was rather a nuisance about the place, and you knew then that the operation had failed ...

... He impishly threw all his papers into convincing people that there would be no war, and his scribes had to write articles to that effect: there was going to be no war, no war. That was actually when I departed from his service because I felt it was preposterous . . .

. . . It's difficult to sum up one's feelings about him. I feel sure that he was a bad man; I feel sure that he was someone who'd sold his soul to the devil; I'm sure that he did great harm to lots of people. But none the less it has to be said that nobody would be able to write the story of the first half of the twentieth century and leave him out . . .

ANTHONY HOWARD: . . . In 1906 Beaverbrook married, and his bride, Gladys Drury, was the daughter of an army general. It was a match made not without a struggle – as Beaverbrook's own daughter explains . . .

JANET KIDD: . . . My grandfather Drury had three beautiful daughters and my father decided that he would like to go and see these three beautiful daughters so he went to Kingston and General Drury was not at all pleased with him. The general thought he was an upstart. So he had to be very careful and there was a great service at the cathedral the next day and he went in behind the VIPs. These three girls had gorgeous hair, right down to their waists, red – not really red but chestnut hair – and they were all three, sitting in front of him and he fell for one. He fell for the back of one . . .

ANTHONY HOWARD: . . . Though the marriage lasted twenty-one years, it was clear even on the honeymoon that it was not all to be plain sailing.

JANET KIDD: As soon as they got to Cuba, Father was off. He was making deals here and selling this there and buying railways and selling land. And my poor mother, instead of holding hands on the beach, realized she'd married a man who was only going to love business . . .

ANTHONY HOWARD: . . . Of all his associations with women one took pride of place – his prolonged affair with Jean Norton, an extra-marital relationship that, initially at least, his wife didn't seem to mind.

JANET KIDD: She liked Jean very much and Jean sort of almost worked into the family if you know what I mean. She loved me and loved Max and loved Peter, my two brothers. She was very good to us and she was very sweet to my mother. So my mother was quite happy about it. In other words she preferred it that way to what had gone on in the past.

ANTHONY HOWARD: But by 1926 the strain of sharing her husband with a *maîtresse en titre* had begun to take its toll.

JANET KIDD: She wanted to get away and we went to Canada and had a very happy time there for a year staying with her brothers, and then we came back and she started to get ill. And I think her illness was due tremendously to being terribly worried because she didn't want a divorce and yet she couldn't . . . She wanted a divorce, I mean, but she couldn't leave him; he was absolutely part of her and so she got terribly worried. And I think that brought on her illness or helped to bring on her illness and she died very, very quickly after that, at the age of thirty-nine.

ANTHONY HOWARD: When she died, you were with your father?

JANET KIDD: Yes, oh yes, yes.

ANTHONY HOWARD: And he was very upset?

JANET KIDD: Well he arrived – he was on his yacht somewhere and I got hold of him and he came in and she was unconscious . . . and after she died he was . . . he walked up and down the dining-room, saying: 'I've lost my harbour. What do I do? I've got no harbour any more.' He was very upset. And he went off to America very quickly . . .


ANTHONY HOWARD: . . . In his old age, other interests gradually came to rival his newspaper. In the 1950s and -60s he wrote two books, *The Decline and Fall of Lloyd George* and *Men and Power*, about the great political events in which he had been engaged as a young man. Charles Wintour had a ringside seat on Beaverbrook the historian.

CHARLES WINTOUR: He didn't regard it as history. He regarded it as chronicle. He would first of all get researchers to amass all the material that existed about the period that he was talking about. Then he would also get somebody else to amass from his own particular private collection of papers – he bought the Lloyd George papers; he bought the Bonar Law papers, and he bought various other groups of papers – and he would see what he could mine out of that particular material. And then the third element would be his own personal diary of events. He would then go through a policy of – a process of 'balancing' as he called it. 'Balancing' was bringing the scene more vividly to life. Whether in the process of balancing accuracy was sacrificed to any degree, I don't know. But he prided himself very much on this process which he regarded as being of equal importance to the original record. And he told me shortly before his death that, in ten years' time, he would be remembered far more for his books than he would ever be for his record as a proprietor of newspapers.

LORD BLAKE: . . . When Bonar Law was on his deathbed, Beaverbrook bought heavily in certain shares which he knew, of course, that Bonar Law had holdings in, in order that the values would go up on the stock exchange and console and cheer Bonar Law in his dying days. It was a very remarkable thing to have done and I can't think of any parallel at all that I've ever heard of . . .

ANTHONY HOWARD: . . . Beaverbrook died on 9 June 1964, just a fortnight after his eighty-fifth birthday. It was from Cherkley that the old crusader's funeral set out just five days later. His former, and last, private secretary was there . . .

COLIN VINES: . . . We went into the drawing-room where there were lots of people – about twenty or thirty, members of the family and one or two cronies including John Gordon, one of the few newspaperman who were there. I couldn't believe my eyes because none of these people, rather, hardly any of them did I actually know. Beaverbrook hadn't seen anything of them and I, of course, stood around waiting for Michael Foot and A. J. P. Taylor and John Junor, because they were the people I thought should be there.

Well, there was no sign of a coffin or a hearse, nothing like that at all. I don't know when the coffin was closed up. I don't know when it was taken out of the house and I don't know in what vehicle it was driven. We got out to the front drive, and at the end of the drive at Cherkley, there's a roundabout and we all sped round this at tremendous speed and proceeded to the crematorium at forty miles an hour at least, dashing to Beaverbrook's funeral. I mean, it was just so typical of Beaverbrook somehow that his funeral should be like this. Not quiet, slow and dignified – nothing like Northcliffe's, whose funeral procession took place right through London with thousands of people cheering or watching or just standing or whatever people do at funerals.

It was a mad house, Beaverbrook's funeral.

# Index